Good Green Jobs in a Global Economy

Urban and Industrial Environments

Series editor: Robert Gottlieb, Henry R. Luce Professor of Urban and Environmental Policy, Occidental College

A complete list of the series appears at the back of the book.

Good Green Jobs in a Global Economy

Making and Keeping New Industries in the United States

David J. Hess

The MIT Press
Cambridge, Massachusetts
London, England

© 2012 Massachusetts Institute of Technology

All rights reserved. No part of this book may be reproduced in any form by any electronic or mechanical means (including photocopying, recording, or information storage and retrieval) without permission in writing from the publisher.

MIT Press books may be purchased at special quantity discounts for business or sales promotional use. For information, please email special_sales@mitpress.mit.edu or write to Special Sales Department, The MIT Press, 55 Hayward Street, Cambridge, MA 02142.

Set in Sabon by Toppan Best-set Premedia Limited. Printed on recycled paper and bound in the United States of America.

Library of Congress Cataloging-in-Publication Data

Hess, David J.
Good green jobs in a global economy : making and keeping new industries in the United States / David J. Hess.
p. cm.—(Urban and industrial environments)
Includes bibliographical references and index.
ISBN 978-0-262-01822-7 (hardcover : alk. paper)
1. Environmentalists—Vocational guidance—United States. 2. Environmental policy—United States. I. Title.
GE60
[.H47 2012]
363.7023—dc23
2012008459

10 9 8 7 6 5 4 3 2 1

Contents

Preface   vii

Introduction   1

I   Background

1   Energy, Manufacturing, and the Changing Global Economy   31
2   Green Jobs and the Green Energy Transition   47

II   Policies and Politics

3   Green Industrial Policy and the 111th Congress   73
4   State Governments and the Greening of Import Substitution   103
5   The Greening of Regional Industrial Clusters   125
6   Localist Alternatives to the Mainstream Transition   147

III   Processes and Explanations

7   Green Transition Coalitions and Geographical Unevenness   171
8   After 2010: Continued Unevenness in the Green Transition   191
Conclusion   213

Appendix: State Government Votes for Green Energy Laws   231
Notes   239
References   255
Index   289
Series List   295

Preface

Sustainability and justice are the central policy issues of the twenty-first century, but they are associated with an even greater challenge: that of finding the political will to implement solutions. Of the many factors that influence the lack of political will, one of the most important is the pressure exerted on political decision making by the sectors of industry that most benefit from the status quo of a fossil fuel economy. Governments and consumers are also complicit in accepting the benefits of a growth-oriented economy based on fossil fuels. The decision to pursue short-term interests at the expense of long-term planetary benefit has become the problem behind the problem.

A realistic prognosis is not necessarily optimistic. Consumption is likely to continue on an upward trajectory until it collides with a series of ecological barriers. Collapse will follow, as has sometimes occurred on a smaller scale when societies have exceeded their local ecological limits. No one knows exactly what collapse will entail, but the metaphor of chaos may be misleading. Instead, for the world's poor, collapse is likely to mean a nasty and short life of subsistence, crime, disease, and violence. We find this existence already in many of the world's growing shantytowns, described in Mike Davis's 2006 book *Planet of Slums*. Those fortunate enough to escape from such a reality may find themselves increasingly subjected to surveillance, criminal predators, limited spatial mobility, and what Andrew Szasz (2007) has called the "inverted quarantine." Unfortunately, this mix of the planet of slums and the inverted quarantine increasingly describes our cities and our lives.

Against this bleak prognosis, an important task for researchers is to explore the structure of political opportunities to find pressure points that might increase the political will to move public policies in a direction that is both more sustainable and more socially fair and just. This book is my third to begin with the assumption that there has been a general failure to address the twin problems of sustainability and justice and that there is a need to understand the pressure points in economic and political systems that might lead to more rapid change.

In the first book, *Alternative Pathways in Science and Industry*, I studied the role of social movements and civil society organizations, in alignment with research programs often found in the subordinate networks of scientific research fields, as avenues for addressing the twin problems. I drew attention to the role of social movements as sources not only of organized political opposition to environmentally harmful industrial technologies but also of ideas and inventions associated with alternative ways of designing our technologies, organizations, and economies. They can serve as laboratories of innovation for new technologies and organizational forms. However, in contrast with the often utopian aspirations of social movement leaders, the historical tendency is not for the laboratories of innovation to become widespread in their original form but instead for them to undergo a process of incorporation and transformation in which mainstream industries selectively accept some of the innovations but modify them substantially in the process. Although such alternative pathways do have historical significance and are associated with long-term industrial change, the changes often fall far short of the original vision of social and environmental reform.

In the second book, *Localist Movements in a Global Economy*, I examined another approach to addressing the power exerted on the political system by large growth-oriented corporations. By shifting consumption and social life to small locally owned organizations—independent small businesses, local food systems, public green energy, community media, and local finance—activists and advocates work toward rebuilding a portion of the economy that has been destroyed by decades of consolidation and globalization. Some of the projects have also been connected with sustainability goals through bioregionalist and relocalization movements, such as shifting some food, energy, investment, and occasionally other economic activity to geographically limited regions with local control. Localist movements have an uneven record on environmental and social fairness issues, and the economic project of restoring local ownership and enhancing the role of smaller enterprises is in many ways quixotic. Nevertheless, the growth of alternative economies represents another strategy for shifting power in the economic and political system away from growth-oriented corporate capitalism.

In this book, I explore a third approach that is emerging for reducing the political power of anti-green coalitions and opening up political opportunities for a more rapid and complete transition: clean energy industries in alliance with labor, environmental, anti-poverty, and other organizations. In the United States the new alliances came together, especially from 2007 through 2009, under the banner of "green jobs," and they scored some policy victories, especially among state and city governments. Much more than the social movements and alternative economies explored in my first two books, the green coalitions operate within the assumptions of the current economic order. Owing to the substantial role of labor and environmental organizations, there is a social-movement component; however, unlike many of the localist groups studied in the previous book, the reform politics of the coalitions studied here tend to accept large corporations and global capital markets as the basis of the global economy. The green transition coalitions advocate the development of industries that could eventually result in a technological and industrial transition that is of sufficient scale to compensate for increases in economic growth. This strategy of building coalitions among labor, environmentalists, green corporations, and other constituencies to open political opportunities is perhaps even more promising than the strategies discussed in my previous two books, but, as I will show, a strong political backlash has also emerged to thwart the reforms.

This book is based partly on research funded by the Science and Technology Studies Program of the National Science Foundation for the grant titled The Greening of Economic Development (SES-0947429). Any opinions, findings, conclusions, or recommendations expressed in this book are my own and do not necessarily reflect the views of the National Science Foundation or others who are acknowledged.

Many people have helped me to think through the issues that are discussed in this book. I want to thank especially the students who were funded by the grant to work on the project during the summer of 2010: David Banks, Bob Darrow, Joe Datko, Jaime Ewalt, Rebecca Gresh, Matthew Hoffmann, Anthony Sarkis, and Logan Williams. Brian Obach, Keith Pezzoli, and an anonymous reviewer also read the entire manuscript and provided many excellent suggestions for improvement. I appreciate the support that editor Clay Morgan and series editor Robert Gottlieb provided. Much of the research on party votes in state legislatures was completed by Jonathan Coley, a talented research assistant and doctoral student in Vanderbilt University's Sociology Department, and I gratefully acknowledge his help and the department's support.

A small portion of the content may have first appeared in a companion research report that was written for an audience of practitioners and political leaders, *Building Clean-Energy Industries and Green Jobs: Policy Innovations at the State and Local Government Level* (Hess et al. 2010).

Introduction

At the 2009 Good Jobs, Green Jobs conference in Washington, the international president of the United Steelworkers, Leo Gerard, described an experience he had had while riding on a high-speed train in China. When a waiter put a glass of water on his tray, Gerard quickly grabbed the glass to keep it from spilling. That reaction was based on Gerard's experiences on slow, jerky Amtrak trains in the United States. The waiter explained that it was not necessary to hold on to the glass, and in fact, as the train sped along at more than 200 miles per hour, no water was spilled.[1]

The anecdote, told to an audience of thousands of union activists and environmentalists at the height of the Obama administration's push for green jobs, is rich with implications. It condenses the multiple problems that the United States and other developed wealthy countries face with respect to the environment, economy, employment, manufacturing, infrastructure, and global political power. In a few decades, China has been transformed from a relatively backward, less industrialized country to a global industrial powerhouse. High-speed rail is just one among other clean tech industries, such as solar and wind, that China has aggressively supported in its bid to become the workshop of the world for clean tech. Notwithstanding the support of many governors and President Obama for green jobs and green technology, the anecdote draws attention to the difficulty that American businesses face in maintaining global leadership, even for high-tech industries such as solar, wind, and high-speed rail. However, for Gerard and his coalition of labor and environmental organizations there is more than a warning in the anecdote; there is a vision of an alternative. Gerard suggests that the United States could rebuild its infrastructure by using technologies that put Americans to work, stimulate the economy, and reduce the country's carbon footprint. The prospect of creating good green jobs at home is therefore raised as a solution to multiple crises.[2]

The idea of green jobs is what sociologists, and increasingly journalists, call a "frame." It is intended to neutralize and overcome the view that pits jobs against the environment. The green jobs frame facilitates an alliance that some large industrial corporations, unions, social justice advocates, and environmental organizations have forged to promote a common ground of environmental reform and industrial development. The frame speaks to the chronic unemployment and underemployment that many Americans face, and it articulates the goal of creating high-quality jobs. An important sector of good jobs is manufacturing, and developing jobs in that sector is a significant challenge. The United States lost about 6 million manufacturing jobs during the first decade of this century. Union leaders such as Leo Gerard see in green jobs a great "win-win" solution to the multiple problems of declining manufacturing, rising unemployment and underemployment, and degradation of the environment.[3]

This book will explore the politics of green energy policies and the prospect of a long-term transition toward an economy that has much lower levels of human impact on the environment. It will argue that the green transition is becoming interconnected with the parallel long-term transition in the global economy that is leading to the relative decline of the importance of the United States and the corresponding rise of other countries, especially China. The idea of relative decline does not imply that the United States is falling apart; rather, it implies that the center of global economic power is shifting to Asia, much as it shifted from Europe to the US 100 years ago. The call for the creation of good green jobs is cast within this crucible of environmental and economic changes that will characterize political life in the twenty-first century. This book seeks to understand the relationship between the two long-term historical changes.

Although supporting and maintaining high-quality domestic jobs is a priority for many countries, this book focuses on the United States. As the world's largest economy and the most stalwart supporter of neoliberalization of the global economy, its successes and failures in building a green transition have global importance. However, there is an additional reason for focusing on the US. The relative decline of the US economy creates the conditions for the country to undergo an ideological shift away from its dominant political ideology of neoliberalism. The general argument that this book investigates is that the United States' pursuit of ongoing trade liberalization and its laissez-faire approach to industrial policy no longer match its position in a highly competitive global economy in which rising economic powers practice aggressive trade and industrial policies. The more specific thesis is that the policy fields in which green energy reforms take place are important sites where the shifts in underlying political ideology are being articulated and contested. As other countries have increased their capacity to compete with the US in high-tech industries such as solar photovoltaics, the US is increasingly showing signs of responding more like an emerging industrial power that embraces developmentalism. Developmentalism remains liberal in the sense of an ongoing belief in capitalism, marketplace competition, and the value of at least some world trade, but the pattern of discourse and policy also contrasts with the support of ongoing trade liberalization and the relatively hands-off approach to industrial policy that characterized post-World War II US policy.[4]

The goal of this book is to provide a better understanding of how the politics of green energy operate within the tectonic shifts of the global economy of the twenty-first century. The goal is neither to evaluate the policies from the perspective of a practitioner nor to provide a normative assessment of whether the emerging pattern of developmentalism in American economic policy is good or bad; it is to make a historical argument that involves describing and analyzing green energy industrial policies in the United States in terms of underlying changes in the global economy and the accompanying shifts in political ideology.

Developmentalism

Developmentalism is defined here as an ideology, that is, a web of underlying concepts and values that both shape and are shaped by actions in the political field. In this view, ideologies are not simple reflections of underlying social differences such as social class; they are cultural systems that transverse agents in the political field and underlie the specific policy positions they adopt. Best understood relationally, the two main contrasting ideologies in the political field in many industrialized countries are social liberalism (sometimes called social democracy or embedded liberalism) and neoliberalism. In the United States, the divisions in ideology are largely aligned with the left wing of the Democratic Party (social liberalism) and the right wing of the Republican Party (neoliberalism). In between are moderates who often achieve legislative compromises that suggest the influence of both social liberalism and neoliberalism.[5]

Social liberalism is based on the historic compact between industrial labor and corporate capital that President Franklin Roosevelt and his allies forged during the New Deal, when owners of large corporations tolerated relatively high levels of regulatory and redistributive intervention in exchange for social peace and economic stability. In the twenty-first century, social liberalism survives in a budget-constrained world as a commitment to social fairness and openness to government regulation to correct market failures such as pollution. Neoliberalism as an approach to economic policy dates back to the 1930s, but it become prominent in the United States as a political force during the presidency of Ronald Reagan. Although macroeconomic policies such as inflation hawkishness, tax cuts, and deregulation are crucial elements of neoliberalism, it is a broader ideology based on ideals of limited government, fiscal prudence, the wisdom of markets, and individual responsibility. Because social liberals didn't disappear with the emergence of neoliberal political leaders, the political field remains a battleground on which supporters of embedded social liberal programs contend with neoliberal reformers. Increasingly, Democrats have adopted policies that borrow from the neoliberal philosophy as a strategic move to win acceptance for policies aligned with commitments to social fairness. For example, in 2011 and 2012 a Democratic president advocated for a job-creation program that involved both directed intervention in the economy and significant tax cuts. Nevertheless, the elements of social liberalism embedded in such policy proposals are still anathema to Republican leaders. In response to the proposal, the Republican Speaker of the House of Representatives articulated a clearly neoliberal alternative that would create jobs by reducing government regulation of the private sector.[6]

Developmentalism crosses the ideological divide by drawing attention to the need for policies that create domestic jobs by protecting domestic businesses from unfair trade practices and helping them with industrial policy. One might argue that developmentalism can be subsumed under neoliberalism as a strategy of adaptation to a liberalized global economy. However, the defensive approach to foreign trade and the economic interventionism of industrial policy are anathema to traditional articulations of neoliberalism. Likewise, developmentalist politics cannot be reduced to redistributive and regulatory policies, the traditional forms of intervention in the economy that are associated with social liberalism. Thus, I suggest that social liberalism, neoliberalism, and developmentalism should be thought of as analytically distinct categories that describe underlying political ideologies. However, specific legislative reforms and public policies are often compromise formations in which the elements of different ideal types are evident.

The political field in the United States is also characterized by marginalized, heterodox ideologies such as socialism, localism, and bioregionalism. There is only one openly socialist senator (in the sense of defending public ownership of economic enterprises and advocating its extension to industries such as health care), and the only significant socialist presidential candidate in recent history was Barry Commoner of the Citizens Party, who ran in 1980. However, in the field of energy policy there is an enduring legacy of public ownership of electricity generation at the federal, state, and city government levels. There is also increasing support for "localism," a political ideology that supports local ownership in the form of independent small businesses, family farms, local nonprofit organizations, and local government enterprises. Localist approaches to policy have also figured in attempts to develop community-based renewable energy. Like localists, bioregionalists encourage the consumption of local foods and materials, but they also advocate for policies that adapt local economies and political systems to regional ecologies.

Developmentalism is situated in this field of political ideologies as an alternative within the political mainstream. It is in the mainstream because it maintains the assumption that the fundamental unit of the global economy is the large corporation, but it departs from the consensus of social liberalism and neoliberalism by adopting a relatively skeptical and more defensive stance toward further trade liberalization and by assuming that an invigorated and coherent industrial policy is needed. Trade liberalization is the doxa of social liberalism and neoliberalism that developmentalism ruptures. At the end of World War II, many political leaders believed that high levels of trade protectionism had not only worsened the trajectory of the Great Depression but also facilitated the war that followed. Furthermore, because the United States was the only large manufacturing economy to remain intact at the end of the war, it could benefit enormously from more open markets for its goods and capital. Since the formation of the General Agreement on Trade and Tariffs in 1948, eight rounds of international negotiations have resulted in many tariff reductions and in a reduction in related nontariff barriers to trade. This is not to say that all industries were open to liberalization. For example, agriculture was mostly excluded from trade negotiations until the Uruguay Round of 1986–1993, in which the United States made some concessions, and the Doha Round of trade negotiations, which began in 2001, floundered on issues related to agriculture. Although some industries have been highly resistant to liberalization, in the United States there has been general support for trade liberalization across the partisan divide.

During the early phases of postwar trade liberalization, the focus was on agreements among developed countries. Less developed countries were allowed to pursue a developmentalist path that included trade barriers, currency devaluation, capital controls, export subsidies, and other forms of support for local industries. Wealthy nations tolerated the developmentalist policies partly because of Cold War rivalry and partly because it was necessary for the West to offer an alternative to both communism and the colonial relationships of the past. However, the economic crisis of the 1970s and the mobilization of less developed countries in favor of a new economic order caused the United States to push the less developed countries to abandon developmentalist policies. With respect to world trade, during the 1980s the United States and other developed countries reversed the tolerance that they had shown toward developmentalist policies and extended the vision of a liberalized global economy to less developed countries. As the communist alternative waned, the West was free to entice and push less developed countries toward greater trade liberalization.[7]

While the United States was pushing newly industrializing countries to open up their markets, it was beginning to institute developmentalist policies at home. The long-term trend of the liberalization of the global economy resulted in a double pincer effect on American manufacturing. The renaissance of industry in Europe and Japan created the first set of pressures; the growth of exports from newly industrialized countries created the second. The US government intervened to protect crucial domestic industries, such as steel and automobile manufacturing, but the broader strategy of the US was to climb up the ladder of technological complexity by substituting high-tech manufacturing for labor-intensive manufacturing. To support the high-tech export strategy, the US pushed for a global intellectual property regime that would protect its high-tech companies while opening up markets for high-tech exports. The liberalization of markets in developing countries that had been behind protectionist curtains improved the profitability of multinational manufacturing companies, which were able to relocate manufacturing to low-wage countries and to increase their sales in those countries.

For American workers, especially those who in unionized manufacturing jobs, the effects of globalization were generally negative. Per capita income in the United States continued to grow after 1970, but real wages for working people and the poor remained stagnant, and in some categories they even declined. As the economists Michael Spence and Sandile Hlatshwayo argue, the American economy became divided into two large groups. In the tradable sectors of globally oriented industries (such as high-tech export industries), wages increased but job growth was limited. In the "nontradable" sectors of retail, health care, and government services, there was job growth but wage stagnation. Overall, inequality increased within the United States.[8]

Although the benefits of trade are intuitive and are mastered even by children who exchange cards and sandwiches, the uneven distribution of those benefits are less intuitive. In the United States the average hourly wage for a nonsupervisory employee in the private sector has been stagnant for decades. In 1964 it was the equivalent of $17.57 per hour in 2008 dollars. By 2008 it was $18.08. For households that earned the much lower minimum wage, the real minimum wage peaked in 1968. At the lower end of the income pyramid, there was either stagnation in wages or a decline in real wages, despite the fact that gross domestic product increased significantly even after adjustment for inflation. Even professional, middle-class heads of households with advanced educations have been unable to achieve the standard of living of their working-class parents, and many people who would like to have a permanent full-time job with benefits have been forced into the temporary workforce. The combination of stagnant wages and the higher expenditures associated with the transition to households with two wage earners has led to higher levels of debt for American households. In 1970 household debt was $500 billion (50 percent of the gross domestic product); in 2007 it was $13.8 trillion (100 percent). The statistics on the declining relative position of at least the lower quintiles of American households dramatize the broad economic shift that has occurred in the American economy since World War II.[9]

By the early years of the twenty-first century, American workers showed increasing skepticism when presented with the proposition that further trade liberalization would benefit them. Although they benefited from lower prices on consumer goods, relatively few workers were able to get retrained and find positions in the export-oriented jobs in the high-tech industries. There were not enough high-tech jobs, and often the workers lacked both the life skills and the technical skills necessary to make the transition. More generally, the liberalized trade regime had allowed China and other geopolitical rivals to climb up the ladder of technological complexity to displace even high-tech jobs such as computer and photovoltaic manufacturing. In the process, China had changed from a backward agrarian country to a global economic superpower with increasing global political influence. Opinion polls have documented the changing perception that trade liberalization has hurt American workers. In 1999 about 30 percent of Americans believed that free trade had hurt the country overall. By 2007 the percentage had grown to 46, and by 2010 it had increased to 53. When the question was phrased somewhat differently ("Have free-trade agreements cost Americans jobs?"), 69 percent of Americans agreed in 2010. Furthermore, opposition to free trade extended across the political spectrum. Among self-identified supporters of the Tea Party movement in 2010, 61 percent thought free trade had hurt the country; among union members, the percentage was 65. The opposition also varies considerably by trading partner. For example, 76 percent of Americans thought increased trade with Canada was good for the United States; only 41 percent thought the same for China.[10]

As the polls indicate, the economic pressures on many American households have cut across the traditional political divide between left and right, a phenomenon that suggests the need for thinking about the political field in a way that also crosses the traditional division between the redistributive and interventionist politics of social liberalism and the anti-regulatory, market-oriented politics of neoliberalism. The term "developmentalism" is intended to capture this emergent phenomenon in American politics and also to draw attention to its similarities to policies pursued by less developed countries. Whereas a national and global economy anchored by large corporations and ever lowering trade barriers has been an underlying area of agreement for both social liberals and neoliberals, the relative decline of the United States in the global economy and the relative stagnation of working-class wages in the US have led some political leaders to advocate a more defensive approach to trade and a more proactive approach to industrial development.

The change is not a temporary response to the global financial crisis that began in 2008 and the high unemployment rates that followed. Rather, it is an adaptation to a general historical shift in the core of the global economy away from the United States toward Asia, especially China. In the long term (50–100 years), the increasing prominence of policies and political positions that are characterized by developmentalism may not be the end of the political story; in other words, one can still envision a transition toward one of the subordinate positions in the political field, such as localism or bioregionalism. However, in the short term (the early twenty-first century), the declining relative position of the United States will be accompanied by an increasing shift toward developmentalist politics and policies.[11]

Developmentalism is an ideology, connected with research fields in the social sciences, that attempts to nail global capital in place to obtain local benefit. Trade restrictions, trade complaints, domestic-content provisions, local procurement preferences, domestic subsidies, regulations tilted against foreign competition, and currency devaluation are among the policy instruments of developmentalism. Often the policies are associated with import substitution, by which domestic energy, such as biofuels and electrical power for vehicles, replace imports such as foreign oil. Because protectionism and import substitution raise the question of which industries should be protected and developed, there is a close connection between developmentalism and an invigorated industrial policy in the sense of industry-specific (even firm-specific) support from government. Developmentalist policies are often associated with the project of building regional industrial clusters, which create local companies and attract nonlocal ones to a regional economy. The regional clusters often have one foot in the global economy and one in the local economy; that is, there are government policies that stimulate local demand for the products of the regional clusters just as other policies help the companies to sell their products in global markets. The phrase "developmentalist liberalism" is intended to capture this Janus-faced quality of American developmentalism. Although developmentalism can take a protectionist form, it can also take a more open form in which there is acceptance of the political mainstream of a liberalized global trade regime, but there is still a defensive approach to further trade liberalization and to the problems of enforcement of existing agreements.

Historical Background

To understand the re-emergence of developmentalist politics in the United States, it is helpful to have a basic understanding of their history. Developmentalism as an industrial and trade policy dates back to the mercantilism of early modern Europe, which enabled England to strengthen its position relative to European competitors and France to improve its political and economic position. Mercantilist policies often improved internal trade (for example, by building roads and canals) while also seeking favorable terms of trade that protected domestic industries deemed crucial for national prosperity. In a sense, mercantilist governments engaged in both import-substituting industrialization and industrial policy in order to accumulate wealth. Although foreign trade involved relations with other mercantilist states, mercantilist governments also sought colonial relationships that resulted in favorable terms of trade, especially for raw materials that could be obtained at low cost in exchange for manufactured goods.[12]

With the gradual dissolution of the mercantilist order, economic thinking slowly began to embrace free-trade arguments. The economist Ha-Joon Chang argues that the British government didn't support free trade until the middle of the nineteenth century, when it dominated world trade. In that situation, free trade became desirable for Britain because it encouraged the flow of raw materials to the imperial center and opened foreign markets to the more valuable manufactured exports made in Britain. Chang describes the strategy as "kicking away the ladder": a country opposes free trade until its domestic industry is strong enough to withstand foreign competition, then embraces free trade in order to gain access to foreign markets and prevent other countries from using tariff barriers to build up competing industries.[13]

Chang further argues that the United States followed the British pattern of first embracing mercantilism and then shifting to free trade. The first secretary of the treasury, Alexander Hamilton, understood the arguments of Adam Smith and other free-trade liberals but rejected them in favor of protectionist policies. Hamilton may have been the first to use the now familiar argument that tariffs were needed to protect infant industries. In his "Report on the Subject of Manufactures," Hamilton argued that the federal government should provide tariff protections and subsidies for domestic industry, tariff reductions for raw materials, infrastructure and patent protections, and other support for domestic industry, at least until it grew robust enough to compete with British and other European imports. Hamilton also attempted to establish what could be called the country's first industrial development corporation: the Society for Establishing Useful Manufactures, which founded the New Jersey city now called Paterson. Although the project failed after a financial crisis affected its financing, it was the first American model of government-supported economic development. Hamilton also advocated government support of industry through other policies, including the construction of infrastructure, funding from a national bank, and even the use of public debt to finance development.[14]

Hamilton's approach had its critics, notably Thomas Jefferson. Political leaders from the Southern states advocated free trade because they benefited from the exchange of agricultural exports for manufactured imports from Europe. In contrast, the Northern states supported trade restrictions in order to protect domestic industry from lower-priced imports from Europe and to capture the South as a market for manufactured goods. After the War of 1812, inexpensive manufactured goods from Britain flooded the country and undermined American manufacturing. In response, Congress approved the Tariff of 1816, the explicit goal of which was to protect domestic industry rather than to generae revenue. However, the tariff was not high enough to protect American industry, and the subsequent increases in protection (especially the Tariff of 1828, known as the "Tariff of Abominations," which raised duties to 62 percent) were highly unpopular in the South. Although Congress reduced the tariff in 1832, the reduction was not enough to mollify the Southern states. The deep tensions between the Middle Atlantic States and the South, with the New England states eventually siding with the industrialized North, led to the nullification crisis and eventually to the Civil War. During that war, when the Northern states no longer had a Southern delegation in Congress to oppose additional protectionism, Congress raised tariffs to new heights. In this respect, Hamiltonian mercantilism was not instituted completely until after the Civil War, when national policies favored manufacturing industries and development based on continental expansion and the railroads. As the economist Michael Hudson has shown, protectionist thought also dominated the profession of economics in the United States, and it remained the leading school of thought in the early years of the twentieth century.[15]

If the federal government had implemented a policy of free trade in the nineteenth century, the United States could have had a relatively underdeveloped, agrarian economy into the twentieth century. The North would have looked like much of Latin America or the American South during the 1930s and the 1940s, and the country as a whole would have been vulnerable to foreign invasion. Instead, by the time of World War I the US had achieved a position of global economic strength with an export-oriented industrial economy. In that situation, Hudson argues, the US increasingly adopted a policy more in line with the free-trade economics of Britain, and advocates of a liberalized approach to world trade gained credibility in the economics profession and at universities. As Chang argues, after World War II the US emerged as the world's dominant economy, and, like Britain in the nineteenth century, it could afford to "kick away the ladder" of import-substituting industrialization. Economists and policy makers who supported the new, liberalized global order saw the Smoot-Hawley Tariff Act and the Buy America Act as examples of misguided policies that made the Great Depression worse by leading to a collapse in world trade. Although the arguments for and against Smoot-Hawley remain controversial, the idea that foreign trade could reduce the likelihood of war had, and still has, tremendous acceptance among political leaders across the political spectrum. Furthermore, with Europe and Japan devastated from the war, the US had little foreign competition in manufacturing.[16]

After World War II, policies associated with Hamiltonian developmentalism could still be found among less developed countries. Some countries didn't undergo trade liberalization until after 1980, when debt-restructuring packages from the International Monetary Fund required liberalization in return for credit. In addition to the stick of the International Monetary Fund, there was the carrot of access to foreign markets. To maximize the benefits and minimize the risks, countries had to join free-trade agreements while figuring out ways to protect their domestic industries in ways that that would not trigger trade retaliation. The result was often the mixed politics of developmentalist liberalism—that is, of joining trade agreements while continuing to provide as much protection for domestic industry as was possible.

Chang argues that countries that have successfully industrialized since World War II (including his home country, South Korea) did so with heavy government support and protection of domestic industries even as they gained access to foreign markets. Other scholars have noted the other side of the coin: for many countries, the experience with free trade has been far from beneficial. For example, the sociologist Alejandro Portes has shown that Latin American countries were, in many ways, better off during the years of import-substituting industrialization than they were after trade liberalization and privatization. As Chang argues, the pathway to successful development requires negotiating access to foreign markets without allowing the destruction of domestic industry, but countries that were forced to accept structural adjustment programs were often required to sacrifice local industrial development.[17]

The policies of trade liberalization that the United States found so beneficial to its interests at the end of World War II—policies that American and European policy makers also believed would be beneficial to global peace and prosperity—have enabled other countries to climb up the ladder of technological complexity, industrial capacity, and economic power. Increasingly, other countries have entered even the highest of high-tech industries, and they have often protected their industries through a variety of developmentalist measures. In this historical context of relative decline for the United States, trade and industrial policy becomes much less consensual than during the period of the Pax Americana. Increasing numbers of Americans don't see a benefit in further trade liberalization, and the stage is set for support for a more defensive approach to the economy that has similarities to the economic policy of the nineteenth century. Although the financial crisis of 2008 precipitated short-term reactions to the credibility of neoliberalism, the long-term change in the global economy is likely to trigger a slow shift in the underlying positions of ideologies in the political field. The confluence of the increasing demand for limited oil supplies and the growing evidence for global climate change has made the policy fields governing green energy a central site for the negotiation of a shift in underlying political ideologies.

Conceptual Framework I: Transition Theory

The conceptual framework used to study the relationship between developmentalism and the green energy transition in the United States involves a synthesis of transition theory and social fields theory. The change to a more sustainable economy requires reshaping the technological basis of the economy, including energy, buildings, and transportation. As a result, the sociology of technology is an important resource for understanding the long-term transition. From the sociology of technology, the primary starting point for this study is Thomas Hughes's work on technological systems—that is, large systems that evolve over the course of decades and that link physical artifacts, natural resources, scientific research, industrial organizations, consumers, workers, and government regulations. A prominent example that Hughes used was the emergence and growth of the electricity system in the US.[18]

Hughes's model of the growth and development of large technological systems relied on a sequencing approach that moved from invention to development, innovation, and consolidation. Hughes argued that systems acquire momentum as they grow, a concept that has similarities to path dependency and lock-in. However, Hughes also argued that technological systems can encounter reverse salients—that is, obstacles that must be overcome in order for the system to expand. Furthermore, large technological systems respond to different environments, which they also shape, and thus comparative analysis can reveal different technological "styles."[19]

Hughes focused primarily on the emergence and the development of technological systems, rather than on "transitions" from one system to another. Transitions are fundamental changes, often lasting several decades, in a sociotechnical system and in the regime or rules that govern it. Relevant examples include the shift from household and workplace power based on human muscles and kerosene to electrical power, the change in the heating of buildings from coal to electricity and natural gas, and the change from horse-drawn vehicles and steam-powered railroads to transportation powered by internal-combustion engines. The projected transition to green energy discussed in this book involves a change in all three systems (electrical systems, heating and cooling of buildings, and transportation) away from carbon-intensive sources of energy. Because new technological systems displace old ones, transitions involve winners and losers. Makers of horse harnesses and carriages didn't fare well in the transition to automobiles, and producers of fossil fuels will not fare well in the green transition in the long term. As a result, there are conflicts among technologies, firms, research programs, government regulators, users, and advocacy groups that are associated with new and old technologies. Often the design distinctions and definitional boundaries that separate new and old are themselves at stake in the conflicts, and agents in mediating positions sometimes create hybrid designs to reconcile difference.[20]

One of the first approaches to the study of the dynamics of change in technological systems was evolutionary; it emphasized variation of technology through innovation and selection by firms based on market conditions and regulatory environments. A group of mostly Dutch scholars has built on the evolutionary approaches and on the work of Hughes and other technology studies researchers to develop a multi-level analysis that breaks down the transition into changes of niches, regimes, and landscapes. Niches are entrepreneurial firms and other organizations in which new technologies are incubated; sociotechnical regimes are the rules that govern the relations between agents and stabilized sociotechnical systems (the tangible elements of large technological systems); landscapes are the "wider exogenous environment," including broad changes in cultural practices, demography, and policy preferences (Geels 2005: 451). The opportunity structure at the landscape level and the strategic actions of advocates and opponents at the niche level are the starting points of a trajectory that enables a niche to become a new regime.[21]

In the study of technology, transition theory has two fundamental advantages over alternative frameworks that emphasize agency-based approaches and microsocial negotiation. First, it places the multi-decade study of large-scale technological change at the center of attention. The framework can provide a basis for encouraging policy makers and industrial organizations to think about technological innovation in much broader terms than they often do. Indeed, in the Netherlands and in other European countries, transition studies provide the basis for policy planning and intervention. Second, transition theory includes macrosocial change as a dimension of analysis, an approach that is broadly consistent with a political sociological approach to science and technology. Although the second dimension is undertheorized, it is present in the conceptual framework.[22]

Some work based on transition theory has already addressed sustainability transitions. The STS scholars Adrian Smith and Rob Raven, who study green energy transitions and policy interventions, argue that a "protective space" is essential for the successful nurturing and shielding of new energy technologies that would otherwise not survive in mainstream energy markets. Smith and Raven break down the concept of niche protection into government regulation, rule exemption, research, location assistance, demand support, trade protection, subsidies, and general political support. Their approach parallels the broader argument in economic development studies that industries in their infancy require support and protection from government. This book will build on their insights by situating such strategies in the broader context of industrial policy and developmentalism.[23]

Another way that this book will build on and extend transition studies is by providing a more comprehensive approach to how sociotechnical systems change. Transition studies have indicated that the growth of niches into regimes is not the only way that sociotechnical regimes and systems change. For example, they may change by hybridization with other regimes, reconfiguration of the existing regime in response to landscape changes, and internal evolution and innovation. There is also general recognition that changes in sociotechnical systems have a dynamic interaction with changes in macrosocial "landscapes." However, the concept of the landscape is very broad and requires disaggregation. It includes both large scale (that is, national or international scale of organizations and events) and long time frames (that is, long-term trends), but the two dimensions don't always coincide. More generally, the framework tends to view societal change from a systems theoretical perspective, which can lead research to underemphasize agency, meaning (understood broadly to include frames and political ideologies), and political conflict.[24]

To some degree the shortcomings are recognized in the transition studies literature. For example, the STS scholar Frank Geels, one of the leading architects of transition theory, has identified the lack of agency and the use of landscape as a residual category as two deficiencies that need to be addressed. With respect to work on sustainability transitions, one corrective to the undertheorized landscape has been to integrate the study of agency and meaning through the analysis of cultural practices associated with technological transitions. For example, the economist René Kemp and the environmental scientist Halina Brown have drawn attention to the study of values, practices, and user behavior associated with greener and more energy-efficient technologies. The social scientists Sabine Hielscher, Gill Seyfang, and Adrian Smith have added to the conversation by showing that community organizations can play a role in encouraging the transition in sustainability practices and values. Their work has also drawn attention to the need to include the study of power and politics in the analysis of landscapes and the dynamics of transitions.[25]

An approach to power that is close to the one that I adopt is found in work on transitions done by the Danish STS scholar Ulrik Jørgensen. His work emphasizes conflicts among "actor worlds" in broader social "arenas." Although not explicitly connected with field sociology, Jørgensen's approach is consistent with the idea that transitions occur in social fields characterized by relations of cooperation and conflict among networks of organizations and other agents. For example, he describes conflicts in Denmark between a community-based, small-scale approach to wind energy and a large-scale approach oriented toward energy supply companies. Conflicts occur between coalitions of agents with unequal power.[26]

In this book, I build on and extend transition theory by making issues of power and conflict between different positions in a policy field much more central. Those issues are especially important for understanding nontransitions. Just as in the scientific field some areas of research are systematically ignored and left undone, so in the technology policy field some types of transitions are systematically blocked. In the United States, green transition policies vary greatly across state governments, scales of government (city, state, federal), and industry-related policy fields (renewable electricity, transportation, buildings). To understand both transition failure and the unevenness of transitions requires a framework that can address the capacity of coalitions to mobilize successfully in some cases and not in others. The concept of stability, with its associations of path dependence and lock-in, provides some analytical leverage; however, to address political power in a systematic way, this book builds on the ongoing extensions and refinements of transition theory by suggesting the value of social field analysis in the study of transitions.

Conceptual Framework II: Field Theory

Social field analysis provides a way to bring together the study of changes in social structure, agency, and meaning in one framework. Social fields are relatively autonomous but interrelated social spaces in which differentially positioned agents engage in relations of conflict and cooperation in the pursuit of their goals and expression of their conscious and unconscious dispositions and ideologies. Within a field, agents form heterogeneous networks that characterize the structure of positions within a field and also link agents across fields. A network of agents in turn can be characterized as having a relatively dominant or subordinate position in a social field based on the level of capital held by the agents associated with it. Fields also generate and allocate specific types of capital that are associated with their partial autonomy. Of particular importance for this study is the number of votes that a coalition can muster in a policy field in support of green energy policy proposals. Although financial capital from the economic field has an important influence on voting in legislatures, it is also possible for social movements to mobilize voters as a countervailing force that has agency in the political field as a result of its partial autonomy from wealth.[27]

Field sociology has the great advantage of enabling a balanced approach to the problem of studying culture, structure, and agency, but there are some shortcomings that are corrected in the version of field theory that I have developed. First, the cultural dimension of field theory cannot be anchored entirely in the concept of the habitus. Dispositions can be studied in a biographical sense (as a personal habitus) and a collective sense (a habitus of a field), but underlying the dispositions are broader cultural currents, such as ideologies, that cut across agents and fields. By studying the deeper level of underlying ideologies, it is also possible to develop a picture of long-term tectonic shifts in fields.[28]

Within green policy fields, political ideologies are associated with different types of policy interventions: social liberalism with social inequality issues that are found especially in urban green corps and justice-oriented weatherization programs, neoliberalism with the creation of green markets and the removal of regulatory barriers to market development for green energy, localism with rooftop solar owned by residents and other forms of community-oriented energy, socialism with municipal control of energy generation and transmission, and developmentalism with support for local and domestic green businesses via trade and industrial policy. Specific policies and the political persuasions of specific actors are often mixes of different ideological streams, and the political position of an ideological stream in a field (as relatively dominant or subordinate) varies with political scale, geography, and policy arena. Thus, the cultural dimension of the version of field analysis used here is located more in the identification of underlying ideologies than in the study of the habitus of individuals and fields.[29]

A second departure from Bourdieu's approach to social fields is to place more emphasis on how fields change. Here, transition theory provides a helpful correction to the focus on reproduction that is commonplace in field theory. Social fields can be studied at varying levels of scale (from organizational and urban scale to national or international scale) and over shorter and longer time periods. As a result, the perspective of multiple scales and durations that transition theory brings to social studies of technological change can be maintained, but it can be shifted into a framework that more directly views those changes as the result of relations of conflict and cooperation in specific social fields. Furthermore, as I have shown elsewhere, there is a tendency for large-scale sociotechnical systems and large corporations to absorb changes by first transforming the design of the systems (e.g., by changing small off-grid solar photovoltaics into large-scale solar farms) and incorporating the organizations (e.g., buying up small firms and absorbing them into large corporations). Thus, in addition to viewing transitions in terms of the niche-to-regime shift or the hybridization of regimes, it is also possible to view them in terms of a long-term process of incorporation and transformation of the alternative pathways.[30]

In the case of the transition of sociotechnical systems associated with energy production and consumption, autonomous market developments don't govern the pace of change. Rather, these heavily regulated sociotechnical systems change largely as a result of the outcomes of policy decisions. Understanding how the agents gain, lose, and exercise power in the political field requires attention not only to the financial and institutional resources that they can accumulate and spend but also to how they frame issues and link them to underlying ideological currents.

This book will focus on the field of public policies because of the capacity of policies to shape the design, pace, and scale of green energy transitions. Within the policy field, the focus will be on three industrial policy sectors (electricity, buildings, and transportation) and three levels of government (federal, state, and local). Thus, transitions are theorized as occurring across multiple fields at different scales, an approach that directly places the problem of uneven transitions at the center of the analytical framework.

The political sociology of the state generally recognizes that in modern capitalist societies government is neither a neutral arbiter of coeval interest groups nor an apparatus of the ruling class. Rather, the state itself is a complex web of fields in which both state and nonstate agents engage in relations of cooperation and conflict to achieve policy goals. In modern industrial societies, the most powerful agents in the policy fields that establish the fundamental parameters of sociotechnical regimes are generally coalitions of political leaders and large industrial corporations. However, because policy fields are partially autonomous social arenas, and because there are often splits among relevant industries (for example, fossil fuel corporations versus green energy companies and diversified industrial corporations such as General Electric), a simplistic concept of a single ruling elite or class can obfuscate awareness of political opportunities opened by divisions among the powerful. Furthermore, in societies in which elections and public policies must be legitimized on the basis of their relationship to the general good, coalitions of less powerful agents can play a significant role in policy outcomes. In some cases, the coalitions can affect political opportunity structures by reframing systemic crises, exploiting divisions within elites, and enrolling other agents located in subordinate positions in the field. With respect to the mixed pace of reform of both partial transition and partial nontransition in the energy system in the United States, the process of long-term change is shaped by unstable and shifting conflicts between, on the one hand, the fossil fuel industries in coalition with conservative political leaders and multinational capital, and, on the other hand, green coalitions of business, environmental, labor, and other groups. The historical outcome is far from predetermined; rather, it is contingent on the interaction of agents in social fields.[31]

At the heart of the green transition coalitions are labor and environmental movements. The once tense relationship between the two movements has given way to a new emphasis on creating green jobs. Researchers who have studied "blue-green" (meaning labor-environmental) coalitions have generally acknowledged that there are differences in habitus that often make labor-environmental coalitions difficult to build and maintain. The organizer and scholar Fred Rose emphasized differences in class culture, and the sociologists Kenneth Gould, Tammy Lewis, and J. Timmons Roberts emphasized class divisions both within the environmental movement (between an ecological and environmental justice orientation) and between the environmental and labor movements. However, Rose and the sociologists Brian Mayer and Brian Obach also drew attention to bridge brokers who could cross organizational and class divisions, and Obach showed that common interests also could serve as a basis for building bridges. In a comparative study of the coalition-building efforts of the Canadian Auto Workers and the United Steelworkers for green jobs policies, the geographer James Nugent also noted that it is necessary to break down broad concepts such as "labor" and "environmentalists" in order to look at coalitions among specific unions and environmental organizations.[32]

Although the labor-environmental coalitions vary by organization and are subject to tensions, several leading unions and environmental groups in the United States have reframed energy and environmental policy from an emphasis on purely environmental goals—reducing pollution, greenhouse gases, toxic exposure, habitat destruction, and so on—to a combination of environmental and economic development goals: the "green jobs" frame. The reframing has helped to enable the labor and environmental coalition to connect with other constituencies. Anti-poverty groups and community development groups have seen potential in the "green jobs" frame as a way of bringing both jobs and housing assistance to the country's poor through programs to retrofit buildings. Furthermore, businesses in green energy industries such as solar and wind, as well as businesses that have articulated sustainability targets as part of their strategic plans, such as in the transportation and consumer products industries, have come to see part of what they do as creating and providing green jobs. The frame of job creation also responds to broad anxieties about job security and job quality that have grown due to outsourcing and global financial instability. The green jobs frame has proved quite successful, particularly in state and city governments dominated by the Democratic Party. Its fate at the national level is less clear.

In summary, the study of the policy fields in which the green energy transition is being forged requires the extension of previous work on blue-green coalitions by including reference to broader alliances, described here as "green transition coalitions," that have emerged in support of green jobs and green industrial development. Although the green transition coalitions have a social-movement component, they are also aligned with the more traditional networks of economic development advocates, green energy businesses, and other businesses that have decided to engage in a transition toward greener products and practices. The coalitions are quite broad and politically powerful, but they are also precarious. There is more agreement about the "anti" (what we should be moving away from) than about the "pro" (the details of defining what we should be moving toward). Owing in part to internal disagreements and in part to resistance from the fossil fuel industry, the outcome of green energy policy in the United States has been uneven. One can look at achievements such as the development of renewable electricity standards in 29 states (a mandate that a certain percentage of energy be generated from renewable sources) and greenhouse gas regulations in the Northeast and California as signs of success, or one can look at them as ongoing evidence that anti-green forces continue to block broad and significant reform. The literature of environmental sociology is sharply divided on this "glass half-full or half-empty" issue. Whereas advocates of ecological modernization theory argue that the transition is significant and is moving forward, advocates of treadmill of production theory argue that the changes so far have been both economically and environmentally insignificant. The approach taken here builds on both sets of arguments by exploring the unevenness of green transition policies. As a result, the question of the depth and significance of the green energy transition is understood as an empirical question that must attend to variation in policies and politics over time. A glass that appears half-full or half-empty depending on one's theoretical framework changes into many glasses, some of which are more full than others.[33]

The analysis of the green transition through the lens of specific policy fields makes it possible to explore the evidence for and against underlying shifts in political culture, such as the thesis that political ideology in United States is undergoing a change toward developmentalism. Specific policy outcomes are compromise formations in highly contested fields, and consequently it is not possible to think about underlying ideological changes as totalizing regimes that can be periodized into a social-liberal period, a neoliberal period, and a developmentalist period. Rather, there is a relative shift of the position of ideologies in the policy field in favor of developmentalism.

Green, Clean, and Issues of Terminology

Because the terminology used in green energy and green jobs policy fields is highly charged politically, it is necessary to provide a brief discussion of how the terms will be used. The phrase "green transition" will refer to the long-term change in the technological basis of the global economy that progressively reduces the environmental impact of human societies. There are two fundamental dimensions: the greening of technology and the reduction of the effects of human consumption on the global ecosystem. The end point of a completed green transition is a reorientation of human societies to a relationship with the global ecosystem understood as "sustainable." The technological transition entails economic and political transformation that will reduce the built-in tendencies of unregulated markets to externalize environmental effects and to engage in growth without regard to environmental implications. The starting points include the incremental policies at various levels of government that will be discussed in detail in this book. It should be emphasized that this book is discussing the starting points of a long-term green transition, and the record of failed political will to enact policies suggests that the green transition is occurring too slowly to stave off the catastrophic collapse of human societies. Forty years have passed since the publication of *The Limits to Growth*, which warned of a possible collapse in the twenty-first century, yet the United States and some other large countries have opted for continued growth in consumption and emissions.[34]

There are major environmental problems on many fronts, including food and water management, ecosystem and habitat destruction, and toxic chemicals in the biosphere. This book focuses only on the energy dimension, which will be termed "the green energy transition" as a subset of the broader green transition. Because the effects of climate change occur over a long period time, it is difficult to convince governments, consumers, and businesses to trade short-term sacrifices for the security of future generations. For better or worse, environmental policy has increasingly been reframed in terms that constituencies do care about in the short term: job security and business development. Thus, the green energy transition has also become a green jobs and green industry transition.

Many related terms ("alternative," "renewable," "sustainable," "green," "clean, "advanced") have been used to describe the energy aspects of the broader green transition, and advocates of one term will tend to view other terms unfavorably. Those aligned most closely with the fossil fuel industry favor "advanced" or "clean" in order to include energy-efficient forms of fossil fuels. Among people associated more with environmentalist politics, the term "renewable energy" is used more frequently, and "sustainable" or "alternative" suggest a potentially broader frame than energy technology. I use "green" as an overarching term, because it is often used generally in a contrastive sense as "greener" than a comparison technology. "Clean" is often used as another umbrella term, and it will be used occasionally here, generally in the context of green technologies that include efficient forms of fossil fuels.

The methodological strategy of using "green" or "clean" in the broadest possible sense should not be interpreted as the absence of a critical perspective. Rather, the terms are understood more in an anthropological sense, as a category used by agents in a policy field. Advocates of hybrid vehicles laud them as green even if they deflect attention from public transportation, transit-oriented development, and the continued use of petroleum; advocates of natural gas claim that it is a cleaner alternative to coal-burning electricity plants or petroleum-powered vehicles; and the coal industry suggests that there are forms of clean coal based on cogeneration (combined heat and power), gasification (conversion of coal to synthesis gas before burning), and carbon sequestration (capturing carbon dioxide emissions and burying them). Likewise, the nuclear energy industry claims that nuclear energy is clean energy because it emits low levels of greenhouse gases, and the biofuels industry argues that the energy is green because carbon emissions from fuel are recaptured in future crops.

If "green" and "clean" are defined to mean carbon reduction relative to some alternative, the opportunities to reframe innovative existing energy technologies as clean or green are indeed open. However, to many environmentalists and environmental scientists the deficiencies associated with fossil fuels, nuclear energy, and biofuels are so great that it is inaccurate to refer to them as green or clean. Their arguments also depend on issues other than carbon emissions, such as mountaintop removal, groundwater pollution, radiation contamination, and the degradation of ecosystems and water resources needed for biofuels production. However, if one's goal is to develop the sociology of the unevenness of the green transition, a normative perspective that automatically dismisses one set of technologies would make it impossible to understand the political conflicts and coalitions that make possible the unevenness that one intends to study. Thus, the approach adopted here is to use the term "green" in the widest sense rather than impose an *a priori* limit on its scope, but also to be attendant to the shades of green that are embedded in different policy directions. Because policy fields are characterized by definitional struggles, or "object conflicts," over what is or is not green, the *a priori* rejection of some technologies as green or clean would limit the capacity of a social scientist to understand and explain those conflicts.[35]

The politics of the green transition involve not only drawing a boundary between what is and is not green but also interpreting some forms of green policy and technology as deeper or lighter shades of green. This issue will be discussed in more detail in chapter 3, but a few introductory remarks are necessary. The deeper forms of green energy focus on the overall reduction in the aggregate environmental impact. The ecological economist Herman Daly systematized this approach by defining sustainability on the basis of the relationship between society and the ecosystem (with variable scale that could include a global level of analysis). Daly argued that the world or a society is sustainable if its use of ecosystem resources is less than the capacity of the ecosystem to replenish consumed resources (or to supply substitutions) and if the environmental "sinks" such as pollution and waste are less than the capacity of the ecosystem to process them. In the metaphor of banking developed by the sociologists Allan Schnaiberg and Kenneth Gould, a society or the global society is sustainable if its "withdrawals" from the ecosystem and "deposits" into it don't overwhelm the capacity of the system to maintain stability. Because in many ways the Earth's human population has exceeded its global carrying capacity, a reduction in the overall ecological effects of human activity is necessary.[36]

One can combine the aggregate reduction approach to include social considerations as well. The concern with equity is expressed in the more common definition of sustainability that appears in the report of the World Commission on Environment and Development (more commonly known as the Brundtland Report), which involves the twin goals of meeting the needs of present generations without sacrificing those of future generations. The Brundtland approach is at least partially consistent with the Daly approach, because meeting long-term needs would require that the Daly criteria apply. Furthermore, the Daly criteria help to avoid approaches to sustainability that result in high local achievements that are based on the "offshoring" of environmental effects. For example, shipping toxic waste to other countries may make the exporting country appear to have achieved sustainability goals, but the environmental effects have been shifted geographically rather than reduced. However, there is also a tension between the two approaches, because current "needs" may be so extensive that it is impossible to achieve the kind of ecosystem balance that Daly's definition requires without a severe collapse in human population, its levels of consumption, or both.[37]

Although there are many pathways toward the goal of meeting the needs of future generations, most are not very acceptable politically. Political and economic organizations are based on a growth logic (government revenues, health-care spending, gross domestic product, corporate revenues and profits) that would require a revolutionary restructuring of social organization to end economic growth. A more realistic solution is to decouple economic growth from growth in ecological impact, and the only effective means of decoupling is a technological transition. As the economist Peter Victor has shown, achieving what Daly calls a steady-state economy does not necessarily require degrowth or zero growth in per capita gross domestic product. In fact, high economic growth in industries that reduce net carbon imprint is necessary in order to achieve a rapid transition. At the same time, attractive investments that have a negative environmental impact must be restricted.[38]

Because there is political resistance to a rapid, thorough, and deep form of the green energy transition, it has taken place slowly and unevenly. The northern European countries have been leaders in pioneering the policies and sociotechnical systems of the green energy transition, and the United States has often innovated with technologies but not with policies. Although the overall pace of the transition at a global level probably is not going to be sufficient to mitigate the worst environmental effects of industrial civilization, a holistic perspective makes it possible to understand that, even though the current pace of the transition toward low-carbon energy is slower than necessary from the perspective of climate change, the growth of green industries has important political ramifications. The growth of new green industries and jobs creates economic and political support within the private sector that can counterbalance the opposition to a green energy transition from coalitions supported by the fossil fuel industries.

Thus, there are important feedback loops between the development of political constituencies that support policies that would deepen the green transition and the growth of green industries, even if the industries appear to be incremental and ineffective from a global ecosystems perspective. At the same time, the incremental policies associated with the lighter shades of green policy can be used to co-opt and block more systemic reform. Thus, the starting points and incremental reforms that characterize much of green energy policy in the United States and in many other countries have two contradictory political implications: they develop constituencies to support deepening of the green transitions, and they can serve as fallback measures that reduce the political will for deeper reform.

Methods and Outline

This book employs a strategy of mostly qualitative social science research methods with the goal of explaining policy change and stasis. The analysis of conference presentations, semi-structured interviews, media and policy reports, historical texts and documents, legislative votes, and other sources provides a comprehensive and holistic view in which information obtained from one source can be checked against that obtained from other sources. Above all, the method is comparative and case based; through the comparison of different policies and policy fields, it is possible to build up generalizations. In turn, quantitative data in chapters 7 and 8 make it possible to refine and develop generalizations.

Some of the research in chapters 4 and 5 is based partly on a training project in the summer of 2010 that involved eight graduate student research assistants who studied in detail state and local policies and completed about fifty interviews with policy leaders in governments and non-governmental organizations. The analysis of policies includes my own review of clean energy policies in all fifty states; attendance at dozens of sessions at ten conferences on green jobs, green business, and green energy; and many background conversations with green jobs leaders and advocates. For chapter 6, the research draws on the base of more than thirty case studies discussed in *Localist Movements in a Global Economy* plus attendance at the annual meetings of the Business Alliance for Local Living Economies, talks before many local business groups in the Northeast, interactions with both local and national living economy leaders, and knowledge gained from the experience of co-founding a "local first" organization.[39]

Chapter 1 provides a historical overview of the role of energy in global geopolitics and the declining relative position of the American economy in the global economy. It shows how protectionist measures and aggressive regional economic development policies emerged in response to the changing position of the country in the global economy, and it discusses green energy policy history in the United States up to 2009. Chapter 2 provides a corresponding introduction to the relative power of the fossil fuel industry, the scope of green transition coalitions, and the complexities of defining green jobs.

Part II consists of four chapters that analyze green energy policies from the perspective of the thesis of an emergent ideology of developmentalism. Chapter 3 focuses on federal government policy in the 111th Congress, which met during the Obama administration's first two years, when green jobs ideas and policies bubbled up from the state governments to the federal government level. After the defeat of cap-and-trade legislation in the Senate in 2010 and the election of anti-green Republicans in November of that year, the political opportunity structure for green energy legislation in the federal government closed down. Action then returned to the state and local governments, which are the focus of the next three chapters. Chapter 4 discusses different definitions of green energy policy in three fields (electricity, buildings, and transportation) and how coalitions can be brought together or fragment over the definitional conflicts. The chapter then discusses how state and local governments engage in import-substituting industrialization by developing demand policies, that is, support for consumer demand for green energy products. Chapter 5 provides a complementary analysis of the "supply side" of industrial policy, which state governments have also developed to support green industrial clusters. Chapter 6 explores the parallel set of changes involved in the small-business sector of retail, services, and agriculture. Building on my previous book on localism, the chapter explores the "local living economies" frame and specific policy reforms that link green energy with local ownership. It then discusses the tenuous convergence of the goals of the "local living economy" movement with those of blue-green alliances. In summary, part II provides a broad picture of the convergence of developmentalist and green energy politics in the United States.

Part III of the book is more analytical and explanatory. Chapter 7 explains the unevenness of green transition policies. A qualitative analysis of the pattern of successes and failures reveals that green transition coalitions played a role as catalysts for some legislative reforms, and a quantitative analysis suggests that support for the Democratic Party is closely linked with the comparative success rate of clean energy policies. Chapter 8 continues the analysis by describing the political landscape of green energy policies at the state government level after the 2010 elections. Although the common perception is that green energy reforms were dead, the chapter argues that the situation is much more complicated at the state government level. There were cases of significant reversals of green transition legislation in some states, but other states continued to push ahead with ongoing reforms. To a large degree the pattern was partisan, but the chapter shows interesting cases of moderately green Republican governors and some bipartisanship in state legislatures. Quantitative analysis suggests that bipartisanship is highest for laws that involve low-cost regulatory reforms, such as permitting. In contrast, reforms that opponents can readily interpret as taxes or financial burdens on businesses, such as system benefits charges, tend to trigger partisan disputes. The changes in the political landscape due to the anti-green backlash suggest that green transition policies may increasingly pass through the filter of austerity politics.

The analysis of the politics of the green energy transition in the United States provides the basis for concluding comments of a more general nature, which situate the policies with respect to the broader political and ideological adjustments that are occurring as the United States undergoes a relative decline in economic position in the global economy. Because other countries have aggressively pursued export-oriented industrial policies, American states and to some degree the federal government are forging a piecemeal green industrial policy that combines protectionist and competitiveness approaches to trade. The changes could mean that the green energy transition in the United States is part of a broader ideological and cultural transition away from the neoliberal thought and policies that have dominated the country since the 1970s, but without a return to the redistributive politics of social liberalism.

I

Background

1

Energy, Manufacturing, and the Changing Global Economy

At the end of World War II, the United States possessed more than two-thirds of the world's gold and most of its functioning manufacturing capacity; however, the US had a significant vulnerability. Its demand for oil was outpacing domestic production, and foreign oil was much less expensive than domestic oil. Access to foreign oil had become central in the country's strategy to maintain its position of global hegemony. The sale of oil and other commodities in dollars, the backing of the dollar with the country's huge gold reserves, and the use of military power to control oil supplies ensured that the American dollar was the world's leading reserve currency.[1]

American dominance of global manufacturing and control of foreign oil via neocolonial relationships could not last forever. Almost as soon as World War II ended, oil-exporting countries began to demand a higher share of oil profits. Although the nationalization of Iranian oil in 1950 primarily affected Britain, the United States began to offer its oil partners a higher percentage of profits from oil revenue. Concern with dependence on foreign oil was high enough in the United States that President Dwight Eisenhower launched the first of many government programs aimed at energy independence. In 1958, the Mandatory Oil Import Program imposed import quotas and preferences for Western sources. In some ways, the policy might be viewed as the first step toward developmentalism in the federal government during the postwar period, because it pursued a path of import substitution for the crucial energy source. However, the resulting program drained domestic sources of oil more quickly, increased the country's long-term dependency on oil, and goaded oil producers into organizing the forerunner of the Organization of Petroleum Exporting Countries. The disastrous first energy-independence program was finally ended in 1973, and by that time the US was even more dependent on foreign oil.[2]

The second long-term change that contributed to the decline of postwar American hegemony occurred during the 1960s, when military spending abroad and deficit spending at home contributed to a balance-of-payments deficit and inflation, which in turn led to a decline in the country's gold stock. Rather than cut spending programs, the United States told foreign creditors to hold their balance-of-payment surpluses in treasury bills. American prosperity came to rest on its status as banker to the world; it could pay for foreign goods with treasuries that other countries held as foreign reserves. Even when the US went off the gold standard, in 1971, the dollar didn't collapse. Countries that held dollars as their reserve currency had an interest in maintaining the greenback's value, and they also needed to buy oil and other commodities that cleared in dollars. Likewise, the rise of oil prices during the 1973 OPEC embargo didn't threaten the dollar regime, because the US government would allow OPEC countries to make only limited purchases of American companies with their new wealth. Instead, their oil wealth recirculated through the banks of the US and Europe to less developed countries as petrodollar loans. It was not until the launch of the euro, in 1999, that a credible, large alternative reserve currency emerged. However, with few exceptions, oil remained denominated in dollars even after the launch of the euro. One exception was Saddam Hussein, who shifted the sale of Iraqi oil to euros in 2000, but the sale of oil in dollars was restored after the United States invaded Iraq. Subsequently, Iran and Venezuela successfully shifted to the sale of oil to currencies other than dollars, but the dollar-oil system remained intact for other countries.[3]

The third major feature of the slow decline in the relative hegemony of the American economy also became apparent during the 1970s, when the United States faced increased manufacturing competition from foreign countries in industries such as textiles, shoes, televisions, and steel. In response, a crucial element of developmentalism began to emerge: new protections for selected domestic industries. The Trade Act of 1974 allowed the US to impose import quotas when foreign competition threatened American jobs and industries, and President Gerald Ford, while on a 1975 campaign tour stop at a steel-manufacturing plant in Ohio, approved the first protectionist measure under the act by establishing quotas for specialty steel.[4]

Japan became a central target of American negotiations involving imports of steel, consumer electronics, and automobiles. Under President Ronald Reagan, the US government obtained voluntary trade restrictions from Japan in 1981 for automotive imports. Japanese companies responded to the measure, which lasted until 1994, by setting up manufacturing operations on American soil. Honda built its first US factory in 1982, and by 1990 other Japanese automotive manufacturers had also established factories in the US. During subsequent negotiations for the North American Free Trade Act, concerns resurfaced. American companies worried that foreign automakers would use Mexico as a beachhead for entry into the American market. As a result, the agreement included another protectionist measure: the complex domestic-content requirements known as rules of origin.[5]

The new forms of protectionism (voluntary export restraints and rules of origin) stirred opposition from advocates of free trade. The neoliberal economist Milton Friedman stated that voluntary export restraints made the Smoot-Hawley Act appear to be benign. In a more measured analysis, the political scientist and industrial policy expert William Nester noted that the voluntary restraints effectively increased the cost of Japanese cars to American consumers, who ended up paying the price of the protectionist measure. "A much more sensible policy," he added, "would have been to impose high tariffs on any foreign automobile maker selling more than, say, 100,000 vehicles in the United States. Thus, the enormous profits reaped by the Japanese under [voluntary export restraints] would have gone to the United States Treasury instead." (Nester 1998: 64) Although economists could argue about the means, the end was now established: the American automobile industries and other crucial American industries would not be allowed to die.[6]

In summary, by the 1980s the broad contours of the new American developmentalism were already evident. Trade and financial liberalization opened new opportunities for American multinational corporations and banks, which were able to locate production and investment in low-wage countries and export back goods and profits back to the United States. However, there was a growing backlash against the effects of trade liberalization and globalization. Domestic manufacturers that sold largely to domestic markets faced severe competition from foreign imports, some of which were from foreign subsidiaries of large American multinational corporations or their investment partners. Likewise, workers and especially unionized labor suffered from job loss, insecurity, and displacement. Although the government responded by enacting protectionist measures for some industries, many manufacturing industries were left to wither away. Workers who had lost good manufacturing jobs could seek retraining to enter the high-tech sector or the more highly skilled service sector; otherwise they ended up in low-wage service-sector jobs. Inequality increased.

In effect, the United States had become hoist by its own petard of trade liberalization. The American dream of home ownership and steady employment was eroding into a divided world of wealthy elites who enjoyed the fruits of globalization and workers who had lost jobs, bargaining power, and opportunities for employment stability and advancement. The first suggestions of a response to increasing inequality and erosion of the standard of living were evident in the decisions to protect selected industries deemed too important to lose, such as steel and automotive manufacturing. As other countries grew in competitive capacity, the United States was driven to take a more defensive and proactive stance.

State Governments' Economic Development Policies

At the level of state governments, economic policy was also undergoing a dramatic change from its configuration during the New Deal era. In 1936, Hugh Lawson White became governor of Mississippi in an election in which he aligned himself with President Franklin Roosevelt, and he inaugurated the Balance Industry with Agriculture program, the country's first modern economic development program. Under that program, cities could seek approval from a state government commission to sell municipal bonds for the purpose of building facilities for new businesses. The program battled a constitutional challenge but overcame it by using arguments based on general welfare considerations that were borrowed from judicial justifications for New Deal programs. Although the next governor of Mississippi stopped the Balance Industry with Agriculture program, it was revived in 1944, when the factory expansion that occurred during World War II had made clear to many political leaders that the relatively small investments of government bonds into industrial infrastructure were very successful.[7]

Southerners in the Jeffersonian tradition resented the "socialistic" implications of government ownership of factories and the use of debt to finance economic development, but Southern states soon overcame their hesitation about government and adopted programs similar to that of Mississippi. In 1946 the Southern Industrial Development Council was founded, and by 1962 nine Southern states and twelve other states had industrial bond programs that enabled city governments to own commercial buildings and to repay their bonds with rental income. The programs were so successful that they aroused opposition from labor unions in Northern states, because the recruitment policies often resulted in job loss when unionized shops in the North moved to non-unionized, lower-wage states. Senator John Kennedy of Massachusetts joined his Northern colleagues in complaining about the "raiding" of Northern factories, and his colleagues in Congress introduced more than a dozen bills that would have made the bonding programs illegal or at least would have ended the tax exemption for municipal bonds and the deduction for rental fees. Southerners resisted the efforts and occasionally made reference to the colonization of their region by the North, and in 1969 Congress approved a compromise measure that set a limit on the size of bonds that could be counted for a tax deduction. In summary, at this point developmentalist programs faced opposition not only from conservative Southerners, whose Jeffersonian views on small government provided an important stream of popular support for rollback neoliberalism during the 1980s, but also from liberal Northerners, who were aligned with unions and manufacturers.[8]

The Southern states also pioneered many of the other emerging policy instruments of the economic development field. In 1935 Alabama offered new industries an exemption from all taxes except school taxes for the first ten years, and other states soon emulated the tax-exemption model. The Southern states also began to set up local industrial development corporations, which could provide loans or loan guarantees from a revolving fund. After 1963, the Internal Revenue Service allowed the organizations to issue bonds provided that they had state government approval. In another innovation, the state of North Carolina inaugurated Research Triangle Park, and by the late 1950s the facility was attracting companies. Likewise, the state of Florida began to attract aerospace firms. State governments also built industrial parks and provided other types of infrastructure support, such as new roads, electricity, water, and sewerage. Finally, Southern states offered training programs and helped guarantee a docile workforce that was not unionized.[9]

Notwithstanding the many innovations that created successful industries and manufacturing jobs, by the 1980s all states faced a much broader challenge: the loss of domestic manufacturing to foreign competition. In response, a new wave of economic development policies emerged that focused more on the high-tech sector. The Mississippi model gave way to that of Massachusetts, and a general economic development policy gave way to policies that were focused on specific industries. Having lost old manufacturing facilities to competition from the American South and abroad, the commonwealth found new sources of industrial and job growth in the emerging high-tech sector. Rather than attempt to regain the labor-intensive factories that had been lost, the state government focused on solving problems for its high-tech sector, such as ensuring an adequate supply of engineers for the defense electronics and minicomputer industries. To that end, in 1982 the state government created the Massachusetts Technology Park Corporation on a 36-acre campus outside Boston. The primary goals of the organization were to pursue economic development and build linkages among academia, industry, and the government, a triad of relationships that later became known as the "triple helix." The organization was also charged with developing a training center for the defense and minicomputer industries, and in the following decade it trained 10,000 engineers in the design of semiconductors and integrated circuits.[10]

By 1991 demand for the engineers had declined, and the legislature responded by creating an expanded economic development mandate that shifted the organization's function to building connections among stakeholders. To reflect the new role, the economic development organization was renamed the Massachusetts Technology Collaborative (MTC). It published studies, fostered networking, developed analyses of the innovation industries in the state's economy, helped to secure funding for companies and universities, and assisted with the formation of start-up companies. New research, such as the work of Michael Porter of the Harvard Business School on regional industrial clusters, helped the organization to develop a goal of cluster development. In 2004 the legislature also created the John Adams Innovation Institute, which invested in businesses and provided matching funds for university grants.[11]

The MTC is a good example of how the economic development policies of state governments changed during the 50 years that followed the founding of the Building Industry with Agriculture Program in Mississippi. The Mississippi program was focused on recruiting industries from the North, and the companies most attracted to the South were in relatively low-tech industries, such as shoe and textile production, for which a reduction in labor costs could make a significant difference in profitability even without technological innovation. In contrast, the Massachusetts program was focused less on recruitment and more on what became known as retention and incubation. Although by no means the only exemplar, the commonwealth of Massachusetts was forging a new model of economic development policy adapted to the competitive global economy that was emerging from ongoing rounds of trade liberalization agreements and other factors driving economic globalization.

The Massachusetts model soon became widespread, including in the American South, because of growing global competition in low-wage manufacturing. As the political scientist and policy analyst Peter Eisinger has argued, there was a dramatic growth of economic development programs at the state government level between 1966 and 1985, and economic development concerns rose rapidly as a policy priority between 1976 and 1981. The new emphasis on economic development was partly a response to the loss of manufacturing in the labor-intensive industries, but, as Eisinger argues, there was also a general change in economic development practices to include a greater emphasis on entrepreneurialism and high technology. Although recruitment-based strategies of economic development never disappeared, the economic development tool kit broadened to include creating an environment that nurtured the growth of new firms. State governments had become, to use Eisinger's term, "entrepreneurial." They were also engaging in industrial policy, because the economic development programs had to be strategic about the selection of industries that matched local research strengths, labor skills, and business expertise.[12]

In addition to the general change in the global economy that was siphoning low-tech manufacturing out of the United States, another factor behind the change in state government economic development policies involved a federal government policy that encouraged state governments to form science-and-technology advisory bodies. Some state governments set up science-and-technology foundations on the model of the National Science Foundation to provide research funding for universities. Although federal funding for state government advisory bodies was limited, and some of the state programs were short-lived, the experiments provided another spur for the second wave of economic development programs. According to Walter Plosila, an advisor and consultant to governors and economic development offices, the full convergence of the science-and-technology orientation with economic development didn't occur until the 1980s, when Texas won competitions to attract the Microelectronics Computer Consortium (MCC), the supercollider, and the Semiconductor Technology and Enterprise Corporation (also known as SEMATEC):

The package that attracted MCC and these other so-called trophy projects included such unheard of elements as endowed university chairs, university linkages and connections, and access to talent pools, in addition to the traditional bricks-and-mortar incentive packages for site improvements, road access, and tax abatements. This winning approach resulted in states' reexamining their efforts and bringing to the table new players and identifying new roles in economic development. (Plosila 2004: 115)

Plosila and Eisinger both argue that the economic development programs that swept across the United States during the 1980s brought with them a new focus on technology, university-industry relations, and entrepreneurialism. Changes in intellectual property rules, such as the Bayh-Dole Act, also contributed to the new emphasis on entrepreneurship, innovation, and technology transfer.[13]

The broad changes in economic development practices have been analyzed further in some of the emerging histories of the field. Like Eisinger, the planner and geographer Amy Glasmeier divides the transitions in economic development programs and practices into a first wave of recruitment and a second wave of retention and incubation. She notes that economic development officials implemented the strategy of recruitment and retention by initiating business support efforts to facilitate technology transfer, encourage entrepreneurship, and provide resources for incubation. They also engaged in demand policy support, such as using public procurement programs to support new industries and help local firms to market their products in foreign markets. During the third wave the goals remained the same, but state and local government officials increasingly served as brokers who helped firms find needed services in the private sector and also helped firms by providing worker training. She suggests that a fourth wave emerged toward the end of the 1990s, when economic development practices shifted toward the identification and development of clusters.[14]

The idea of a "cluster" is an elusive one, partly because there is no standard definition that delimits the scope by industry and geography. For the present purposes a vague definition (an industry limited to a geographical region that is at the size of a metropolitan region) is sufficient. The old industrial clusters in American cities—steel and glass in Pittsburgh, automobiles in Detroit, rubber and tires in Akron, aerospace in Seattle—were vertical in the sense of having a supply chain of supporting firms that fed one or more large manufacturers. The recruitment of a large manufacturer established conditions for the growth of new companies in the supply chain. In contrast, the new industrial clusters consisted more of horizontal linkages among established manufacturers, start-up companies, the service sector, venture capital, universities, industrial associations, and government agencies. The model was Silicon

Valley, not Detroit; flexible production, not Fordist manufacturing; high-technology, not smokestacks; and entrepreneurial networks, not vertically integrated supply chains. Not all regional economies had the resources to emulate Silicon Valley or Route 128, but the vibrant innovation economies of the two bay areas increasingly became models for economic development policy and practice. In this context economic development organizations saw their role as brokers who facilitated networking and helped to identify training, funding, and other needs.[15]

Although the changes in economic development practices were implemented in various "waves" and in varying degrees across the many state and local economic development offices, the broader point is that emerging historical scholarship on economic development policy has documented that a significant transition did occur. Recruitment strategies never disappeared, and in fact they remain a major part of economic development policies and practices for the green energy industries. Likewise, retention and incubation were not completely new. However, there was a significant shift in the overall strategy.

In summary, a second strand of developmentalism emerged in state governments. Whereas during the 1980s federal government policy showed increasing signs of protectionist measures in support of selected industries faced with pressure from the global economy, at the state government level the policy response was to shift toward industrial policy based on the construction of regional high-tech clusters. The products of the regional clusters were consumed partially in-state and could serve as substitutions for products imported from other states and countries, but the products were also sold on national and global markets. The central feature of the cluster was to provide a geographical advantage to colocation due to access to special resources, technology transfer, and industry-specific labor and services. Even if companies eventually decided to locate some of their manufacturing elsewhere, they often retained ownership and management locally. In this way, a regional economy was able to participate in the benefits of a global economy while also attempting to anchor capital in place.

The Emergence of Green Industrial Policy

The economist Michael Hudson notes that after the Trade Act of 1974 was passed, representatives of various industries soon asked for trade protection. President Ford turned down the shoe industry, the auto industry, and other industries before finally accepting the steel industry's request for protection. By making determinations about which industries could be left to wither on the vine of global competition and which were going to be protected, political leaders such as Ford and Reagan were in effect engaging in an industrial policy. Likewise, when state governments made a decision to recruit a company or build an industrial cluster, they were also engaging in an industrial policy in the broad sense of making a selection of which industry was worth supporting.

Industrial policy has long been weaker in the United States than in other countries. For much of the twentieth century, the US sat at the apex of the global economy, and many of its industries dominated world trade. Industrial policy is more appropriate for a country that is attempting to build up the global position of businesses in industries that are dominated by firms headquartered in other countries. Furthermore, as Eisinger argued, the continental size of the US has coincided with the geographical dispersion of industries, so that industrial policies tend to get caught in the crossfire of sectional politics. There is industrial policy in the US, but it is piecemeal and the result of the pervasive influence of industrial contributions and lobbyists.[16]

The first green industrial policies in the United States were forged during the 1970s amid increasing worries about foreign oil prices, rising trade deficits, and declining competitiveness of American manufacturing. In response to the oil embargo of 1973, President Richard Nixon called for energy independence, and President Gerald Ford carried out the initiative. During the 1960s the primary form of alternative energy was nuclear energy, but under Ford something more recognizable as clean or green energy began to receive attention. Project Independence included energy-efficiency standards for federal buildings, credits for insulation, and support for synthetic fuels. Energy laws passed during the Ford administration mandated the first fuel efficiency standards for automobiles and authorized $2 billion in loan guarantees for investments in conservation. The first fuel efficiency standards, set up to measure an average across the fleet of an automaker, implicitly protected American manufacturers, because at the time Japanese manufacturers had only smaller, more fuel-efficient vehicles. Subsequently, President Jimmy Carter also used his energy program to limit rebates on fuel-efficient cars to domestic ones.[17]

Carter's National Energy Plan, launched in 1977, recognized the need for a long-term transition to energy technologies that were not dependent on fossil fuels. Although the plan supported renewable energy, it also reserved a role for domestic coal under the broad rubric of energy independence. The subsequent National Energy Act and Energy Security Act of 1978 articulated energy independence as a goal but didn't provide a full set of mechanisms to bring about the transition. The Carter administration launched some investments in renewable energy and synthetic fuels, but the policies were mainly on the supply side, and they failed to support demand for the new energy sources. When the price of oil declined in response to flagging demand, there was no mechanism in place to support the experiments in clean energy. Likewise, the $88 billion invested in synthetic fuels produced an expensive product that could not compete in markets, and the project is often used as an example of why industrial policy is risky and potentially wasteful.[18]

In California, Governor Jerry Brown led a more successful articulation of supply-side and demand-side policies in support of the development of green industries. His administration pursued the green energy transition as part of a broader environmental agenda that included the country's first energy-efficiency standards for buildings and appliances, multiple initiatives for improved air quality, adding more than 1,000 miles of rivers to the federal Wild and Scenic River system, and opposing offshore oil drilling. With respect to renewable energy, Brown initiated a tax credit and reduced hurdles for solar energy installations, required solar water heating in large state buildings, and supported the development of geothermal, wind, and biomass. The 1978 Mello Act, arguably the country's first renewable-electricity standard, set a goal of 1 percent of the state's energy from wind by 1987 and 20 percent by 2000. The goal was backed by a state government tax credit for wind, new federal government regulations that required utilities to pay the avoided cost to small wind producers, and a decision by the state's Public Utilities Commission to set the rate of wind generation at 7 cents per kilowatt hour (in comparison with 1–3 cents in other states). The combination of policies led to the state's wind rush, which lasted until the federal and state incentives ended during the middle of the decade. Brown's policies, like those of Carter, are seen as ahead of their time, but they were substantially different from Carter's. According to the political scientist Max Neiman, whereas Carter focused on individual sacrifice and lower consumption, Brown focused more on efficiency standards and demand creation for renewable energy.[19]

The policies of the Carter and Brown administrations could have developed into a fully articulated green industrial policy that would have established the United States as the leader of a global green energy transition and as a manufacturing mecca for green tech. Instead, the country took another direction. President Reagan's 1981 National Energy Policy Plan rejected green industrial policy for a market-based approach, and under his leadership budgets for energy conservation and renewable energy were slashed by more than half. Reagan also accelerated the deregulation of petroleum prices. Although the effect of his policy may not have been as important as the general decline in demand that had accompanied oil price hikes, prices at the pump declined and undermined the national sense of crisis. More generally, inconsistencies between Democratic and Republican administrations have tended to create boom-and-bust cycles for manufacturers and producers of renewable energy.[20]

Although the United States didn't build on the Carter and Brown reforms, which might have led to a more complete suite of green energy policies such as those found in northern Europe, there were some incremental developments in the federal government during subsequent decades. Because energy legislation at the federal government level tends to emerge in omnibus bills that are compromise formations among diverse interests, even during the administrations of pro-oil Republican presidents there was some support for green energy. For example, the Energy Policy Act of 1992, passed during the presidency of George H. W. Bush, included support for energy-efficiency measures and renewable energy. The law also laid the groundwork for extensive competition among wholesale generators and among retailers. The 1978 Public Utility Regulatory Policies Act (included in the National Energy Act of that year) had required utilities to buy electricity from private generators if the cost of purchasing electricity from them was lower than the avoided (marginal) cost. Although intended to help renewable-energy-generation companies, the change also triggered the growth of small-scale, combined-cycle natural gas generation. The further restructuring of energy markets that followed the 1992 legislation made possible retail competition and more generation of renewable energy, but the extent to which state governments used the reforms to pursue a green energy transition varied substantially.[21]

Legislation during the administration of George W. Bush also provided some support for the renewable-energy and energy-efficiency industries. The Energy Policy Act of 2005 is perhaps best known for having exempted natural gas and oil drilling from clean-water regulations, a change that opened the door to hydraulic fracturing technologies by disabling regulatory oversight. In general the tax subsidies of the 2005 law favored the fossil fuel industries and nuclear energy, and the law also repealed the Public Utility Holding Company Act of 1935, which President Franklin

Roosevelt had supported to break up the utility holding companies. However, the law also authorized incentives for the development of hybrid vehicles, tax breaks for energy improvements in homes, and grants and subsidies for production of renewable energy. Likewise, the law required public utilities to offer net metering if requested by customers, a change that helped to overcome a significant barrier to distributed renewable energy. The Energy Independence and Security Act of 2007 authorized a suite of grant and loan programs for energy efficiency and renewable energy and the controversial mandate for the phase-out of incandescent light bulbs. As a result of the legislation, by 2008 the Department of Energy was issuing solicitations for loan guarantees for advanced energy technologies, a broad category that included fossil fuels and nuclear energy. The law also provided the first major advance in fleet fuel efficiency standards for automobiles in decades, but the change was introduced largely to derail a higher standard that the state of California had developed and other states planned to follow.[22]

Although Republican presidents have generally been skeptical of renewable energy for electricity, support for biofuels development has tended to be bipartisan. The best explanation for the bipartisan pattern on this issue is that the obstacle of competing sectional interests identified by Eisinger is less prominent in this policy field, because agricultural industries are so widely dispersed geographically in the United States. After the oil embargo of 1973, interest in ethanol reemerged, and the Energy Tax Act of 1978 provided a tax exemption for fuel blended with at least 10 percent ethanol. The Energy Security Act of 1980 provided loan guarantees for biofuels, the amendments to the Clean Air Act in 1990 made possible the use of ethanol as a fuel additive, and the Energy Policy Act of 1992 set up goals and mechanisms for the use of alternative fuel vehicles in government fleets. The Energy Policy Act of 2005 initiated a renewable fuels standard of 7.5 billion gallons by 2012, and the subsequent Energy Independence and Security Act of 2007 set a goal of 36 billion gallons of renewable fuel by 2022, with a cap of 15 billion gallons for corn ethanol and a minimum of 16 billion gallons from cellulosic ethanol. The legislation also set goals for petroleum reduction in federal fleets. In summary, across both Republican and Democrat administrations, there has been a cumulative industrial policy in support of biofuels.

In addition to developing an industrial policy in support of biofuels, the federal government has also used trade policy to support the industry. Agricultural subsidies, including for corn, have long proved resistant to trade negotiations, and the ethanol industry receives other, more direct support from the federal government. The federal government provided a tax credit, the Volumetric Ethanol Excise Tax Credit of about 50 cents per gallon for ethanol blenders, and a tariff of about 50 cents per gallon on imported ethanol. The latter basically compensated for the tax credit, so that the tax credit didn't go to foreign ethanol producers. The primary foreign producer of ethanol, Brazil, opposed the ethanol tariff, and in 2010 it removed its own 20 percent tariff on ethanol in order to bring pressure on the United States to remove its ethanol tariff. Domestic ethanol producers battled the Brazilian ethanol lobby over the tax credit and tariff, arguing in favor of an import-substitution policy and against the free-trade proposals of Brazil. Wesley Clark, co-chair of the American lobbying group Growth Energy, summarized the industry's view: "Ethanol is America's fuel: It's made here in the US, it creates US jobs, and it contributes to America's national and economic security." (Mulkern 2010) In January, 2012, the federal government allowed the tax credit to expire, but the tariff remained in place.

In summary, the history of green industrial policy in the United States has been relatively piecemeal for electricity and energy efficiency, but it has been more coherent for biofuels. It was not until the 111th Congress and the administration of President Barack Obama (whose policies will be discussed in chapter 2) that anything approximating a coherent green industrial policy emerged at the federal government level. However, the same cannot be said for state governments. Even during the Reagan years, when the federal government was pulling back from the beginnings of a green industrial policy, the state electricity commissions were promoting energy efficiency and conservation. California and Iowa were also pursuing renewable-electricity standards.[23]

Because federal energy laws are often compromise measures, with pork shared among diverse constituencies, policy goes in all directions at once. There tends to be support for green energy industries, even when the dominant direction of the legislation supports continued use of fossil fuels. But other than the case of biofuels, support for green industries is highly uneven and piecemeal, so that policy emerges differently according to presidential administration, industry, and scale of government. As of early 2012, the federal government has not enacted a national standard for renewable electricity, a national standard for energy efficiency, or a policy for the reduction of carbon emissions. Although there is a green industrial policy in the United States, it is uneven, and in many ways it is behind the policies of other industrial countries.

Conclusion

Fundamental changes in the global economy that were evident by the 1970s precipitated several shifts in energy, trade, and industrial policy. One shift was the emergence of protectionist measures for industries deemed crucial for the survival of the national economy, such as steel and automobiles. Although trading partners sometimes accepted the protectionist measures as "voluntary" restraints, they often did so under the threat of facing potentially more stringent forms of protectionism. Another shift was the reinvigoration of industrial policy that was especially evident in the transition of state governments' economic development strategies toward the development of high-tech clusters, which were intended to replace manufacturing operations that utilized low-skilled labor and were moving abroad. A third shift was the growing dependence of the United States on foreign oil due to the growth in demand for liquid fuels and the lack of low-cost domestic supplies. The half-century dream of energy independence has never been realized, but it has helped to frame and to legitimize national and state industrial policies in support of biofuels.

To extend Eisinger's argument, the pattern of sectional rivalries has also characterized green industrial policy. The coal, oil, and natural gas resources of the United States are concentrated geographically, and the industries are not afraid to display their economic might by influencing legislative change. The industries view the greening of electricity in the United States as a threat, because new renewable-electricity generation could either displace existing fossil fuels or retard the growth in their consumption. Fossil fuel interests have tended to block the greening of electricity at the federal government level, and the green transition for electricity has moved forward mainly at the state and local level in states that don't have strong oil, coal, or gas industries.

Support for biofuels is more evenly dispersed geographically, partly because almost all states have active agricultural interests and partly because there is a broad national benefit from at least some import substitution of imported oil with domestic biofuels. Furthermore, because farming states are often swing states, both political parties tend to support biofuels policy. The use of corn and soy for biofuels is highly controversial from environmental and food-and-justice standpoints, but those concerns are less important in the calculus of political support than local industrial power and votes from agricultural states. Furthermore, investments into biotechnology and biofuels promise a next generation of biofuels that address at least some of the environmental and equity problems. As a result, although the United States has failed to enact cap-and-trade legislation and a renewable-electricity standard at the federal government level, it has established a renewable fuels standard.

A primary challenge for the green energy transition in the United States, both as a policy problem and as a research problem for transition theory, is the unevenness of the transition. Policy changes are uneven in multiple ways: across industries (electricity versus biofuels), across state governments (Massachusetts versus Wyoming), in government scale (federal versus states versus cities), and by political party (Democratic versus Republican presidents and governors). The highly pitched anti-green politics seen in the post-2009 Tea Party movement is reminiscent of President Reagan, who removed from the White House the solar panels that President Carter had installed. In view of the broad resistance to green energy policy in the United States, it is not surprising that advocates have increasingly linked policy development to job creation, business opportunities, and economic development.

2

Green Jobs and the Green Energy Transition

In the 1970s, when green energy policies first emerged in the United States, the supporting political constituencies were mainly environmentalists and green businesses. The utilities took seriously the utopian claims of environmental and progressive activists, who envisioned a time when the power lines would come down because all energy would be generated by on-site solar panels. Opposition from utilities softened slowly as a result of structural changes in the industry (changes that separated generation from distribution) and in the technology. Technological changes facilitated grid-based forms of renewable energy (for example, large-scale solar and wind farms) and distributed generation. After state government legislation mandated some production of electricity from renewable energy but allowed utilities to recuperate costs, utilities found that they could live with the change. However, the industry continued to prefer generation from coal, natural gas, and nuclear energy, because of the difficulties in managing the intermittent generation of wind and solar energy.[1]

The second long-term change in the political landscape occurred when some environmental organizations developed a more positive working relationship with the unions. The historian Robert Gottlieb showed that during the 1920s the unions were involved in environmental issues such as environmental health in workplaces and communities, and the sociologist Brian Obach noted that unions also supported the Clean Air Act of 1970 and the Clean Water Act of 1972. During the 1980s, labor-environmental coalitions worked with state governments on environmental health policy for the workplace and communities, but there were also tensions in the relationship—especially with respect to nuclear energy and timber harvesting, which unions supported because of the jobs. More generally, Obach notes, "job loss fears during the 1980s prevent[ed] unions from fully embracing environmental concerns, and the mainstream environmental movement adopt[ed] some conservative and defensive tendencies during the period as well" (2004: 53). After the passage of the 1990 amendments to the Clean Air Act, the United Steelworkers joined the National Clean Air Coalition, but the United Mine Workers opposed the amendments. During the 1990s, unions and some environmental organizations found common ground in opposition to the North American Free Trade Agreement, which both constituencies saw as leading to a race to the bottom in labor and environmental standards. Through the Alliance for Sustainable Jobs and the Environment, some unions and environmental organizations also found common cause in protests against the meeting of the World Trade Organization in Seattle. However, the AFL-CIO opposed ratification of the Kyoto Protocol, and when Senators John Kerry and Ernest Hollings proposed an increase in the Corporate Average Fuel Economy standards for vehicles in 2001, the United Auto Workers mobilized against the reform. In 2002 unions were also split on President George W. Bush's proposal to drill for oil in the Alaska National Wildlife Refuge.[2]

Although unions and environmentalists had an uneasy relationship, after 2000 several of the leading unions and environmental organizations developed a closer working relationship under the frame of "green jobs." The frame facilitated additional coalitions with faith-based, anti-poverty, civil rights, progressive, and community organizations that wanted to connect low-income job development with the retrofitting of buildings. By then, the green business sector had also matured into a "green-tech" industry that attracted investments from venture capitalists, from mutual funds, and from large corporations. In addition, some large corporations had adopted principles and plans in support of a long-term greening process. In short, beyond the development of the labor-environmental relationship into a coalition, there were emerging green transition coalitions that included not only other social movement organizations but also venture capitalists, green businesses, and large corporations that had embraced sustainability as part of a long-term strategy.

The growing strength of the green transition coalitions also produced a backlash from fossil fuel companies in coalition with conservative political leaders, foundations, think tanks, and media outlets. They influenced the political field by supporting climate-change deniers and anti-green political candidates. This chapter will provide a general background on the fossil fuel industry and green transition coalitions, then it will discuss the category of "green jobs" as the main frame of the green transition coalitions.

The Economic Power of the Fossil Fuel Industries

In the United States, fossil fuel companies are not government enter-prises, and they exert tremendous political influence. On the one hand, they fight a rear-guard action by attempting to reverse existing policies and to stop efforts for deepened reform. On the other hand, they engage proposed reforms by positioning the cleaner forms of their technologies as players in the long-term green transition. The second strategy generally includes the idea of clean coal, natural gas, and hybrid vehicles as bridge technologies that are necessary stages in the long-term green transition. Although the concept of "bridge technology" can be brought into align-ment with the idea of a multi-decade transition to low-carbon energy sources, it can be used to favor short-term advancements in incremental improvements that slow the pace of the green energy transition.[3]

The economic and political power of the fossil fuel industries is sub-stantial and in many ways overwhelming. During the first two years of the Obama administration, the Metro trains in Washington hosted adver-tisements that reminded Washington politicians that that the oil and gas industries represented 9 million jobs. The number is backed by an indus-try report, but in 2009 the president of the American Petroleum Institute claimed that the oil and gas industries were responsible for only 6 million jobs: 1.8 million in direct jobs and another 4 million in "induced" jobs. Furthermore, because about half of the 1.8 million are employees of gas stations, 1 million may be a more accurate estimate. If one adds to the million oil and gas employees the coal industry's estimate of 174,000 jobs (including electricity generation), the total number of people directly employed in the oil, gas, and coal industries is about 1.2 million.[4]

What are the comparable statistics for renewable energy and energy efficiency? A study by the Pew Charitable Trusts estimates that there were 770,000 clean energy jobs in the United States in 2009, but of that number only 162,000 were renewable-energy and energy-efficiency jobs. Using their comparison for consistency, the ratio of fossil fuel jobs (1.2 million) to renewable-energy and energy-efficiency jobs (162,000) is about 7 to 1. If one takes industry self-estimates of employment, the numbers of people employed in the three leading renewable-energy industries are 100,000 in solar, 85,000 in wind, and 70,000 in ethanol (including 45,000 in agriculture), and the energy-efficiency services sector has been estimated to have 114,000 jobs. If one adds another 50,000 for direct jobs in hydropower, biomass, biodiesel, and geothermal, the total industry self-estimate of employment for renewable energy and energy efficiency comes to about 419,000. When compared against the industry's own estimate for coal, oil, and gas (2.1 million plus 174,000), the ratio is 5.4 to 1. A third approach is to use the narrow category of electrical power generation, where the ratio of employment in oil and natural gas generation to jobs in hydropower, wind, and solar is 6.5 to 1. (See table 2.1.) In short, different approaches lead to the similar conclusion that from 5 to 7 times as many people are employed in the fossil fuel industry as in renewable energy and energy efficiency.[5]

The claim that the wind energy industry employed 85,000 people prompted a flurry of comments in the blogosphere based on the mistaken assumption that wind energy jobs had outpaced coal jobs; however, wind energy jobs were being compared only with coal mining jobs, which were estimated at only 76,000. A journalist checked the estimate with the coal industry and found that the trade association claimed about 174,000 direct jobs. However, as table 2.1 indicates, there are some areas where an argument of parity could be made. For example, more people are employed manufacturing equipment for wind and solar combined than in manufacturing equipment for mining and for the oil and gas industry.[6]

Because of the size differential, the fossil fuel industry has greater resources with which to influence government policy than green business associations and corporations have. Industrial influence operates directly through lobbying and campaign donations and also through conservative

Table 2.1
Comparative industrial strength of the United States. Source of data: IBISWorld 2011.

Industry name and code	Revenue	Employment
Electric power generation industries		
Coal and gas power (22111a)	$96 billion	75,000
Nuclear power (22111b)	$33 billion	34,000
Hydroelectric power (22111c)	$6 billion	10,000
Wind power (22111d)	$4 billion	1,400
Solar power (22111e)	$0.1 billion	<200
Manufacturing		
Mining, oil, and gas machinery (33313)	$20 billion	53,000
Wind turbine manufacturing (33361b)	$13 billion	32,000
Solar PV manufacturing (33441c)	$4 billion	34,000

think tanks and political networks. The energy industry has one of the highest rates of spending on lobbying, and within the energy industry spending in 2011 by oil and gas companies ($75 million), electric utilities ($75 million), and mining ($16 million, mostly coal) far outpaced lobbying by the industry associations for biofuels, clean energy, solar, and wind ($10 million for the ten largest donors). With respect to anti-green conservative politics, an analysis of one important meeting held by the billionaires David and Charles Koch—well known for their funding of candidates associated with the Tea Party movement—showed that their coalition included supporters from more than a dozen representatives of the oil, coal, and natural gas industries. Even in states with small fossil fuel industries, such as New Hampshire and Wisconsin, the industry has reached into environmental and industrial policy through organizations such as Americans for Prosperity.[7]

Constituencies for the Green Energy Transition

Although in 2009 and 2010 it appeared that federal government policy had reached a tipping point in favor of green energy reform, the defeat of the proposals for a cap-and-trade system for carbon emissions and a national standard for renewable electricity revealed that the political power of the green transition coalitions was not able to overcome anti-green industrial resistance. However, some state and local governments supported green transition policies both before and after the cresting of momentum in the federal government. As a result, there has been a slow accretion of green industrial development and a positive feedback loop by which the creation of green jobs leads to the growth of constituencies that support green transition policies. This section will describe the main constituencies in green transition coalitions.

Blue-Green Coalitions
The new blue-green coalitions that emerged after 2000 developed from meetings led by Jane Perkins, who worked on environmental policy for the AFL-CIO. Through the Climate Change Working Group, the unions and environmental organizations attempted to develop shared principles in which job preservation and environmental goals could be maintained together. According to Brian Obach, "Continued resistance from several unions within the federation ultimately forced the end of the AFL-CIO's direct sponsorship of the effort. Several of the more committed unions

and environmental groups went on, however, to form the BlueGreen Alliance to continue their work." (2004: 79) Leo Gerard, the president of the United Steelworkers and in many ways the leader of the labor-environmental coalition, frequently jokes that the Steelworkers and the Sierra Club had been "dating" for 30 years, and the creation of the BlueGreen Alliance in 2006 represented a formalization of the relationship.[8]

On the environmentalist side, the Natural Resources Defense Fund joined the alliance; on the labor side, the American Federal of Teachers, the Communication Workers of America, the Service Employees International Union, the Laborer's International Union, the Unity Workers Union of America, and other unions joined. By 2011 the alliance claimed, on the basis of the memberships of the constituent unions and environmental organizations, to represent 15 million members. The alliance actively supported climate-change legislation that was debated (but not approved) in Congress in 2009 and 2010; it also supported state and federal renewable-electricity standards, trade reform to support environmental and labor concerns, employee "free choice" legislation (which would facilitate unionization), the reform of transportation policy to include high-speed rail and more public transit, and the reform of toxic chemical regulation. There was some potential for a powerful next generation of progressive politics that extends from the unions' traditional working-class base to include middle-class voters concerned with quality-of-life and environmental issues. The potential number of voters in the BlueGreen Alliance (15 million) is larger than even the highest estimate of fossil fuel employment (9 million); however, the capacity of the labor-environmental coalition to mobilize wealth to sway elections is lower. The reinvigoration of the country's left based on cross-class, cross-sector coalition politics may also account for the increased virulence of anti-union politics from the country's right, as evidenced by attacks on public workers' unions after 2010.[9]

The Apollo Alliance was a closely related organization that provided research support and policy guidance for the blue-green coalitions. Founded in 2003, the organization's board included prominent leaders from labor unions, environmental organizations, think tanks, and corporations. Drawing on the vision of the Apollo space program launched during the Kennedy administration (a metaphor that President Obama grabbed by comparing green transition politics to the Sputnik event and launching a solar energy "sunshot" program), the Apollo Alliance called for a similar investment in the transition to the green economy. To that end, in 2009 the organization launched the New Apollo Program under the slogan "clean energy, good jobs." The economic development plan included energy efficiency for buildings, an increase in production of renewable energy, development of a "smart grid," efficiency improvements for power plants, transportation infrastructure, alternative fuels and vehicles, clean energy research, and educational programs. The organization claimed that its policy vision influenced the green business development provisions of American Recovery and Reinvestment Act of 2009 (the "stimulus" act). Because the law included provisions in support of the development of clean tech and green jobs, it represented a temporary but significant step toward a comprehensive green industrial policy at the federal government level. In 2011 the Apollo Alliance merged with the BlueGreen Alliance to become the Apollo Alliance Project of the new BlueGreen Alliance.[10]

Among the blue-green coalition organizations, the adjective "good" is often used with the term "green jobs." For example, the name of the conference supported by the BlueGreen Alliance is "Good Jobs, Green Jobs." Likewise, the Apollo Alliance (2008a: 3) defines green-collar jobs as good jobs in the sense of "well-paid, career-track jobs that contribute to preserving or enhancing environmental quality." The project compares green-collar jobs to traditional blue-collar jobs, which have a range of skills and include opportunities to advance from entry-level positions to higher-skill, higher-wage positions: "Put simply, if a job improves the environment but doesn't provide a family-supporting wage or a career ladder to move low-income workers to higher-skill occupations, it is not a green-collar job." (ibid.) The emphasis on the quality of the jobs is also common in other statements from organizations associated with the labor-environmental coalitions.

Although the definitions are flexible enough to recognize that good jobs can be non-union jobs, such as jobs in small service companies and nonprofit organizations, "good" often has overtones of unionization. The meaning of the adjective became obvious to me only when I sat in the plenary audience of the "Good Jobs, Green Jobs" conference and noticed that most of the participants were from labor unions from across the country. Several of the prominent labor unions saw in the green energy transition an opportunity to regain manufacturing jobs, which are often unionized, and to create unionized jobs in other industries, such as transportation and services. The call for good green jobs is hardly anti-business; in fact, there is a close relationship between the unions and unionized businesses that produce green products and energy or have undertaken a general greening strategy. Plenary speakers included not only union leaders and government officials but also the CEOs of unionized companies. Many of the business leaders spoke highly of unions, because they ensure a skilled workforce that helps the firm maintain its reputation for quality products. Although there was a great deal of interest in manufacturing, many of the other unions that appeared at the conference (such as transportation, communication, and utilities unions) were not directly in manufacturing industries, and some of the workers represented were professionals (such as the architects).

In short, the categories of "good," "unionized," and "manufacturing" jobs don't overlap completely. It is possible to have a good job (that is, one that has benefits, family-supporting wages, and potential for career development) that is not unionized and not in manufacturing, and it is possible to have a unionized job that is neither "good" nor in manufacturing. But manufacturing jobs generally pay better than blue-collar service-sector jobs, and many of the traditional manufacturing jobs have been unionized. As a result, the vision of the BlueGreen Alliance is to reinvigorate domestic manufacturing as part of a broader strategy to strengthen unionized labor in both manufacturing and the service sectors that contribute to a green transition.

This is where the labor perspective on developmentalism comes in. The vision of reinvigorating manufacturing through the green energy transition faces a significant challenge, because green manufacturing, like other types of manufacturing, has moved offshore as a result of trade agreements. By 2009, more than 50 percent of wind turbines, 75 percent of photovoltaic components, and 70 percent of renewable-energy systems and components were manufactured outside the United States. The coalitions of labor and environmental organizations, led by the steelworkers, continually drew attention to the loss of manufacturing and the need to link green jobs development with green manufacturing. Because the United States had steadily lost manufacturing jobs to other countries, they argued, only aggressive policy support could stop the hemorrhaging of jobs. Indeed, in response to federal government policy, there were some signs of progress toward regaining jobs in the wind turbine and battery manufacturing industries, although less so for solar photovoltaic manufacturing. Thus, a major implication of the new wave of integrated trade, industrial, and environmental policy is that it draws attention to the highly desirable jobs in manufacturing. As a result, trade relations, especially the issue of green manufacturing in China, are inexorably linked with green jobs.[11]

Although the focus of this book is on the United States, it is worth noting that other industrialized countries have confronted a similar problem. In 2011, France's Minister of the Environment, Nathalie Kosciusko-Morizet, stated that the country's environmental policies should be set up to "create jobs in France, not subsidize Chinese industry" (Einhorn and Patel 2011: 45). As Europeans became more aware that their subsidies for solar panels benefited Chinese firms rather than European manufacturers, governments became more motivated to reduce their subsidies. Without the link to domestic job creation, the demand policies for renewable energy were at risk of losing political support.

Green Businesses

The CEOs of unionized green businesses were welcomed into the blue-green coalitions, and they also had a leading position in the plenary sessions of the Good Jobs, Green Jobs conferences. However, there are other categories of industry that support the greening of the economy but are not necessarily completely in alignment with the vision of good, green jobs that is linked to organized labor. The other types of industry can find common ground with the blue-green coalitions on specific issues; hence, the term "green transition coalition" is used to refer to the networks that extend beyond the labor-environmental coalitions. Two significant political players from industry are the renewable-energy industry's associations and leaders of the financial and industrial fields that have invested in clean tech.

The renewable-energy industries have their own trade associations, which have had a lobbying presence in Washington since 1974. Although the associations lack the lobbying strength of the fossil fuel industry, they have a coherent message and have had some influence on specific policy outcomes. Because the associations include non-unionized manufacturers among their members, they connect with blue-green coalitions more on the issue of demand policies than on that of "good" jobs. For example, the American Wind Energy Association, the Solar Energy Industries Association, and the Geothermal Energy Association support a national standard for renewable electricity, climate-change legislation such as a cap-and-trade policy for carbon emissions, reforms to improve electricity transmission, a clean energy development agency, increased research funding for renewable energy, and various production and investment tax credits that support renewable energy. There are differences among the associations, but the differences rest on the specificities of the industry. For example, the wind industry is especially interested in improved access to production of renewable energy on federal lands (that is, rights to build solar and wind farms on federal lands), the solar industry is interested in national net metering and interconnection standards (that is, technical changes that allow homes and businesses to connect rooftop solar to the grid), and the geothermal industry advocates for policy reforms for leasing, permitting, and drilling. The differences are relatively minor in comparison with the common front of support for an invigorated demand policy. In some cases, such as cap-and-trade reform and renewable-energy credits, the policy instruments help to create new markets and can be interpreted as consistent with a neoliberal approach to policy reform. In other cases, there is strong support for a broad industrial policy that is consistent with developmentalism.

There is also a segment of the financial industry that has embraced green investments as a strategic goal and therefore is in alignment with the green industrial associations on demand policies. The term "clean tech" first emerged as an investment category, and the business and investment world tends to prefer the term "clean" to "green" as the umbrella term for businesses, policies, and investments associated with the green energy transition. The Cleantech Group, a leading organization for industry analysis, defines "green tech" as an "old economy" approach. According to the organization, green tech or "environmental technology" represents end-of-pipeline technologies driven by regulation such as smokestack scrubbers (in my terminology, technology associated with the older regime of social liberal mandates). In contrast, clean tech is defined as "new technology and related business models that offer competitive returns for investors and customers while providing solutions to global challenges" (Cleantech Group 2009). The competitiveness and innovation emphasis provides a somewhat different approach to the global economy than the emphasis on domestic manufacturing among the unions. Thus, there is potential that coalitions built on demand and industrial policies may fracture on the issue of global trade policy, with the unions more inclined toward a protectionist stance and the clean tech businesses and investors more oriented toward policies that preserve access to export markets. However, because investors have often placed bets on American companies that are manufacturing in the United States, they have an interest in protecting their investments from predatory industrial policies of other countries.

Whereas the Clean Tech Group emphasizes venture capital and enterprise development, another segment of the financial industry focuses on investments in existing publicly traded companies. One approach to green investment focuses on environmental sustainability goals as part of a broader strategy of improving the social and environmental responsibility of large corporations. The portion of the industry dedicated to socially responsible investment (SRI) is considerably larger than green venture capital, with more than $2 trillion invested in the United States. In this segment of the investment industry, the term "environmental" tends to be favored over "clean tech," and the definition is very loose and flexible, usually in the form of an environmental screen that is only one of a broader set for SRI screens. Whereas the SRI firms tend to focus on the investment categories of "environmental" and "sustainable," a second approach can be found in investment funds that have a sectoral strategy of investing, such as investments in energy-efficiency firms or in renewable-energy firms. Here, rather than "environmental" or "sustainability," the terms "green," "clean," and "alternative energy" tend to be more common, depending on the relationship to nuclear energy and fossil fuels.[12]

It would make sense that investors who have a portion of their portfolios in clean, SRI, or green financial instruments would have a personal interest in supporting policies that deepen the green energy transition. We don't know how the greening of investment portfolios affects the political support of small investors for green transition policies. However, there is some evidence for the linkage between investment strategies and policy support among prominent investors. For example, in 2006 John Doerr, a partner in the firm of Kleiner, Perkins, Caulfield, and Byers, joined with other business leaders to lobby for California's Global Warming Solutions Act of 2006 (AB 32), a law that laid the groundwork for cap-and-trade legislation. The law was subsequently subjected to a ballot "recall" proposition that was spearheaded by out-of-state oil companies, and California venture capitalists provided a significant portion of the countervailing funding that led to a successful defense of the legislation. Doerr has also advocated for a national mandate of ethanol pumps similar to that in Brazil. Together with Jeff Immelt, the CEO of General Electric, he advocated for a national cap-and-trade policy; for a national renewable-electricity standard for utilities; for a national smart grid; for clean energy standards for buildings, cars, and appliances; and for a national Clean Energy Deployment Administration. The latter would have provided the mandate for a national green bank, which would have provided financial support for the green energy transition. Another prominent venture capitalist, Vinod Khosla, has criticized oil companies for making it difficult to obtain E85 fuel (an 85 percent–15 percent blend of gasoline and ethanol) at the pump. He called for policy solutions that require all cars and 10 percent of all fuel pumps to be E85 compatible; he also backed price supports for ethanol when gasoline prices plummet below a minimum level.[13]

In addition to the role of individual venture capitalists in green policy fields, the National Venture Capital Association established a Clean Tech Advisory Council and published various policy papers on clean technology. Many of the recommendations that they made for the Obama administration—including higher levels of research and development funding, more attention to green buildings, and the need for a long-term carbon policy—were consistent with the policy directions that were supported in the ARRA and in the proposed climate-change legislation that was defeated in 2010.[14]

In 2010, a group of business leaders led by John Doerr, Bill Gates, and Jeff Immelt also founded the American Energy Innovation Council and published a plan for government subsidies for the conversion to a green energy future. The report called for an independent national government energy strategy board to develop an energy plan and oversee spending, an increase in federal government subsidies from $5 billion per year to $16 billion per year, national centers of excellence funded at $150–250 million per year, support for an "Advanced Research Projects Agency-Energy" (ARPA-E) modeled on the Defense Advanced Research Projects Agency, and the formation of a public-private partnership to oversee pilot projects. The report noted that the $16 billion annual expenditure would be minuscule in comparison with the federal budget and the daily expenditures of $1 billion on foreign oil, and it also noted that American spending on energy research and development lags that of other countries on a percentage basis. Some of the proposals did have policy traction; for example, the proposed budget for 2011 included $550 million for the Advanced Research Projects Agency-Energy, a DARPA-like program for energy that subsequently made investments in a portfolio of next-generation energy technologies.[15]

One can see from the description of the specific policy proposals that the green business leaders emphasize different policy priorities from those of the blue-green coalitions. The business leaders are much more concerned with competitiveness and innovation, and they also recognize that innovative supply-side policies such as ARPA-E will go nowhere without strong demand policies such as a national cap-and-trade program and a renewable-electricity standard. In general the focus is on building a coherent and effective green industrial policy. Although the blue-green coalitions welcome green industrial policy, they draw more attention to trade policy and the need to protect American manufacturing jobs, concerns that are less salient for business leaders of global corporations such as General Electric. These two sides of developmentalist politics—industrial policy and defensive trade policy—can be brought together under the broad tent of green energy policy, as can the different constituencies, but there is also significant potential for political fracture.

Anti-Poverty and Progressive Organizations
A third major constituency in support of green energy policies is built from organizations that have addressed issues of poverty and social inequality. Although the organizations lack economic power, they can mobilize voters and provide support for the progressive wing of the Democratic Party. Here, the party's traditional political ideology of social liberalism, with its redistributive programs of providing support to the most vulnerable populations, is merged with the broader developmentalist politics discussed in the previous sections. Whereas the blue-green coalitions focus on unionized green jobs and manufacturing jobs, and the green businesses and investors focus on policies that support business innovation and consumer demand, the anti-poverty organizations draw attention to the service-sector jobs of weatherization, the greening of buildings, and rooftop solar installation. The buildings-related jobs have been especially important in urban green jobs programs, where they address the needs of the unemployed or underemployed who often have modest or low skills. This type of green jobs policy often has strong support from urban mayors and their political constituencies, because the programs reduce energy bills for low-income residents while also providing them with jobs.

A leading organization that has defended the use of weatherization and building services jobs as an avenue for combining environmental politics and poverty reduction is Green For All, which Anthony Van Jones launched in 2007 at the Clinton Global Initiative. Van Jones was the co-founder of the Ella Baker Center for Human Rights, a nonprofit organization located in Oakland, California. The center began with a focus on the civil rights issue of police abuse of the largely African American and Latino urban residents, and after 2005 it expanded into environmental politics. Green For All advocated for policy reforms, including the Green Jobs Act of 2007, the inclusion of green jobs training in the ARRA, and federal climate-change legislation. The organization also hosted conferences and educational programs, including the Green

For All Academy, which was offered in partnership with former vice-president Al Gore's We Campaign for leaders in low-income communities. Van Jones attained national recognition in 2008, when he published *The Green Collar Economy*, and in the following year he served for a brief period as the Special Advisor for Green Jobs, Enterprise, and Innovation in the White House Council on Environmental Quality. He resigned after a wave of attacks from right-wing media outlets, but he subsequently continued to advocate for green jobs and continued to speak across the country in favor of the "triple play" of environmental, equity, and economic benefit.

Although Green For All is arguably the leading organization in support of this approach to green jobs, there are other important organizational bases for the constituency. Many urban mayors who are connected closely with constituencies of neighborhoods with high unemployment rates and substandard housing have found the combination of building retrofitting and job creation attractive. In some cases, there are grassroots efforts such as the Chicagoland Green Jobs Alliance, which partnered with the city and the Partnership for Communities (a fund of the Chicago Community Trust) to support green jobs training for public housing residents. In Newark, Mayor Cory Booker partnered with the Apollo Alliance to develop a plan for green jobs for his largely low-income constituents, and, as chapter 7 will show, other cities and states have launched "high road" agreements that combine building retrofitting with good jobs for underserved populations.[16]

There is also general support for this strand of green jobs policy from progressive organizations, which united in 2009 to form a coalition in support of the "new economy." Although the boundaries of what is and is not included in the new economy are fuzzy, the term is used generally to refer to businesses that embrace the triple bottom line of economic success, environmental progress, and social fairness. Among the policies advocated by such organizations are living wage campaigns and "green banks," which would provide support for new economy businesses in the green sector.[17]

Faith-based organizations have also supported programs that combine the greening of buildings with anti-poverty initiatives. In 2009 a coalition of Christian, Jewish, Moslem, Hindu, and anti-hunger organizations led a one-week mobilization under the slogan "fighting poverty with faith: good jobs, green jobs." The organizations called for economic recovery policies that linked green industrial development to energy savings and job training in disadvantaged communities and to policy reforms that ensure that green industries offer "good jobs." The one-week educational campaign resulted in some press coverage and drew attention to the goal of connecting the transition to a greener economy with poverty alleviation. The lasting effect of the mobilization is difficult to determine, because it percolated through various faith-based organizations and because specific legislative goals were not articulated. However, the campaign should not be underestimated, because the total population represented by the signatory organizations far exceeds the millions represented by the labor and environmental organizations.[18]

Organizations that support building weatherization combine a focus on the conservation and efficiency sides of the green energy transition with traditional job-creation programs that are in a direct political lineage with the anti-poverty programs of the Great Society and the work programs of the New Deal. Although the urban justice and religious organizations cut across partisan, ethnic, religious, and class divides, they promote the view that the federal government has a responsibility to help the least advantaged groups in society. Ideally, the new green jobs are also "good" jobs. In a definition that is consistent with those of the Apollo Alliance, the Ella Baker Center argues that green jobs should be "good, living wage jobs in enterprises and industries that are environmentally positive" (Ella Baker Center 2009). However, the emphasis is less on unionized workplaces and more on assistance to persons with "barriers to employment." The phrase appears occasionally in discussions of the green jobs programs in urban areas, and it is used to refer to a mixture of factors that include a history of incarceration, lack of a high school degree, lack of skills, and recent history of being out of the workforce. Many of the government-sponsored green jobs programs in urban areas target residents with barriers to employment and offer them training in entry-level positions. Some of the programs also offer more advanced training and access to a "career ladder" to more advanced positions.[19]

With funding from the ARRA that began in 2009, many cities put into place programs that train persons hampered by employment barriers. In some cities, such as Chicago, programs already existed, and some state governments (notably California and New York) established programs to support green jobs training. Numerous nonprofit organizations across the country also expanded their job training programs to help persons with employment barriers find work in energy efficiency, retrofitting, and solar panel installation.

Although the approach to green jobs that is linked to poverty reduction seems like an ideal banner under which Democratic urban political constituencies can find common ground, the programs faced significant challenges. One challenge is the skill set needed for jobs in home energy auditing, weatherization, and solar panel installation. Some of the work requires math and carpentry skills that go beyond the skill sets found in many entry-level positions. A second problem is that green jobs in this sector can involve potential exposure to toxic materials, thereby calling into question the category of a green job. For example, concerns have been raised about chemical exposure for workers who install blown-in insulation, and the recycling industry is notorious for occupational health and safety issues at the material recovery facilities. A third issue is that the training programs must lead to jobs, and consequently governments must ensure that there is the demand for services that the newly trained green-collar workers are ready to provide. Federal government programs tend to undergo a boom-and-bust cycle, and there is a need for long-term and stable demand programs.[20]

Another tension in the poverty-oriented side of green jobs is the relationship with unions. The Laborers' International Union of North America has been involved in green jobs training programs in building retrofitting, and the unions are generally supportive of the job training initiatives in the services sector. However, weatherization jobs in small contracting businesses are not necessarily unionized jobs, and there can be tensions with unions, especially with the traditional trade unions. For example, in some states electricians have obtained rulings to require that solar panel installation is completed only by electricians. Although good for electricians, the rulings squeeze out certification programs for solar installation that were available to persons with lower skill sets.[21]

It would be easy to overestimate the tensions between the anti-poverty approach to green jobs based on finding work for persons with employment barriers and the manufacturing and more highly skilled jobs sought by some of the unions. The two types of jobs are not only complementary but also symbiotic. In other words, the energy-efficiency industry produces demand for products such as caulking and insulation (both of which are still manufactured largely in the United States) and high-tech items such as programmable thermostats. An industry study estimated that more than 90 percent of caulk, foam, insulation, furnaces, and replacement windows were manufactured by domestic companies. For water heaters and some other appliances, the range for domestic manufacturing was 62–78 percent. Thus, the retrofitting programs create green jobs not only in the retrofitting service industry but also in associated manufacturing industries.[22]

What Is a Green Job?

If "green jobs" (understood broadly to include support for both business development and demand policies) is the unifying frame of the diverse constituencies that constitute green transition coalitions, what exactly is meant by "green job"? Because the federal government's Bureau of Labor Statistics doesn't track the category, the various reports on green jobs must construct their own definitions. Some people in the field argue that all jobs should become green jobs, because there is the potential for all industries to undergo a greening process in which materials are less toxic, manufacturing externalities are closed, and there is extended producer responsibility over the entire product life cycle, including take-back programs for the end of a product's life. A more common approach to the concept of a "green job" is to define it as employment in a business that engages in some kind of green activity. From this second perspective, any of the following could be a green job: a person with a conventional skill set who is working for a green business (such as an accountant in a green firm), a person with a traditional skill set that has been augmented to address the green transition (such as an electrician who installs solar panels), or a person in a completely new job category that is in some way "green" (such as a home energy auditor).

Most approaches to defining green jobs use a catalog of industry sectors to explain the concept. For example, Raquel Pinderhughes, a professor of urban studies at San Francisco State University who studies green jobs organizations, identified both entry-level and advanced greencollar jobs in ten sectors: energy, water, green buildings, woodworking, green space, food, transportation, nontoxic printing, nontoxic cleaning, and waste stream diversion. In the energy sector, entry-level jobs include construction and installation; more advanced jobs include solar electrician and project manager. Another approach to defining green jobs, led by Michael Renner of the Worldwatch Institute in coordination with the United Nations Environmental Program, breaks down green jobs into energy supply alternatives (e.g., renewable energy), buildings, transportation, basic industry and recycling, food and agriculture, and forestry.[23]

More general than industry-based classifications are the broad sectors of services, manufacturing, and management and research. For skilled workers without advanced education, manufacturing jobs are generally preferable to the service and maintenance jobs, because they pay up to double the hourly wage. From an economic development perspective, manufacturing jobs also have higher economic multiplier effects; that is, they create more jobs than service-sector jobs. The multiplier for a manufacturing job in the auto industry is as high as 10 (that is, ten indirect and induced jobs for every automotive assembly job), and even jobs in the automotive supply chain, which generally involves manufacturing as well, have an estimated multiplier of 4. In contrast, multiplier effects for service jobs are generally much lower, between 1 and 2. Manufacturing may be a small percentage of total jobs, but because of the relatively high multiplier effects the gain and loss of manufacturing jobs exert powerful ripple effects across the economy. In the long term, laid-off workers in the manufacturing sector are able to find positions in other sectors, but the new jobs may not pay as well unless the workers are able to obtain higher levels of education and training.[24]

Although manufacturing jobs are desirable and important, a report prepared for the United States Conference of Mayors estimated that they represent fewer than 10 percent of all green jobs. Likewise, a report by the California Community Colleges Economic and Workforce Development Program projected that most green jobs in the state will continue to be in service industries such as solar installation, wind turbine technicians, and green construction, rather than in manufacturing. A study of green jobs in California by the industry organization Next10 also found that manufacturing jobs accounted for only 21 percent of all green jobs, in comparison with about 45 percent for services. Of the remaining categories, supplier and installation were the largest and could be aggregated with their category of services. The convergence among the diverse studies about the relative dominance of service-sector jobs is not surprising, because it represents an economy-wide pattern.[25]

Even the high estimates for manufacturing jobs suggest that they are not more than a third of all green jobs. In 2010, the California Employment Development Department came up with much higher numbers than the somewhat more narrowly defined numbers in the Next10 study, which had estimated that the number of core green jobs in the state was 159,000 in 2008. In the state government study, an estimated 300,000 Californians spent at least half their employment time in a job related to green products or services, and another 171,000 spent less than half their time in such a job. The largest category was manufacturing (93,000 jobs), followed by construction (68,000), a mixture of scientific and administrative jobs (43,000), waste management and remediation

(39,000), and wholesale trade (34,000). Although manufacturing was the largest category of green jobs in this study, if one interprets construction, waste management and remediation, and wholesale trade as constituting a single category of largely service jobs, then manufacturing was again the smaller category. The study also estimated that the total number of green jobs was about 3.8 percent of the workforce, a relatively high number from a national perspective and even high with respect to estimates of about 3 percent in other West Coast states. Although not all green jobs in these studies are clean tech jobs, it is interesting that the general estimates of green jobs in California—either 159,000 in the Next10 study or 300,000 in the state government study—compare favorably with an estimated 52,000 jobs in the state's biotech industry and 220,000 in the software industry.[26]

Also important for understanding definitions of green jobs is their growth rate. The Next10 study on California found that between 1995 and 2008 green jobs grew at a rate of 36 percent—that is, 3 times the average growth rate for all jobs in the state. At the national level, the above-mentioned study by the Pew Charitable Trusts, which focused on a relatively narrow definition of green jobs in what it termed the "clean energy" sector, also found a higher than average growth rate for green jobs. The statistics showed that green jobs were growing at a rate of 9 percent per year between 1998 and 2007, in comparison with 3.7 percent for other jobs. Of special interest in the Pew report is the relative growth rate among types of green jobs. The report found the largest category of jobs in remediation, recycling, and waste and water treatment (65 percent), but those jobs were growing at a relatively slow rate of about 3 percent per year. In contrast, jobs in biofuels, hybrid-vehicle manufacturing, and construction were only 7 percent of all green jobs but growing at a rate of 67 percent per year, and jobs in clean energy generation, maintenance, and energy efficiency were about 20 percent of all clean energy jobs and growing at a rate of 20 percent per year. In short, growth was driven primarily by jobs in clean energy, energy efficiency, biofuels, and hybrid-vehicle manufacturing.[27]

A subsequent study by the Brookings Institution found a growth rate of 3.4 percent from 2003 to 2010, in comparison with a national average of 4.2 percent. The most plausible explanation for the lower growth rate for green jobs is that the Brookings study defined the clean economy more broadly than the Pew study. Because the Brookings study counted almost 3 times the total number of jobs, it probably had a heavier weighting of the green industries with slower growth rates. Consistent with other studies, the Brookings study found that industries such as wind, solar, biofuels, conservation, and green buildings were growing at a more rapid rate than the rest of the economy, in some cases more than twice the average growth rate for jobs of 4.2 percent. Furthermore, during the peak recession years of 2008 and 2009, the clean economy grew at 8.3 percent. The study suggested that the relatively high growth rate during the recession may have been due to federal funding from the American Recovery and Reinvestment Act.[28]

One conclusion from the comparison of studies is that it is not a straightforward matter to calculate the number of green jobs in the country and their growth rate. At the low end, the Pew study estimate was 770,000, or less than 1 percent of the national workforce, and at the high end, such as the definition that the California government used in its study, the estimate for the total number of green jobs at the national level would be 6 million, or about 4 percent of all jobs. The Brookings Institution study used a middling figure of 2.7 million in 2011 (about 2 percent of all jobs), which it compared with 1.2 million direct jobs in the fossil fuel industry (again, not counting gasoline stations). Thus, when one uses broad definitions of green jobs rather than a narrow definition of direct renewable-energy and energy-efficiency employment, it is possible to make the case that a tipping point has arrived in which the "green" economy has become larger than the "carbon" economy, especially in states that don't have strong coal, oil, and natural gas extraction industries.[29]

However, in order for the relative ratios of green jobs and fossil fuel jobs to translate into policy, the people who are counted as having green jobs would have to see their future as enrolled in the green transition. The translation may occur in the narrow subset of renewable-energy and energy-efficiency jobs, but it is much more problematic for many of the other categories that are included in estimates of total green jobs. Furthermore, it is clear that even the most optimistic estimates of the total number of green jobs and their growth rates would not solve persistent problems of unemployment, which reached more than 14 million people during the recession that followed the financial crisis of 2008. The clean economy is only about 2 percent of employment, in comparison with the largest sector of employment, health care, which is 10 percent of all jobs. In a discussion about wind turbine and electric vehicle manufacturing in his state, Mitch Daniels, the Republican governor of Indiana, commented:

We are excited about green jobs. We are chasing them everywhere we can, and we are enabling them as creatively as any state. There aren't enough of them by any count to replace one-for-one jobs that have been lost or at risk. They're not of high enough quality. There are some great jobs in some important new sectors, but we haven't seen any evidence that they should be sought at the expense of the traditional economy or the traditional energy that powers that economy. (2009)

The relatively small number of green jobs and their service-sector weighting suggest that there are limits to an economic development strategy that would solve short-term employment and underemployment issues with heavy reliance on green job creation. However, the high growth rates of some types of green jobs suggest that in the long term there is potential for green jobs to be a much more important factor in overall employment. The mayors' report articulated a scenario for 2038 based on the assumptions that 40 percent of the country's electricity would come from renewable energy, there would be a 35 percent reduction in electricity consumption based on retrofits to buildings, and at least 30 percent of transportation would come from alternative fuels. Under that scenario, green jobs would constitute about 10 percent of all new job growth. Furthermore, when one relaxes the definition of green jobs to include industries outside the energy sector (such as green chemicals, recycling, remediation, organic agriculture, broadband communication, and public transportation) that have roles to play in the green energy transition, the number of jobs that could be designated as green increases significantly.[30]

To facilitate the creation of more green jobs, economists have estimated that for every $100 million in venture capital investment about 2,700 new green jobs are created—that is, at a cost of about $37,000 per job. In the 2008 presidential election, candidate Barack Obama promised to spend $150 billion dollars over ten years to create 5 million new green jobs—that is, at a cost of $30,000 per job. Other estimates of the actual average cost of creating one green job have been as high as $50,000. Although the estimates vary, they suggest that a trillion-dollar investment (somewhat larger than the total expenditure of the ARRA, but spread out over many years) would be needed to create from 20 million to 30 million new green jobs. Such levels of investment would be well beyond the private-sector venture capital that is available in the United States for clean tech investment, even over a ten-year period. Ongoing government policy support would be necessary, and that prospect tends to trigger ideological fault lines, because it violates a premise of neoliberal ideology.[31]

Furthermore, if the United States were to embark on a full-fledged green transition with an investment of $1 trillion, the 20 million to 30 million new green jobs probably would change not only the country's "environmental footprint" but also its political landscape. Because green is mostly blue in the United States, a surge of 20 million to 30 million new green jobs could translate into more Democratic voters. Within the Republican Party, one might also see the resurgence of relatively moderate and green Republicans such as George Pataki and Arnold Schwarzenegger. But under either scenario—a shift in power toward Democrats or a realignment within the Republican Party—there would be a significant change in the political landscape.

Conclusion

In the broader history of environmental policy in the United States, the convergence of constituencies in favor of green businesses and jobs represents a significant change in the history of both environmental and industrial policy. The political scientists Daniel Mazmanian and Michael Kraft argue that environmental policy went through three historical periods: the command-and-control regulations of the 1960s and the 1970s, the balancing of environmental and market-oriented approaches during the 1980s, and the focus on sustainable communities during the 1990s. In terms of the underlying political ideologies, the first phase was consistent with the interventionist politics of social liberalism, the second with the early phase of Reagan-Thatcher neoliberalism, and the third with the devolutionary politics of the softer, Clinton-Blair form of neoliberalism. Extending the analysis of Mazmanian and Kraft into the twenty-first century, I suggest that the merging of sustainability policies with developmentalist concerns for job creation and industrial development represents a fourth phase of environmental policy. In the book *Emerald Cities*, the urban studies researcher Joan Fitzgerald also noted the change when she argued that in American cities "sustainability and climate change strategies could also be engines of economic development" (2010: 1). Hatched and nurtured largely in state and local governments, the policies percolated up to the federal government level, at least temporarily, during the first two years of the Obama administration.[32]

Although "green jobs" is the popular frame in which this fourth wave of policies is presented to voters, the network of reforms could be summarized as a more defensive approach to foreign trade and an invigorated industrial policy. Green industrial policy entails government intervention in the economy, but not in the traditional social liberal mode of correcting for market failures or redistributing wealth. Instead, the intervention involves support for new industries by instituting both supply-side and demand-side policies. In response to the developmentalist policies, conservatives draw on neoliberal philosophies of government by arguing that developmentalist strategies bet on some industries rather than others, a role that they argue is best left to markets. They also oppose protectionist measures, again by arguing that a free-market approach is best. As a result, the prospect of creating green jobs and developing green industries becomes caught in the crossfire of broader ideological differences about the proper role of the government in the economy. The four chapters that follow will analyze in detail how the policy developments associated with green jobs are connected with underlying ideological differences.

II
Policies and Politics

3
Green Industrial Policy and the 111th Congress

The 111th Congress met in 2009 and 2010, during a historic moment of severe financial crisis and recession. Strong Democratic majorities in both houses and Barack Obama's campaign promise of "change you can believe in" increased expectations that significant legislative reform would occur. Among the promises was the link between green energy policy and job creation that had mobilized green transition coalitions. Many independent voters who were concerned with job security found the framing of green energy transition policies appealing, and they joined with union members, environmentalists, green businesses, "new economy" progressives, and anti-poverty groups to support a presidential candidate who promised 5 million green jobs. However, by 2010 the high levels of expenditures by the fossil fuel industry to defeat cap-and-trade legislation and the subsequent setbacks for Democrats in the elections that year meant that the political opportunity structure at the federal government level opened by the electoral support of Democrats in 2008 appeared to have closed. The word "appeared" is used purposefully. As the remainder of the book will show, the polarized nature of American politics implies that the underlying pattern of unevenness in the green transition at the state and local level was going on well before the election of Barack Obama to the presidency and continued even after the anti-green backlash of late 2010.

This chapter will analyze the developmentalist aspects of federal government policy, with a focus on green energy, during the first two years of the Obama administration. It will begin with the argument that the rise of China as a rival in global economics, politics, and even ideology has created the perception of a severe challenge to the new dependencies in manufacturing and threats to American industry that are engendered by trade liberalization. The first section will show the range and depth of concern with Chinese "mercantilism." The next two sections will examine the emergence of defensiveness in trade law and federal government legislation. The last section will explore the state of green industrial policy in the federal government during the two-year period. Together, the sections on trade and industrial policy will constitute a general exploration of the thesis that developmentalism is of growing significance in American politics.

Green Industrial Policy and Perceptions of China

It might have happened that the political discourse and policy measures aimed at combating the perceived mercantilism of the Chinese government were quite separate from green energy and green jobs policies. However, in this section and the next I will argue that the two issues became closely linked, because some of the most striking conflicts between the United States and China over trade involved the green industries. Unlike Japan in the 1980s, China in the twenty-first century was a rival superpower that neither accepted American hegemony in the world nor shared Western traditions of parliamentary rule. As the new superpower rivalry emerged, traditionally liberal and Democratic issues, the environment and jobs, were linked to the more bipartisan concerns of American power on the global stage.

One of the most commonly referenced examples of the perception of China as a mercantilist threat to the United States is an essay by Paul Krugman, who drew attention to the artificially high value of the Chinese renminbi and its effect on the prices of manufactured goods. Krugman, a Keynesian economist and a *New York Times* columnist, linked the Chinese threat and American job losses in statements such as the following: "For the next couple of years Chinese mercantilism may end up reducing US employment by around 1.4 million jobs." (2010) He argued that the United States would lose little if China were to dump its hoard of American dollars, and he suggested that a trade confrontation might be beneficial for the United States. Furthermore, on the issue of developmentalism he raised a fundamental question about the belief that protectionism is bad for the economy:

There's the claim that protectionism is always a bad thing, in any circumstances. If that's what you believe, however, you learned Econ 101 from the wrong people—because when unemployment is high and the government can't restore full employment, the usual rules don't apply.

Let me quote from a classic paper by the late Paul Samuelson, who more or less created modern economics: "With employment less than full...all the debunked mercantilistic arguments"—that is, claims that nations who subsidize their exports effectively steal jobs from other countries—"turn out to be valid." (ibid.)

Although Krugman preferred to solve the problem by instituting exchange-rate adjustments, he left open the door for protectionist policies as an American response.

Krugman's advocacy of a more aggressive posture with respect to China's developmentalist policies reflects a growing recognition within the United States that the Chinese government's attitude toward foreign companies had changed. The country that had once courted foreign investors had shifted to increasingly cold and hostile inspections of American companies. Leo Hindery, chairman of the US Economy/Smart Globalization Initiative of the New American Foundation, argued that the United States should pay attention to China's "mercantilist" (his term) policies, including the following:

(1) regulations to block non-Chinese firms from selling their products to Chinese government agencies,

(2) technical standards that prevent or at least greatly hinder the Chinese government and Chinese businesses from buying non-Chinese goods, and

(3) rules that force Western companies to give up technological secrets in exchange for access to China's markets. (Hindery 2010)

The last point referred to the Indigenous Innovation Production Accreditation (IIPA) Program, which the Chinese government launched in 2009 to limit its procurement to foreign companies willing to transfer their intellectual property. Hindery explained:

This program is far more restrictive than any other buy-domestic program in the world, and its adverse impacts are already being felt across all industries that seek to export to China, but especially in computers and consumer electronics, green technologies, autos, aviation, and specialty materials. And if this wasn't blatant enough, embedded in the IIPA Program is the demand that in order to sell things in China not yet manufactured there, foreign companies must first transfer and license, to Chinese companies, their latest technology for "co-innovation" and "re-innovation." (ibid.).

Furthermore, Hindery pointed out, foreign companies that complain about any forms of unfair treatment are subject to harassment.[1]

Another source of concern came from export-oriented American manufacturers that are not large enough to benefit from global manufacturing operations. Often these companies are family-owned and privately held businesses. Whereas the Chamber of Commerce is aligned with multinational global corporations that generally support greater trade liberalization, the United States Business and Industry Council advocates for family-owned and privately held manufacturing businesses, which have been especially hurt by competition from Chinese manufacturing. The website of the public education arm of the Business and Industry Council includes dozens of references to Chinese mercantilism. William Hawkins, a senior fellow for national security studies at the council, is a prominent critic of what he calls the "new mercantilism" of China. He defined mercantilism as the "drive for exports and a large reserve of hard currency," and he worried about the build-up of Chinese sea power and rise of Chinese bilateral agreements. The organization prefers to replace trade dependency with import substitution—in other words, the production of goods in the United States. Peter Morici, an economist associated with the Business and Industry Council, writes:

To jump start the economy, the trade deficit—which is almost entirely the deficits with China and on oil—must be addressed. That requires confronting China's undervalued currency and mercantilism, and finally developing America's abundant oil and gas resources. (2011)[2]

For this organization, the focus is on developing domestic industries, and hence the operational category is domestic energy rather than domestic green energy.

Unions are another source of criticism of trade policies that have decimated American industries. American exports to China are concentrated in the industries of raw materials, food, and materials for industrial manufacturing, whereas Chinese exports to the United States are mostly manufactured products from consumer goods to industrial equipment. For many Americans, especially those who have jobs in the manufacturing sector, the obvious remedy is a return to the developmentalist policies that worked so well for the US in the nineteenth century. At green jobs conferences, one often hears labor leaders say of the Chinese "They're cleaning our clock" or "They're eating our lunch." Like domestically oriented American manufacturers, labor leaders are aghast at how readily the US has surrendered its manufacturing capacity to China and other countries. From their viewpoint, the US should stop the hemorrhaging of its manufacturing sector through stronger protectionist measures.[3]

Union leaders are often the most outspoken opponents of the open and unprotected approach to trade policy that the United States has pursued. For example, the United Steelworkers leader Leo Gerard commented: "In the free for all twenty-first [century], it all sounds terrific—free markets, free trade, and free commerce. But really, it's lies, traderous [*sic*] lies, and statistics." (2008) Gerard added that in 2000, when China joined the World Trade Organization, Americans were promised hundreds of thousands of jobs, but instead millions of jobs moved to China, including jobs for scientists and engineers. He suggested that free trade be replaced with fair trade, in which all countries respect labor, environmental, and product safety laws. More generally, the BlueGreen Alliance has argued that environmental, manufacturing, and trade policy are all linked:

The US must develop and implement a national manufacturing policy aimed at leveling the playing field between domestic and foreign companies. When all countries abide by a common set of trade rules, companies, workers, and the environment all benefit. If the US is going to be a leader in the clean energy economy, we not only need the right policies and investments, but we need to ensure that there is a level playing field. (2011)

Much of the sentiment in favor of a defensive approach to trade is based on the perception that some trading partners, above all China, pursue a mercantilist strategy. The framing of Chinese trade policy as mercantilist deflects criticism from the economics profession and from advocates of free trade among business and political leaders, because the argument is not so much about the benefits of trade or the value of free trade in principle as much as it is about the claimed manipulation of trade agreements that has damaged American industries and jobs. The expression "unilateral disarmament" sums up the view that the United States has opened up its manufacturing markets to foreign competition without providing the same levels of subsidies and support found in other countries. In this sense even the protectionist side of developmentalism doesn't break entirely with the common ground of mainstream social liberals and neoliberals in support of free trade. As the statement from the BlueGreen Alliance indicates, arguments are formulated within the framework of existing trade agreements and the mechanisms for remediation rather than openly calling for high tariffs and isolationism.[4]

However, it is possible to find comments in support of a more extreme form of developmentalism, in which the current world trade regime would be ended. Union leaders occasionally express a desire that the World Trade Organization be abolished or that the United States withdraw from it, but only a few people have thought through the implications of a different global economic order. Ambrose Evans-Pritchard, the historically minded International Business Editor of the *Daily Telegraph*, suggests a scenario in which the United States retreats behind a new wall of protectionism:

The risk—or solution?—is that the US will opt for a variant of Imperial Prefer-ence, the pro-growth bloc created behind tariff walls by the British Empire with Scandinavia, Argentina, and other like-minded states in 1932. This experiment has been air-brushed out of history by free trade hegemonists.

One can imagine how this might unfold. North America would clamp down on dumping, at first gingerly, before escalating towards a cascade of Smoot-Hawley tariffs and barriers. Mexico and Central America would join. Brazil and Mercosur would find it irresistible because that is where the demand would be, and BRIC [Brazil, Russia, India, and China] solidarity would wither on the vine. (2011)

Robert Samuelson, a contributing editor for the *Washington Post* and *Newsweek*, suggested similar implications. Although he argued that the high unemployment rates of 2008 and later could not all be blamed on China, he also suggested that the loss jobs to China (2.8 million by his estimate) during the first decade of the twenty-first century was slowing the American recovery, especially because many of the jobs lost were in manufacturing. He added:

No one should relish threatening China with a 25 percent tariff. It would be illegal under existing WTO rules; to save the postwar trading system, we'd have to attack it. This would risk an all-out trade war when the world economy is already tottering. There's no guarantee that China would respond as hoped. Initially, it might retaliate. Cooperation on other issues would collapse. Prices of Chinese exports (consumer electronics, shoes) that we barely make would prob-ably rise. Other countries might adopt protective measures.

All this is dangerous stuff. The policy's only recommendation is that it might be slightly better than the alternative: condoning China's ongoing assault on our industry. In the past, it's been clothes and furniture; in the future, it will be cars and commercial aircraft. China's policies assail other countries, too, and its trade surpluses destabilize the global economy. There's already a trade war between them and us; but only one side is fighting. (2011)[5]

The scenario of the collapse of trade with China is perhaps unlikely, and at present American developmentalism involves a much more com-plicated balancing act that includes support for a global regime of free trade but is qualified by increasing defensiveness with respect to the developmentalist policies of China. It is less likely that the United States will return to the developmentalist mercantilism of the nineteenth century (or, as Evans-Pritchard envisions, of a broader circle of limited trading partners) than shift toward an increasingly defensive and pragmatic approach to trade that leads to deepening disputes with China and other trading partners.

The sample of comments on Chinese mercantilism provided here indicates that people with a wide range of political persuasions—from avatars of social liberalism such as Krugman and the unions to conservative business manufacturing associations—agree that free trade, especially with China, has been damaging to American manufacturers, if not to the economy and the country as a whole. The protectionist sentiment has the capacity to cut across ideological lines and potentially to create shifts in the underlying landscape of political ideology with respect to the free-trade consensus that a wide range of economic and political leaders in the United States have shared since the end of World War II.

Trade Complaints and Green Industries

The defensive posture with respect to trade is not limited to public discourse in the political field; it is also embedded in policy action. Since 2000, the US government has imposed tariffs on a wide range of imported products, including steel pipes, coated paper, and tires, and many of them were imposed in response to the Chinese government's subsidies and trade policies. In the case of steel pipes, which are used in oil drilling, during the period 2006–2008 imports from China quadrupled from $681 million to $2.8 billion, prompting charges of dumping. Partly in response to American tariffs on steel pipes, China's Tianjin Pipe Group decided to construct a $1 billion factory in Corpus Christi, Texas.[6]

As the case of steel pipes suggests, one outcome of the defensive posture with respect to trade is for Chinese companies to open factories in the United States, much as Japan did during the 1980s. American jobs are created, and both labor and manufacturing constituencies are mollified. Although foreign direct investment from China into the United States remains small in comparison with investment from Canada, Japan, and some of the European countries, it has been growing. Notably, in 2011 China's ENN Group announced a plan to invest $8 billion in clean energy projects in the United States.[7]

During the first two years of the Obama administration, the most prominent trade dispute with respect to green technology was the complaint that the United Steelworkers filed with the Office of the United States Trade Representative, under section 301 of the Trade Act of 1974, on September 9, 2010. The union alleged that China was engaging in unfair trade practices that threatened the future of the renewable and clean energy industries in the United States. The steelworkers argued that China had engaged in hundreds of billions of dollars of illegal trade practices that caused serious damage to American green energy manufacturing industries such as wind turbines and solar photovoltaics. Six weeks after the complaint was filed, the United States Trade Office agreed to investigate the complaint. Although the US government didn't file a complaint, it did pursue a subset of the issues, and by July 2011 it had achieved one concession: China agreed to eliminate subsidies to wind turbine manufacturers that use domestic content.[8]

In defense of retaliatory measures, the Steelworkers' vice-president, Tom Conway, commented that the United States was "losing its leadership of this sector" and that China planned to "control" the industry by "breaking every rule in the book" (United Steelworkers 2010b). Although many American firms that have manufacturing operations in China agreed with the union's claim about violating trade agreements, they were afraid to complain publicly. As a result, the report was issued both in a public version and in a private version that discussed in more detail the issues that specific firms face. The public document[9] identified several main areas of trade violation; I summarize them here:

• China controls the world production of many rare-earth metals, and it has restricted access to those metals through export quotas and taxes that are in violation of World Trade Organization rules.

• China provides subsidies that are only available to clean energy exporters (a violation of trade rules), and it also provides export credits that violate the rules of the Organization for Economic Cooperation and Development.

• China has domestic-content requirements and preferences for its wind farms, and it excludes foreign firms from access to carbon credits.

• China requires that joint ventures include technology transfer from foreign companies, a provision that is in violation of World Trade Organization rules.

• Chinese subsidies for the green manufacturing sector were double those of the United States and caused loss of market share for American companies in China and Europe.

Although subsidies are permitted under trade law, export subsidies tagged to specific industries are not allowed, and subsidized companies cannot be required to use domestic content. Furthermore, if one country can show that its domestic industry has suffered "serious prejudice" because of another country's industry specific subsidy, then the subsidy becomes actionable under trade law.

Congress supported the petition with two letters, one from 181 Congressional representatives and another from 43 senators. The Congressional letter argued that the United States "must take urgent and decisive enforcement action to secure a level playing field for fair competition for green-technology manufacturers" (US Congress 2010). The representatives also asked for the president to establish a dedicated China trade enforcement team.

Not all Americans agreed with the defensive approach to trade with China, and some political leaders continued to defend the benefits of trade liberalization. For example, during a visit to China for the meeting of the C40 (the mayors of the world's top cities), Mayor Michael Bloomberg of New York commented:

Let me get this straight: There's a country on the other side of the world that is taking their taxpayers' dollars and trying to sell subsidized things so we can buy them cheaper, and have better products, and we're going to criticize that? (Stein 2010).

Bloomberg accused the political leaders who were supporting protectionism of being uninformed:

If you look at the US, you look at who we're electing to Congress, to the Senate— they can't read. I'll bet you a bunch of these people don't have passports. We're about to start a trade war with China if we're not careful here. (ibid.)

The defensive approach to trade has also divided green transition coalitions, because Chinese imports benefit American consumers by bringing down the price of renewable energy, such as solar photovoltaics. Although the Chinese government's subsidies harm American manufacturers, they benefit American consumers of green energy products such as solar panels.[10]

The Chinese response was consistent with that of other trade disputes: the government rejected the trade accusation as false and claimed that the United States was hypocritical. Turning the protectionist rhetoric back on the United States, a spokesperson from the Chinese embassy in Washington called the investigation "unwarranted and protectionist in nature" (Chan and Bradsher 2010). Zhang Guobao, vice chairman of China's National Development and Reform Commission and head of the National Energy Commission, argued that American politicians were scapegoating China rather than examining domestic causes for America's poor economic performance. He added that the United States also has substantial subsidies and domestic-content provisions:

What America is blaming us for is exactly what they do themselves. Chinese subsidies to new energy companies are much smaller than those of the United

States government. If the United States government can subsidize companies, then why can't we? (Wines and Yang 2010)

Li Junfeng, Deputy Director of the Energy Research Institute of the China National Development and Reform Commission, noted that the United States lost its leadership in solar photovoltaic manufacturing first to Germany and Japan and only later to China. He added that the poor performance of the American solar industry was due to inconsistent policies across political administrations rather than unfair trade policies from China. He argued that in bidding competitions in China foreign companies did well on the technology score but were not competitive on price. He also denied that China has export subsidies for solar manufacturers and that the government requires technology transfer for joint ventures. More generally, the Chinese government claimed that 50 percent of the materials used in the manufacture of its solar panels are imported, and half of the imported materials are from the United States. The country also claimed that about half of the solar photovoltaic manufacturing equipment is imported from the United States.[11]

Although China rejected the allegations, it could not deny that a change in the location of solar photovoltaic manufacturing had driven many American manufacturers out of business and led to a global consolidation of the industry, even among Chinese companies. China went from manufacturing only a small percentage of the world's solar photovoltaics in 2000 to dominating the world market by 2010. The United States was able to maintain a trade surplus with China in the solar industry, but only because of its exports of silicon feedstock and secondarily of solar manufacturing equipment, not photovoltaic panels. In effect, the US had become a raw materials exporter to China. Although it still maintained an advantage at the high end of capital goods manufacturing, it was possible that China would soon displace capital goods manufacturing as well. If that were to occur, the capacity for next-generation solar research in the US would be crippled by the lack of local technology transfer capacity.[12]

American companies complained that opportunities to earn contracts for large-scale installation projects in China declined after China built up its own solar energy industry. To earn contracts, American companies must work with Chinese companies and also surrender intellectual property to Chinese firms, thereby transferring investments by the US government in future technology to Chinese companies. Carolyn Bartholomew, chair of the United States-China Economic and Security Review Commission, complained:

The Chinese government is offering extensive subsidies to the world's green-technology manufacturers to encourage them to move production to China. And when the manufacturing leaves America, the research-and-development operations are sure to follow. After all, the manufacturers want their researchers and engineers on site to work out problems and suggest work-arounds. This one-two punch has been a successful strategy for China in the automotive sector, where battery and fuel cell research formerly conducted in America is being conducted alongside auto assembly lines in China. (2010)

This comment connects the protectionist and competitiveness aspects of green industrial policy. From a protectionist viewpoint, China is using trade policy aggressively to break down intellectual property protections for American industry. Some of its policies may be in violation of trade law and therefore actionable. From the competitiveness viewpoint, the US government has failed to keep up with the subsidies that the Chinese government offers its clean tech businesses. American companies are therefore lured to China not only because of the market size but also because of the country's generous subsidies, and in return they surrender intellectual property to Chinese firms. In the short term, the American companies benefit because there are very low restrictions from the United States when they export manufactured goods back from China. It becomes impossible to resist the benefits of moving to China, both because of access to the Chinese market and because of the ability to sell back into the American market with goods manufactured in China.

An example of the complex relationships that have emerged for green energy manufacturers is the Spanish wind manufacturer Gamesa, one of the global leaders in the industry. The company agreed to a contract to manufacture in China, but it had to use Chinese suppliers, which it helped to train and develop. However, the Chinese government and the local suppliers worked with new Chinese turbine manufacturers to displace Gamesa. The government offered its own turbine manufacturers generous loans, construction contracts, and inexpensive land that were not available to Gamesa. In 2005 China began to require that 70 percent of the components in turbines for Chinese wind farms had to come from Chinese companies. The Spanish company's market share in China plummeted from 33 percent in 2005 to 3 percent in 2010, while the local companies grew to have 85 percent of the domestic market share. However, because the Chinese market for wind energy was growing so rapidly, Gamesa didn't suffer an absolute decline in sales in China. Furthermore, in order to maintain its access to Chinese markets, the company didn't complain about the trade violations. But was the long-term strategy good for the global manufacturer? In effect, it had transferred technology to Chinese companies, which began exporting and soon grew to have 50 percent of the global market.[13]

With respect to the similar growth of solar photovoltaic manufacturing in China, the United States and several European countries investigated allegations of dumping of solar panels at below-cost levels, a situation that could trigger retaliatory trade measures. The American company SunPower and European companies accused China of unfair trade practices because of its 50 percent subsidies of solar manufacturers, and in 2009 they sought investigations of anti-dumping practices that could lead to trade protection by the US government and by the European Union. Under world trade law, even a legal subsidy can become actionable if it causes a disruption in another country's industry. China provided $30 billion in credit to its solar industry, an amount that was estimated to be 20 times that of the United States. As will be shown in chapter 8, the issue resurfaced in 2011 as a result of the bankruptcy of the American solar photovoltaic company Solyndra.[14]

Another dispute—one related to the conflict over clean energy manufacturing—concerns the mining and production of rare-earth metals. They are important constituents in various clean energy technologies, including batteries, solar photovoltaic panels, and fuel cells. The United States had been self-sufficient in the mining and production of the metals, but its mines were closed down during the 1990s because of competition from lower-priced Chinese products. China became the center of 97 percent of the world's processing of rare metals, and mining and manufacturing elsewhere closed down. A Chinese company purchased one of the last American companies in the business and moved the technology to China. In 2010 the Chinese government cut export quotas of rare metals by 72 percent, a decision that has implications for high-technology equipment in many industries, including clean energy technologies and weapons. In 2011 a panel of the World Trade Organization ruled that China's export quotas and duties on rare-earth metals could not be justified on environmental grounds; and in 2012 the trade organization ruled more broadly against China's export restrictions on metals.[15]

Although the United States has won some concessions from China, the broader challenge is that China's investments in research and development for green industrial policy are higher than those of the United States. China's twelfth five-year plan, for the period 2011–2015, included an increase in investments in clean energy research and development, reductions in energy intensity, and increases in consumption of renewable and non-fossil-fuel energy. The planned increased investment in clean energy was on a base that had already exceeded the United States in 2009, when China invested $34.6 billion in clean energy industries and the United States invested only $18.6 billion.[16]

Protecting Green Manufacturing

After 2008, Congress responded to growing concerns about the loss of manufacturing jobs and the sense of unfair competition with legislation designed to protect American businesses and to enhance their competitiveness. Laws approved under the Democratic Party's slogan "Make It in America," which sometimes had bipartisan support, included the following:

• the United States Manufacturing Enhancement Act (HR 4380), which reduced tariffs on imported goods not made domestically in order to lower costs for American companies (perhaps counter-intuitively, the law protected American businesses by reducing trade barriers, but only on goods not produced domestically)

• the Protecting American Patents Act (HR 5874), which provided additional appropriations for the United States Patent Office to reduce the backlog of applications

• the Preventing Outsourcing Act (HR 1586), which closed tax loopholes that encourage American companies to shift jobs overseas.

The Currency Reform for Fair Trade Act of 2010, passed by the House but not the Senate during the 111th Congress, would have allowed the US government to impose tariffs on countries that systematically undervalue their currency. In 2011 the Senate passed a similar bill with bipartisan support (79 votes in favor).[17]

The most overtly protectionist and most controversial measure passed by the 111th Congress was the domestic-content provision that appeared in the 2009 American Recovery and Reinvestment Act (ARRA). Domestic-content provisions date back to the Buy American Act of 1933, which required 50 percent domestic content in manufactured goods purchased by the federal government. Beginning in 1978, "Buy America" requirements were added to transportation and highway laws, and in 1994 the United States added domestic-content labeling requirements for automobiles. Most of the domestic-content requirements allow for exceptions in the case of excessive cost or lack of availability.[18]

Because the ARRA provisions applied to items purchased by the federal government or built with government assistance, they were not economy-wide measures and were allowed under general World Trade Organization law. However, some countries have signed a side agreement to limit such favoritism. Forty trading partners have signed the Government Procurement Agreement (GPA), which was designed to end domestic-content provisions even for government purchases. Importantly, China, India, and Brazil had not signed the GPA at the time of ARRA. As a result, domestic-content policies could operate within World Trade Organization rules but protect job loss to China and other newly industrialized countries. Furthermore, the GPA applies only to state governments that have signed it. Thirty-seven state governments signed the agreement, but some included exceptions, such as for the steel industry in Pennsylvania. Federal legislation that involves shifting expenditures to state and local governments (as occurred with much of the funding in the ARRA) allows some of the funding to be spent by state and local governments that do not adhere to the GPA. Here, one can see a trade benefit from the neoliberal policy known as "devolution" of spending to state and local governments.

Strongly supported by unions, the domestic-content provision of the ARRA applied to iron, steel, and manufactured goods in public works. Because the provision didn't draw a clear line between domestic assembly and manufacture and between subcomponents and final assembly, its effects on foreign trade were not clear. For example, because a wind turbine has more than 8,000 components, and because (like automobiles) wind turbines are manufactured by global companies, determining the level of "domestic content" of a wind turbine is a complicated task. To accommodate complexities and shortages, the provision allowed for a waiver under specific conditions, such as non-availability, lack of consistency with the public interest, and unreasonable cost (defined as greater than 25 percent of the entire project). Enforcing the act created challenges for the Department of Energy, which formed partnerships with both the unions and manufacturing associations to process requests for waivers and to identify domestic manufacturers. The processing of waivers also created headaches for state and municipal governments, but it did identify new manufacturing opportunities for domestic companies.[19]

The "buy American" provisions also provoked opposition from the US Chamber of Commerce, which issued a study and statements that argued that the rules would be self-defeating. The organization argued that the rules would slow down "shovel-ready" projects by immersing them in red tape and that the rules would cause trading partners to invoke retaliatory measures, which in turn would harm American jobs in the export sector. Instead of a "buy American" plan, the Chamber advocated a "buy American, sell American" approach that would be less threatening to the globally oriented corporations that it represented. The Chamber also issued a study that combined an analysis of the domestic-content provisions in the ARRA with research on the forthcoming free-trade agreements with Colombia, Panama, and South Korea. The Chamber argued that 176,000 jobs would be lost if the domestic-content rules resulted in the loss of only 1 percent of foreign trade. More specifically, economists at the Peterson Institute argued that at best the "buy American" provision would create only 1,000 jobs for steelworkers, and they suggested that more jobs could be lost because of the possibility of trade retaliation.[20]

The Alliance for American Manufacturing countered the Chamber of Commerce with an opposing study, which the United Steelworkers endorsed. The manufacturers' report noted that the domestic-content provisions were consistent with trade law and that rather than encourage countries to retaliate, the provisions might encourage countries to join the GPA, a change that would open more markets to American products. Furthermore, the study argued that the stimulus package as a whole would create 3,675,000 jobs, of which 408,000 would be in manufacturing, and that the "buy American" provisions would increase new jobs in ARRA projects by about one third. The manufacturers' report also criticized the Peterson Institute study for ignoring indirect job creation. A subsequent report by the manufacturers' alliance added that in the years 2007–2009 the United States had lost 2.1 million manufacturing jobs, and the US economy had lost 5.5 million manufacturing jobs between 2000 and 2010, or about 32 percent of all manufacturing jobs. The alliance noted that polls found that more than 80 percent of Americans support "buy American" provisions and that the provisions received strong favorable and bipartisan votes in the House of Representatives and Senate. Furthermore, the study noted that more than 500 communities and state governments in the United States had adopted their own version of "buy American" provisions.[21]

The implementation of the ARRA provisions and other support for American manufacturing provoked additional controversies. In 2009 a consortium of Chinese and American companies announced a decision to build a 600-megawatt wind farm in west Texas, with planned support from the ARRA. The wind farm was trumpeted as creating 2,800 jobs, but subsequent reports indicated that the project ended up creating only

15 percent of the jobs in the United States, with many of the other jobs going to China. Furthermore, investigative reports in late 2009 and early 2010 indicated that for an ARRA clean energy program that gave grants of 30 percent of cost to companies to build new renewable-energy facilities, more than 80 percent of the funds went to foreign companies, mostly wind manufacturers. Some senators called for a moratorium on the ARRA program until the flaws were addressed, but the proposal alarmed the wind industry. The American Wind Industry Association argued that a moratorium would cost 50,000 American jobs and that the federal government should instead implement a federal renewable-electricity standard, which would create 274,000 American jobs. One can see in these exchanges how much they are made in reference to the developmentalist concern of making and keeping jobs and industries in the United States.[22]

Domestic-content provisions and other support for domestic manufacturing, especially demand policies at the state government level, appear to have helped some manufacturing industries to regain lost steam. A report by the American Wind Energy Association in 2009 indicated that domestic content for wind manufacturing grew from less than 25 percent in 2005 to nearly 50 percent in 2009, and the president of the same association noted that the number of wind manufacturing companies grew from a few dozen in 2004 to more than 200 companies in 2010. A broader industry report even suggested that the suppressed dollar and rising labor costs in China were associated with a general repatriation of manufacturing to the United States, but the argument was based only on a few cases.[23]

Whether caused by policies such as the ARRA provisions or general economic changes, the potential repatriation of manufacturing to the United States could be accompanied by greater foreign ownership of domestic manufacturing operations, much as occurred with the automobile industry during the 1980s. Of the leading global wind manufacturing companies, many are European and Asian, and counts of domestic manufacturing jobs don't distinguish between wind manufacturing by General Electric or foreign companies. Chinese firms are also opening manufacturing operations in the United States: the large Chinese firm Suntech opened a plant in Arizona, and the wind-power company A-Power planned to open a factory in Nevada. Rail manufacturing represents another area of heavy, steel-intensive manufacturing that is likely to grow provided that high-speed rail receives continuing funding, but again the leading manufacturers in the United States tend to be foreign companies.

For blue-collar workers the difference is not so important (European companies may even be more willing to work with unions), but for an innovation economy, the split between ownership and manufacturing means that the high-end research-and-development jobs remain close to corporate headquarters in other countries, and consequently the potential for research to be translated into local innovation is reduced.[24]

Supporting Green Businesses

In addition to defending domestic industry in trade disputes and legislation, the other main developmentalist response to global competition is to provide government support to those industries. The Obama administration selected green industries for special federal government support, and *Bloomberg Businessweek* labeled the president "venture capitalist-in-chief" because of the government's clean energy investments. Calling Obama's focus on green energy industries a "new American industrial policy," the magazine also expressed skepticism, noting that "adventures in industrial policy by governments around the world have squandered tens of billions of dollars chasing fashionable but ill-conceived ideas" (Doring 2010). Among the corpses of failed industrial policy, *Bloomberg Businessweek* noted, was the $80 billion investment in synthetic fuels that President Carter had supported. However, the article also recognized other cases of successful industrial policy in the United States, such as the railroad industry during the nineteenth century and the Internet during the 1990s. The Obama administration hoped that the investments in cutting-edge clean energy technologies would recall the Internet or the semiconductor industry more than the ill-fated program of the Carter administration.

Although *Bloomberg Businessweek* was calling attention to the novelty of American green industrial policy, a comparative perspective suggests that President Obama was playing catch-up to other countries. The Pew Charitable Trusts tracked the industrial policy of the United States for "clean power" in comparison with that of other countries and found that the level of investment by the US as a percentage of gross domestic product was well below that of other G-20 countries. Moreover, some countries invested at a relative rate that was more than 5 times that of the US, and in absolute figures China surpassed the US in 2009. The lack of demand policies, such as a cap on carbon emissions and a renewable-electricity standard at the federal government level, further contributed to the ineffectiveness of government support for green tech. The Pew study suggested that by 2020 China, Indonesia, Japan, and South Korea would account for 40 percent of clean energy investments among the G-20 countries. Countries that invest most heavily in clean energy technologies and clean energy emissions policies are likely to have the most robust manufacturing sectors. According to the report,

[the] G-20 countries with the most robust policy frameworks (China, Germany, and Brazil, for example) appear to have the strongest clean energy sectors relative to the size of their economies, while those with weaker policy frameworks (such as the United States, Australia, and Japan) lag behind. (Pew Charitable Trusts 2010a: 11)[25]

Although industrial policy for clean energy industries in the United States is relatively weak in comparison with that in other countries, because of the size of the US economy the absolute level of support is still impressive. The remainder of this section will survey the elements of industrial policy for clean energy in the US as another aspect of green developmentalism. Although there is no coherent, integrated industrial policy to substitute foreign imports with domestic products and, conversely, to make green energy industries in the United States globally competitive, there is a patchwork of policies that together constitute a quasi-industrial policy.

Demand Policies

In the 111th Congress, the foundation stone of demand policy was the 2009 American Clean Energy and Security Act (HR 2454), which included a combined energy-efficiency and renewable-electricity standard (20 percent by 2020), a cap-and-trade system that would lead to an 83 percent reduction in greenhouse gas levels relative to the 2005 levels by 2050, and other measures aimed at increasing energy efficiency and conservation. The title of the bill reflected attempts to frame the reform policies as a security or defense issue in addition to environmental and job-creation dividends. When the House of Representatives approved the law, the country was on its way to having landmark legislation in green energy policy that would have supported investment by providing a stable policy landscape.

However, the Senate was unable to pass legislation similar to the House bill. The Senate bill's co-sponsors, John Kerry and Joseph Lieberman, carefully framed the Clean Energy Jobs and America Power Act (S. 1733) in terms of energy independence, jobs, and a healthy environment as part of a strategy to build strong support for the bill. Kerry characterized the bill as follows:

This is a bill for energy independence after a devastating oil spill, a bill to hold polluters accountable, a bill for billions of dollars to create the next generation of jobs, and a bill to end America's addiction to foreign oil and protect the air our children breathe and the water they drink. (2010)

To gain support for the bill, Kerry and his colleagues made concessions on nuclear energy, offshore drilling, and clean coal. Friends of the Earth criticized the concessions by claiming that the law would provide "subsidies to expensive, unsafe and environmentally damaging technologies such as nuclear reactors and carbon capture . . . for coal plants, not to mention ambiguous incentives for biofuels" (2009). Although Kerry, Lieberman, and other senators who supported the legislation lost support from some environmentalist organizations, they were able to put together an impressive green coalition that included executives from some energy companies, large corporations, centrist environmentalists, unions, and military officers. Even with the compromises and the support, they were not able to secure enough votes to win passage. When the bill was shelved, many environmentalists and progressive activists were not disappointed.[26]

Republicans claimed that the Clean Energy Jobs and America Power Act amounted to a "$751-billion national energy tax" (GOP.gov 2010) and was a continuation of the big-government, tax-and-spend policies of social liberals. Their reply also included a statement of the alternative that the Republican Party supported:

Republicans and the American people continue to support an "all of the above" energy policy that promotes energy independence, job creation, and a cleaner environment through greater efficiency; developing nuclear, renewable, and alternative sources; and the expanded, environmentally responsible development of America's energy resources. (ibid.)

Alternative legislation put forward by Senator Richard Lugar proposed a broad system of permits that included "diverse domestic power," such as carbon-sequestered coal, nuclear, and energy-efficiency technologies. Lugar's approach also relied on voluntary measures that were vaguely consistent with a more market-oriented philosophy. On the one hand, Republicans reframed the developmentalist rhetoric of Kerry and Lieberman as old-school social liberalism; on the other hand, they re-appropriated the developmentalist rhetoric of energy independence and job creation with policies made safe for nuclear energy and fossil fuels. As a result, the Republicans didn't oppose the broad goal of domestic industrial development; the debate focused on the means and the relative emphasis on renewable energy versus other forms of "clean" energy.[27]

Resistance from the fossil fuel industries to the Kerry-Lieberman bill was also strong, but there were splits among large corporations. Between January 2009 and June 2010, oil, gas, and utility companies spent more than $500 million in opposition to green energy policy, and the Chamber of Commerce filed a court petition demanding that the Environmental Protection Agency hold a public debate on climate-change science and the effects of emissions on public health. Although the government agency regarded the science as complete, the Chamber wanted to hold a Scopes-style trial for climate-change science. In protest against the Chamber's anti-green policies, several major companies—including Apple, Nike, Excelon (a utility company that owns nuclear reactors and would benefit from carbon regulation), Pacific Gas and Electric, and PNM Resources (New Mexico's largest utility)—left the Chamber or resigned from the board of directors. In a similar move, Duke Energy left the National Association of Manufacturers over its efforts to stop climate-change legislation. In December of 2009, Greenpeace joined the fray when activists draped the headquarters of the US Chamber of Commerce with "climate crime scene" banners. During the same month, a group of 40 large companies urged President Obama to move forward with a global climate-change agreement. The signatories included consumer-products, electronics, and utility companies as well as the Solar Energy Industries Association and Business Council for Sustainable Energy.[28]

In July 2010, Senators Harry Reid and John Kerry announced that they didn't have enough votes to pass the energy bill in the Senate. Although Kerry promised to introduce similar legislation in the future, the battle in the 111th Congress was over. By the end of the year, the lame-duck Congress had managed to pass only very meager reforms in support of green industrial development: an extension of energy-efficiency incentives and a tax grant program for renewable-energy companies that were elements of the Middle-Class Tax Cut Act of 2010.

Although the defeat of the Kerry-Lieberman legislation revealed the weakness of green coalitions with respect to anti-green Republicans, the Chamber of Commerce, and the fossil fuel industry, the battle over climate-change legislation revealed an important change within large capital. The coalition of supporters had gone well beyond green energy businesses, labor unions, environmentalists, and anti-poverty groups to include large corporations that had accepted the need for policy reform to guide the green energy transition. As the struggle within the US Chamber of Commerce indicated, some very powerful corporations, even ones not closely connected with green industries, had shifted allegiance toward policies in support of a long-term green energy transition. The failure to pass climate-change policy at the federal government level indicated that the relative strength of the coalition had not yet reached a tipping point, but the failure should be placed in a longer-term perspective that indicates growing support in the private sector for climate-change legislation. Furthermore, public opinion was strongly supportive of the regulation of greenhouse gases.[29]

The passage of a renewable-energy standard and a carbon cap would have potentially transformed energy markets in the United States by creating predictable, long-term expectations for demand. It probably would have shifted financial projections for fossil fuel energy toward a much higher risk category and accelerated the point at which solar and other renewable energies reached grid parity. The reform would have been the basis not only of a green transition in environmental terms but also of a green industrial policy, and the legislative defeat made it more likely that the United States would be unable to gain or maintain global leadership in most green industries. Instead, the US would be more likely to have to import greater amounts of renewable-energy technology. In turn, the loss of manufacturing leadership would weaken the efficacy of the country's still formidable research sector.

Another defeat for demand policy during the 111th Congress involved energy-efficiency goals for buildings and appliances. A report by the American Council for an Energy-Efficient Economy estimated that energy-efficiency standards for buildings and lighting saved $34 billion in 2010 and would save $68 billion in 2030. Translating the numbers into the obligatory estimate of jobs, the study estimated that as of 2010 efficiency measures had created 340,000 jobs. To support this area of green energy policy, the ARRA provided $3.2 billion in energy efficiency and conservation block grants and $5 billion for weatherizing households with modest incomes. In 2010 a coalition of labor, business, and environmental organizations supported the proposed Home Star legislation (HR 5019), also known as "cash for caulkers." The legislation would have provided rebates for building retrofits and also developed certification for contractors and standards for building improvements. Again, the legislation failed to pass in the Senate. Contractors did not like the requirement of certification by the Building Performance Institute, which was located in New York. Because at the time more than 80 percent of the certified contractors were located in New York and New Jersey, the benefits of the legislation would not have been distributed widely.

Furthermore, contractors disliked the bill's requirement to have them pay the up-front costs of the retrofits and receive reimbursement later.[30]

Another form of demand support for the greening of buildings is through labeling programs and standards for government buildings. As of 2011 the government had piloted only voluntary labels for the efficiency of buildings, such as the Home Energy Score for energy upgrades to buildings and the Energy Smart Home Scale for new buildings. However, the federal government did set standards for energy efficiency for its own buildings. Because the federal government owns nearly half a million buildings, its own energy standards can provide a significant boost to both the manufacturing and contracting industries. Consistent with the goal, as of 2010 new federal government buildings and substantial renovations were required to be certified at the gold level, the second highest category of the certification scheme of the Leadership in Energy and Environmental Design (LEED) program of the United States Green Building Council.[31]

With respect to transportation and energy, there was some support in the ARRA for electric vehicles, and the Obama administration continued to deepen the country's more bipartisan and longstanding support for biofuels. As the level of ethanol sold at the pump as a blend with gasoline gradually increased in line with the goal for 2022, the blend limit of 10 percent created a limit for the renewable fuels standard, and the Renewable Fuels Association argued that it was desirable to increase the blend to 12 percent immediately and then to 15 percent. Midwestern governors also pushed for similar changes in the federal government's standards and rules for ethanol blends. For example, Governor Chet Culver of Iowa, the state with the highest level of biofuels production, supported a 15 percent increase in the federal mandate for ethanol, a change that he claimed would create about $24 billion in import-substitution revenue for the country. In 2009, 54 manufacturers of ethanol petitioned the Environmental Protection Agency to increase the blend limit. In October 2010 and January 2011, the Environmental Protection Agency issued rulings that cars and light trucks manufactured after 2001 could safely use E15 fuel. An industry study estimated that increasing the percentage of ethanol in the blend from 10 to 15 would create 12,000 direct jobs and 136,000 additional jobs. To some degree, job creation for biofuels involves shifts within agriculture and from petroleum refining, but many of the jobs would be new, domestic jobs due to import-substitution benefits. No matter how dubious corn-based ethanol is as a green energy source, the calculus of jobs and potential for import substitution created a strong political coalition in favor of its further development.[32]

Supply-Side Policies

One might assume that the higher labor costs of the United States cause green energy firms to site their manufacturing elsewhere, but wind and solar manufacturing can be found in high-wage European countries, and industry analysts state that other factors are more important when choosing a site for manufacturing. In a study of the comparative costs of manufacturing solar panels in the United States and China, differences in labor costs only accounted for about 5 to 10 percent of the differences in overall costs; a much larger factor was lower materials costs. Furthermore, companies commonly mention that their decision to shift manufacturing abroad often takes into account better tax subsidies and lower electricity costs. Asian countries often offer ten-year tax holidays and subsidies for product development, neither of which are available in the United States.[33]

Energy subsidies from the federal government tend to favor the fossil fuel industries over renewable-energy industries. For example, between 2002 and 2008 the federal government provided $72 billion in tax credits and grants to the fossil fuel industries and only $29 billion for renewable-energy industries, of which about $17 billion went to corn ethanol. The relative support for nuclear energy and fossil fuels is continuous across political administrations as different in energy politics as George W. Bush and Barack Obama; however, there were differences in emphasis. In the budget proposal for the Department of Energy for fiscal year 2009, President Bush cut funding for the Office of Energy Efficiency and Renewable Energy from $1.7 billion to $1.2 billion and increased funding for fossil fuel energy from $904 million to $1.1 billion and for nuclear energy from $1 billion to $1.4 billion. Within Energy Efficiency and Renewable Energy, solar energy received $157 million, wind $52 million, and geothermal $30 million. Two years later, the budgetary proposal of President Obama shifted the figures toward energy efficiency and renewable energy, but the budget maintained high levels of support for fossil fuels and nuclear energy. The budget included a request for $2.4 billion for the Office of Energy Efficiency and Renewable Energy, that is, double the request of the Bush administration. For fossil fuels and nuclear energy, the proposed budgets were $760 million and $912 million respectively. In other words, Obama proposed reductions in the Bush administration's budgets, but far from a 50 percent cut. The Obama budget also doubled the support for renewable energy: $302 million for solar, $220 million for biomass, $123 million for wind, and $55 million for geothermal energy. Although the numbers represented increases in support for energy efficiency and renewable energy over the levels found in the Bush administration's budget, the overall ratios of support for nuclear and fossil fuels to renewable energy remained tilted in favor of the former.[34]

A temporary but significant injection of federal government support for green energy industries appeared in the ARRA. The 2009 law provided $64 billion in spending and $21 billion in related tax incentives for energy, climate change, and transportation, including Advanced Research Projects Agency for Energy (ARPA-E), electric vehicles, alternative fuels, renewable energy for electricity, and smart-grid development. The ARRA also amended the loan guarantee legislation in section 1705 of the 2005 act. One of the foremost subsidies in the ARRA was $2.3 billion in funding for the Advanced Energy Manufacturing Credit (also known as Section 48C of the Internal Revenue Service code), a program that allocated a 30 percent tax credit for qualified investments for clean energy. The original program received 500 applications for a total of $8 billion in requests for assistance (well above the cap of $2.3 billion), and in response the administration tried to increase the support in subsequent budgets. The America Competes Reauthorization Act (HR 5116), passed in 2010, also supported the ARPA-E program, new regional innovation clusters, and goals for science research and education.[35]

Another area of government support for green energy businesses is green jobs training programs. The Green Jobs Act of 2007, which Green For All and the Apollo Alliance supported, had authorized up to $125 million in funding for green jobs training programs and was aimed primarily at persons with employment barriers. Funding was not appropriated immediately, but under the ARRA $500 million was allocated to green jobs training, including the "Pathways Out of Poverty" training grants, state government partnerships for training, and business and labor partnership training grants. The Department of Labor also continued to fund about 122 job corps across the nation for at-risk youth, and many organizations diversified into training for green jobs. Although the programs focused on underserved and at-risk workers, some of the grants for the state government partnerships made possible broader training and planning. The Environmental Protection Agency also provided funds for job training.[36]

Additional legislation, which was approved by the House or the Senate (but not both) during the Obama administration, revealed increasing awareness of the need to support policies for green energy industries but also a failure to convert the policy proposals into law. (See table 3.1.) Had the suite of laws been passed, there would have been a much stronger case for the argument that the 111th Congress had launched a new era of green industrial policy.

A more successful aspect of supply-side policy support is federal funding for basic and applied research, an area of historic strength of the United States. During this period the Department of Energy budget for scientific research was $5 billion, but federal government investments in green energy research could also be found in the Department of Agriculture, the Department of Defense, the Environmental Protection Agency, and the National Science Foundation. Although research contracts to companies can constitute an actionable trade-related subsidy, in general trade agreements don't restrict funding for basic research.[37]

Increasingly, federal funding through the Department of Energy to the national laboratories has supported renewable-energy research. Although the National Renewable Energy Laboratory is a focus of such research, several other national laboratories have developed specialties in green energy research and testing. In the North, Illinois is home to the Argonne National Laboratory, which is the leading national laboratory for transportation research and is a partner in the Kentucky-Argonne Battery Research and Manufacturing Center in Lexington, Kentucky. In New York, the state's battery energy and transportation consortium has worked with Brookhaven National Laboratory, which conducts energy-efficiency research and has testing facilities for research related to fuel cells and advanced materials. In the South, Oak Ridge National Laboratory conducts cellulosic ethanol research and is home for the Solar Technologies Laboratory, Center for Advanced Thin-Film Solar Cells, and other research centers and facilities related to solar energy research. Also in the South, the Savannah River National Laboratory claims to have the largest concentration of hydrogen experts in the country. Although known for weapons research, the laboratory also conducts research on hydrogen storage and metal hydrides, and it works with local governments, universities, and companies on hydrogen fuel cell research. In the West, the Sandia National Laboratories perform solar testing, manage the Concentrating Solar Power Program, and help the state of New Mexico to build its solar industry. Solar energy, biofuels,

Table 3.1
Green and manufacturing legislation in the 111th Congress. Sources: Brown 2010, Matsui 2010, Pelosi 2011,Solar Energy Industries Association 2009.

Title	Number	Description
Strengthening Employment Clusters to Organize Regional Success Act	HR 1855	Coordination of workforce training in specific industrial sectors, including clean energy
Clean Energy and Security Act	HR 2454	Included a proposal for the Clean Energy Development Administration, which would be funded with $10 billion to support a $100 billion revolving loan fund and a clean tech business competition grant program
America Works Act	HR 4071	Training and certification for American workers
National Manufacturing Strategy Act	HR 4692	Increase domestic manufacturing and promote clean energy exports
Clean Energy Technology Manufacturing and Export Assistance Act	HR 5156	Support the relatively low performance of American clean energy manufacturers in exports
Security in Energy and Manufacturing Act	HR 5041	Strengthen the 48C tax credit and change it into grants to help start-ups that do not have tax liability
Rare Earths and Critical Materials Revitalization Act	HR 6160	Response to the Chinese decision to limit exports by providing support for the revitalization of the American mining industry for rare-earth metals
Investments for Manufacturing Progress and Clean Technology Act	S 1617	$30 billion revolving loan fund to help small and medium-size manufacturers convert to clean energy manufacturing

and smart-grid research is also conducted at the Pacific Northwest National Laboratory, which has collaborations with regional universities and the Bonneville Power Administration. In California, Lawrence Livermore National Laboratory has become a center for research on net zero energy buildings (that is, buildings that create as much energy as they use) and for other areas of green energy research.[38]

In summary, research funding and the research strengths of the United States remain strong bases for the supply side of industrial policy. However, without other support policies and strong demand policies a comprehensive industrial policy is impossible. Furthermore, without the connection to manufacturing strength the relationship between research and new technology development is severely weakened.

Conclusion

By 2000, the United States was facing severe economic pressures on its manufacturing industries from newly industrializing countries. China became both the symbol of the shifts in the world economic system and a target of claims that its gains were based on the manipulation of trade agreements to the benefit of its export industries and the detriment of American manufacturers. The rivalry with China intensified in a pattern of trade disputes and defensive laws. China's strategy of geopolitical rivalry was to engage in protectionism, to invest heavily in targeted industries, and to violate trade agreements. Although violations of trade agreements were sometimes caught and remedied, they created temporary benefits that made possible long-term shifts in industrial dominance.

Although the rivalry with China went well beyond the issue of green manufacturing, one should also not underestimate the importance of energy transitions to global economic hegemony. In a 2006 book titled *Global Energy Shifts*, the sociologist Bruce Podobnik suggests that the change in the economic center of the world system from Britain to the United States during the early twentieth century was associated with the energy transition from coal and steam power to petroleum and the internal-combustion engine. Although changes in energy regimes don't cause a change in position in the world system, they have coincided in the past and may coincide in the future. To extend Podobnik's argument, China's substantial investments in green tech may well coincide with the broad transition of global economic power from the United States.

To counter the loss of position of green energy industries, the United States has made some efforts to remedy trade violations and develop a green industrial policy. As this chapter has indicated, for the green energy industries there are supply-side policies of subsidies, tax credits, jobs training, and research. By supporting domestic manufacturing and research, the US government encourages companies to locate and keep their research, development, and some manufacturing operations at home. The support helps level the playing field against foreign countries that offer strong incentives for relocation. Demand policies, in contrast, have been controversial, and the crucial proposals of the 111th Congress didn't become law.

Trade and industrial policy is Janus-faced because it is rooted in the differing constituencies and their perceived interests. Supporters of continued trade liberalization believe that the United States can maintain its global position by climbing up the ladder of technological complexity to high-tech products that can be protected with intellectual property agreements and exported throughout the world. This side of developmentalist policy is more in the outward-oriented, free-trade, competitiveness mode. In contrast, there is also an import-substitution dimension that is embodied in the calls for energy security, the protection of good jobs, and the revival of American manufacturing. A price on carbon is an implicit import-substitution policy, because it would favor domestic transportation energy such as biofuels and electric vehicles over imported petroleum. Likewise, about 15 percent of the natural gas used in the US currently is imported. However, calls for energy independence and security don't automatically align with the green energy transition, because new technologies of extraction may enable the US to become energy independent for natural gas, and the replacement of foreign petroleum with electric vehicles in turn relies on an electricity grid that is dominated by coal and natural gas. Instead, the protection of domestic manufacturing on the grounds of long-term innovation capacity and security is probably a more sound basis for anchoring the import-substitution argument.

In conclusion, green industrial policy during the 111th Congress was more concentrated than in any other session of Congress since the 1970s, but it remained limited, especially on the demand side. The failure to pass laws that mandated a renewable-electricity standard and a carbon cap indicates that green transition coalitions failed a crucial test of strength. The many steps toward such a policy, especially in the provisions of the ARRA, suffer from short-term funding horizons. However, the conclusion that green energy transition policies in the United States are piecemeal is only partially true. Some state and local governments have stepped into the void by vigorously pursuing their own green industrial policies. Thus, a full understanding of the politics of the green energy transition in the United States requires attention to the patterns of change at the subnational level of government.

4

State Governments and the Greening of Import Substitution

Although the federal government has only a limited industrial policy in support of the green energy transition, state governments have forged more comprehensive policies. Between 1996 and 2000, fifteen states included a public benefits fund in electricity restructuring legislation, and by 2000 eight states had also developed a standard or a goal for renewable electricity. Although the motivation behind some of the policies was environmental, for states that imported their energy from other states or from abroad, the policies also had economic dividends, because they created jobs from locally produced energy. As the economic implications became clearer, state and local political leaders became more articulate about the convergence between green energy and economic development policies. This chapter will discuss the demand side of state-level developmentalism, beginning with a general discussion of the various shades of green energy policy that are relevant at the levels of state and local government. After sections on electricity, buildings, and transportation—three of the most significant areas of demand policy at the state government level—the chapter will explain the trade-like implications of state governments' demand policies, including import substitution and procurement preferences.[1]

Shades of Green Energy Policy

An inquiry into the politics of green industrial policies among state governments requires a preliminary discussion of the politics of definitions, that is, how the different approaches to the problem of defining what is and is not green lead to fractures in green coalitions. As was mentioned in the introductory chapter, the category of green or clean embraces a wide range of options, and there are political disputes over what should or should not be counted as acceptable. This section will review the range of policy strategies currently in play.

Electricity Generation

Because coal and natural gas represent more than half of electricity generation in the United States, the fossil fuel industry can legitimately argue that the best way to reduce greenhouse gas emissions is to reduce carbon emissions from coal and natural gas. The phrase "clean coal" can mean improved technologies of electricity generation, such as combined heat-and-power or gasification plants with state-of-the-art pollution-control devices. However, carbon capture and sequestration will be required to burn coal in a way that approximates the goal of carbon-neutral energy. The technologies are not yet available at a commercial scale, but the pilot projects have received funding support from the federal government. Because carbon sequestration technologies are still in their research-and-development phase, safety issues remain unanswered. For example, a soil survey of a farm that sits on top of a carbon sequestration site found elevated levels of carbon dioxide in the soil. Furthermore, a comprehensive approach to clean coal would also require returning to extraction by mining rather than mountaintop removal. Thus, there is potential for even clean forms of coal to create opposition on safety and environmental grounds.[2]

Similar questions have emerged about natural gas and nuclear energy. Natural gas is considered the cleanest of the fossil fuels, but it still generates greenhouse gases, and it has become controversial because of the environmental side effects in communities where hydraulic fracturing is located. Likewise, the generation of nuclear energy involves low levels of greenhouse gases, but it remains controversial because of the high overall cost, vulnerability to terrorist attacks, risk of a meltdown, contamination of neighboring land, pollution at mining sources, nonrenewability of the fuel source, and storage of waste. The Fukushima disaster also underscored the risks associated with extreme weather events.[3]

The argument that coal, natural gas, and nuclear energy should be included under the broad tent of green transition technologies is complicated, because opposition from those industries can end any hope of political success. Likewise, to some degree green investors include clean forms of traditional energy sources as part of their portfolios, so fractures can emerge in green transition coalitions. In some cases, state governments have opted to construct renewable-electricity standards in ways to include fossil fuels and nuclear energy. For example, Pennsylvania's "alternative" portfolio standard allows "clean" forms of fossil fuels to be counted, such as waste coal and natural gas from coal or coal beds, and Ohio's standard includes both renewable sources and "advanced" energy sources such as clean coal and nuclear energy. Likewise, Virginia allows utilities to subtract their nuclear energy generation before calculating the base for the renewable-electricity standard.[4]

Although wind, solar, geothermal, biomass, and hydropower are generally the main forms of renewable energy that are described in renewable portfolio standards,[5] even the greener forms of green energy have their shortcomings. The best wind, solar, and geothermal resources all tend to be located in regions of the country that are distant from population sources. Building new power lines takes considerable investment and planning, and proposed new lines tend to incur political opposition. The solution may be to shift to a smaller scale of energy generation (such as microturbines, rooftop solar, and building-scale geothermal), but distributed renewable energy poses significant management problems for utilities and system operators in addition to higher cost for consumers.

Large-scale solar and wind farms can also divide green transition coalitions on environmental issues and on livability issues. Some of the earliest wind farms in the United States were located on the flyways of migratory birds, and bird death became a concern. However, subsequent wind farms have taken flyways into account and have also changed the turbine technology to make it easier for birds to avoid the blades. Opposition to wind farms has also emerged in scenic areas, such as the mountains of Vermont and the coastline of Cape Cod. Studies have shown that "viewshed" concerns are only one among many; nearby residents are concerned with a broad range of economic and environmental impacts.[6]

There has also been some opposition to solar farms. A plan to use the Mojave Desert in California as a site for solar and wind farms drew opposition from environmentalists and Native American groups, and in response California Senator Diane Feinstein introduced legislation in 2009 to protect a million acres of the desert from solar and wind farms. The proposed legislation would require that the military services, the Bureau of Land Management, and the Forest Service review millions of acres of land in California, Nevada, and Arizona for the purposes of renewable-energy development. Feinstein's proposal to use military lands may provide a general solution to siting issues faced by solar and wind farms throughout the country. The bill also provided support for transmission lines.[7]

The manufacture and disposal of photovoltaics raises issues that suggest another fault line in green transition coalitions. The manufacture of photovoltaic panels can expose workers to silicon, cadmium, and other toxic materials, and some of the waste products escape into the air and water. In China, where environmental regulations are more lax than in the United States, there is evidence of unsafe disposal of chemicals in the areas surrounding manufacturing facilities. The next generation of nanotechnology-based photovoltaics will increase the efficiency and decrease the cost of production, but there are many unanswered questions about the safety of nanomaterials. Solar photovoltaics last only 25 years, and at the end of the life cycle they present disposal problems similar to those for other electronic waste. For that reason the Silicon Valley Toxics Coalition has called for an extended producer responsibility system that requires manufacturers to take back used photovoltaic panels. The steam-based energy of concentrating solar probably presents fewer risks of toxic exposure throughout the life cycle, but it requires high levels of water, which is often at a premium in the arid regions where concentrating solar is most common.[8]

Other forms of electricity generation that are sometimes included in a state government's renewable-electricity standard are biomass (power plants that burn wood waste) and hydropower. Biomass is renewable, but burning it generates greenhouse gases and particulate matter, and incineration from waste has also been the target of environmental justice mobilizations due to concerns with toxic chemicals released during burning. In North Carolina, powerful hog and fowl industries managed to get their animal waste included in the renewable-energy portfolio standard. Freshwater hydropower in the United States has run into limits, partly because public opposition from coalitions of local residents, white-water enthusiasts, and environmentalists has made it increasingly difficult to build large-scale dams. Instead, interest is growing in tidal power, which has some advantages over other forms of renewable energy (e.g., its less intermittent nature and its proximity to population centers).

In summary, developing demand policies for green electricity may seem like a simple matter of setting in place a strong renewable-electricity standard, but the boundaries of what is and is not clean or green are the subject of intense negotiations when defining state government standards for green electricity. Although green transition coalitions have rallied under the banner of renewable energy, even renewable-energy projects have stirred opposition, and the complicated politics of drawing boundaries can trigger fault lines in broad green transition coalitions and rally opposition from the coal, natural gas, and nuclear power generation industries.

Buildings and Energy Efficiency

Because the growth in energy consumption can outpace reductions in greenhouse gases based on the shift to cleaner forms of energy generation, a parallel set of policies is needed to reduce overall consumption. The problem, known in the literature as the rebound effect, can be addressed through good policy, that is, a comprehensive approach that both reduces consumption and shifts energy sources to those with a lower level of environmental impact. State governments recognize the benefits of both renewable-energy generation and energy-efficiency measures by having developed a suite of interlocking policies. This section will focus on energy efficiency.[9]

One of the primary means for reducing demand is through the greening of buildings, which contribute about 40 percent of the world's energy consumption. Most residential and commercial buildings have their own heating systems powered by natural gas, oil, and electricity, and many also have air conditioning powered by electricity. Thus, buildings generate greenhouse gases from two sources: on-site heating (such as natural gas supplies to furnaces and hot water heaters) and electricity consumption.

The "deepest" form of the greening of buildings is to redesign them so that they will produce net zero energy—that is, over the course of a year they produce as much energy, usually from solar power, as they consume. Although there a few policies in effect for net zero energy, they represent an experimental niche. The other approach is to redesign buildings so that they are closer together and use a common source of heat, such as in the district heating system of St. Paul, Minnesota. However, it is both economically and politically difficult to bring about a rapid transition that would tear down existing buildings and essentially redesign urban and suburban spaces. The challenges are especially acute for single-family homes, where cultural practices make unattractive the prospect of tearing down neighborhoods and replacing them with compact multi-family units. As a result, mainstream design operates within the constraints of a technological regime based on separate buildings with their individual energy generation systems. The result is a focus on energy efficiency.

Energy-efficiency measures for buildings are often referred to as the "low-hanging fruit" of the green energy transition, because they are inexpensive and have a relatively short payback period. For heating and air conditioning, examples of efficiency improvements include adding insulation, replacing windows and doors, caulking leaky windows, installing programmable thermostats, and shifting to high-efficiency furnaces, boilers, and boiler mates. For electrical appliances and lighting, the main goal is to replace older items that consume higher levels of electricity with newer appliances and to switch to compact fluorescent light bulbs. Proposals for energy-efficiency policies can obtain broad political support because they appeal to the frugality of conservatives, and they can also be connected with the needs of low-income and working-class households to reduce their energy bills. The programs can also create jobs for relatively unskilled workers and opportunities for unionized labor, and they can appeal to utilities that wish to manage peak loads and avoid the economic and political costs of the construction of new facilities for electricity generation. In brief, if energy-efficiency policies are configured as cost-saving measures that benefit the poor and address peak-load concerns, they can overcome political opposition. At the state and local government level, energy-efficiency programs are widespread.

Smart-grid technologies represent an extension of energy-efficiency approaches that go beyond weatherization and retrofitting, but they represent a much greater challenge politically than retrofitting. The new technologies promise to encourage conservation through improved feedback and variable pricing, and they also contribute to efficiency by enabling customers and the electricity suppliers to manage peak load. However, several concerns have been raised, including vulnerability to computer attacks, the potential for the invasions of privacy because of the capacity to interpret the signature of individual products, knowledge of when the building is occupied that could be used by criminals, and concern with the health effects of electromagnetic fields. Fairness issues have also emerged, because the savings associated with programming appliances to run during the middle of the night will likely be most available to large businesses and high-income customers. Likewise, customers with special needs, such as people with medical conditions who need higher room temperatures in the winter or lower temperatures in the summer, may find that they are penalized because the electricity provider knows that they have set the room temperature outside an acceptable range. The many challenges facing smart-grid technologies suggest that a politically successful deployment will require careful planning to ensure that concerns with hackers, privacy, system resilience, health, and social fairness are addressed. Again, it is not simply a matter of building a system that works technically. The system designers must also develop a new regime that enables the system to address the needs of the networks of providers and consumers. In California, many cities and counties, including ones known for their green politics, contested the state's policy of mandatory smart meters.[10]

Transportation

The third general area involves the greening of transportation. As in the case of electricity generation and energy consumption in buildings, a shift to clean or green transportation power can have little environmental benefit if there is continuing growth of consumption. The deeper shade of green in this policy field involves the transition to a denser built environment with higher levels of public transportation. For cities that already have extensive public transportation networks and a dense built environment, the main challenge is to expand public transportation and make it greener. In some cases, the greening of diesel buses has also become a civil rights issue because of the effects of diesel exhaust on asthma rates.[11]

Because many people, especially in suburbs, will continue to use automobiles, and there is continuing demand for trucks, efficiency technologies provide a complementary approach to strategies aimed at reducing petroleum-based transportation. Although American automobile manufacturers resisted the transition to electric vehicles during the 1990s, the bailouts that they received after the recession of 2008 softened their resolve against the transition, as did ARRA funds and other government support. Furthermore, by 2008 the Japanese automakers had proved the viability of hybrid vehicles. The hybrid vehicle is generally considered a bridge technology to two other long-term technologies: vehicles powered completely by electricity or by fuel cells. When one plugs an electric vehicle into an electric outlet, the source of energy in most American states is still largely coal and natural gas, just as a common form of hydrogen production is natural gas reformulation. Nevertheless, an electric vehicle that draws on electricity from a coal-fired power plant emits a lower level of greenhouse gases than one powered by petroleum, as does a fuel cell vehicle for which the source of hydrogen is natural gas reformulation. In a complete green transition, the source of energy for electric and fuel cell vehicles would be renewable energy. At this point, most metropolitan transit agencies have begun the greening of their transportation by shifting to hybrid diesel-electric buses and by building light rail transit lines.[12]

Another area of state and local government policy is the conversion of government fleets to use more biofuels. Whereas the greening of public transportation and automobiles presents opportunities for broad coalitions among environmentalists, unions, civil rights groups, and manufacturers, the growth of biofuels is more divisive. Farmers, biotechnology firms, and green venture capitalists are aligned in favor of biofuels, and environmentalists and social justice organizations raise concerns about their negative effects. In the United States the production of ethanol from corn requires high levels of fossil fuels embedded in pesticides, fertilizers, farm vehicles, refining, and transportation to market. One can easily draw the conclusion that ethanol is merely a liquid storage medium for fossil fuels with a little solar energy embedded in the crop base. There is a corresponding controversy in the literature about the "energy return on investment," that is, the energy available in ethanol after subtracting non-renewable-energy inputs such as coal and petroleum used in the production and transportation of the fuel. A meta-analysis that employed consistent assumptions across studies indicated that there was a small positive return on energy invested for corn ethanol. However, the greenhouse gas emissions are only slightly lower than those of gasoline, depending in part of the type of fossil fuel energy used in ethanol refining. Almost all analysts agree that the carbon reduction benefits of corn ethanol are marginal. Furthermore, when one takes into account other environmental side effects of corn ethanol, such as the effects on cropland and watersheds, many conclude that the fuel doesn't deserve consideration as a green energy. The societal implications for corn ethanol are also highly problematic. In the United States the percentage of corn grown for ethanol was approaching 50 percent and affecting the price of food. At a global scale, the growth of biofuels has contributed to monocropping and toxic pesticide drift, both of which have forced small farmers with relatively sustainable practices to leave their land.[13]

Ethanol is more defensible technically and socially if one assumes changes in the current technological regime of production and refining. With respect to production, cellulosic ethanol has much more favorable metrics of energy return on investment, land-use effects, and greenhouse gas emissions. A similar argument can be made for the transition from soy-based to algae-based biodiesel. On the plus side, algae don't have to be grown on cropland, and consequently the need for pesticides or herbicides is reduced. Furthermore, algae production uses land 3 times as efficiently as corn and 5 times as efficiently as canola. On the negative side, researchers have argued that the production of algal biofuels will probably consume more water and more energy than cropland-based biofuels, including ethanol from corn and biodiesel from canola. Whereas farmers can solve the problem of nitrogen depletion for crop-based biofuels through rotation, the growth of algal biodiesel in shallow pools requires fertilizer, which in turn requires petrochemicals. The biodiesel could be derived in a more sustainable way, but the algae pools would need to be placed near wastewater streams, and the carbon dioxide would need to come from flue gas from a fossil fuel burning electricity plant.[14]

By using wind or solar energy to power part of the refining process, biofuels would become partially a storage medium for the greener forms of energy. Much greener forms of biofuels are possible, if the biotechnology-based refining technologies and use of cellulosic material are combined with renewable energy to replace the embedded fossil fuels in fertilizer, pesticide applications, refining, and transportation to markets. Notwithstanding the many limitations of biofuels, it is likely that policy reforms will continue to include biofuels under the umbrella of green energy technologies because of the wide political support from farming interests. The level of political controversy associated with biofuels could decline with the shift to biotechnology, reduction of direct competition with food sources, and integration of renewable energy into the production process.

Demand Policies

State and local governments forge their green energy policies in this field of competing definitions of green or clean technology and the differing constituencies that rally in support of one or another definition. A review of the policies quickly shows how geographically uneven the green transition policy field is at the state government level. This section will follow the order of the previous section by discussing three general areas of green energy policy.

Electricity Generation

In the United States, the primary policy mechanism to support the greening of electricity generation is the renewable-electricity standard. By 2012 about half of the states had enacted a renewable-electricity standard, ranging from a mandate (utilities must produce or purchase a percentage of their electricity from renewable sources by a specified date) to voluntary goals. Figure 4.1 shows the relative volume of activity at the state government level. The tally includes the establishment of new mandates for renewable energy, increases in existing mandates, and the articulation of goals. Activity peaked in 2007, that is, before the 2008 presidential election when the issue was at its height of popularity and was achieving bipartisan support in some states. However, the graph also indicates that even after anti-green backlash that emerged in the 2010 elections, there was still some activity.

At the high end of renewable portfolio standards, New York has a long-term goal of 80 percent renewable energy by 2050, and California has a short-term goal of 33 percent by 2020. The short-term goals may have a stronger effect on planning for new generation facilities than the long-term goals of a transition by 2050; however, both long-term and short-term goals together constitute a favorable environment for planning by utilities and generation companies. Some states also have a

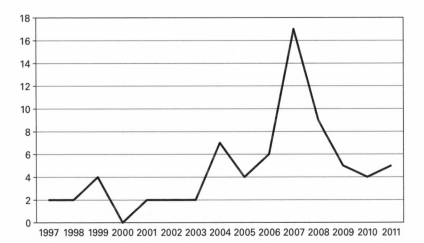

Figure 4.1
State governments' actions to initiate or modify renewable-electricity standards and goals (based on individual state reports in Database of Incentives for Renewables and Energy Efficiency 2011b). The data include both the original establishment of standards and the increases (either by legislatures or by public utility commissions). Because actions by public utility commissions and other bodies are counted, the number is higher than the number of strictly legislative activities described in the appendix.

carve-out for solar energy, usually from 2 to 5 percent. At the weaker end of the spectrum, some states have only voluntary standards.[15]

Generally, a renewable-electricity standard requires electricity service providers to purchase renewable-energy certificates from qualified producers. Utilities recover the increased costs either through a surcharge or an increase in the base charge for ratepayers. Under the mandatory programs, there are penalties for noncompliance. There is usually price competition among producers of renewable energy, but in a few cases there is a feed-in tariff, which establishes a fixed price for the generation of renewable energy.

The public benefits fund, another pillar of state government support of the greening of electricity, provides financial support for renewable-energy generation and energy efficiency. As of 2012, about twenty states had public benefits funds, and those states also had a renewable-electricity standard. Most of the funds were authorized during the late 1990s as part of electricity restructuring legislation. Public benefits funds are generally financed by a system benefits charge (a small surcharge on utility bills), but funding can come from other sources, including revenue from greenhouse gas trading programs. Because system benefits charges function as a transfer from general customers to those who are willing to invest in energy-efficiency projects or renewable-energy projects, some legislators and governors have criticized them as an unfair tax. The charges can be made fairer if a portion of the revenue is dedicated to a compensating low-income energy-assistance program.

Another source of revenue for renewable-electricity and energy-efficiency projects is the Regional Greenhouse Gas Initiative (RGGI) in the Northeast. It began in 2009 and was predicted to result in a 10 percent decrease in carbon dioxide emissions by 2018. Although the European experience suggests that loopholes in cap-and-trade policies can significantly reduce their environmental benefits, in the United States the system is effective at generating revenue for the state governments that is reinvested in demand programs and green industrial development. By the end of 2010 the RGGI program had raised nearly $1 billion, which was invested mainly in renewable energy, energy efficiency, and low-income assistance.[16]

Other regions and states were also planning carbon trading schemes. Legislation in California (AB 32) in 2006 established a process for developing a carbon trading program, and in 2007 the governors and premier of Manitoba signed the Midwestern Greenhouse Gas Accord, which was a first step to a regional cap-and-trade system. Under the Western Climate Initiative, Western states and some Canadian provinces planned a cap-and-trade system for carbon dioxide emissions that was scheduled to begin in 2012. In 2008 the state of Florida approved HB 7135, which authorized the state's Department of Environmental Protection to develop a cap-and-trade program and a plan to reduce greenhouse gas emissions in the electricity sector to 1990 levels by 2025. The proliferation of regional and state-level systems helped to motivate attempts to develop a national policy that would standardize the rules. However, with some exceptions, support for regional initiatives evaporated after the 2010 elections.

An alternative to carbon trading is a carbon tax, which is more transparent, more easily applied across energy sectors, and less susceptible to manipulation than a cap-and-trade system. However, in the United States the word "tax" generally is not popular with voters, and opponents complain of government interference in the economy. The Carbon Tax Center (2010) explains the importance of framing the issue as follows: "The key is to steer around the pitfall of having a carbon tax framed as yet another way to raise taxes; the secret is a clear insistence on *earmarking revenues from carbon taxes to provide equal rebates to all US residents or to reduce existing regressive taxes.*" The Carbon Tax Center advises that a carbon tax can be used to reduce payroll taxes and sales taxes, both of which are regressive in structure. Nevertheless, carbon taxes are unpopular and can be found only in a few places in the United States. For example, in 2006 the city of Boulder passed the country's first carbon tax, which was levied on electricity consumption to fund energy-efficiency programs. In 2008 the nine counties of the San Francisco Bay Area passed a carbon tax; it covers businesses that emit carbon through smokestacks, including for building heat. Montgomery County of Maryland also passed a carbon tax in 2010, but it covers only the county's 850-megawatt coal plant.[17]

State governments have developed many other demand policies, such as contractor licensing, certification for renewable-energy equipment, interconnection standards, and net metering. Only a few states have put in place close to the full suite of policies that represent a comprehensive, demand-side portion of a policy to green the electricity industry. The states that have the most developed suite of policies also tend to import fossil fuels from other states. The substitution of electricity from fossil fuels with electricity from renewable energy creates local businesses and jobs, because it captures revenue that is going out of state. Although the term "import-substituting industrialization" is rarely used, it is a good description of the economic implications of the industrial policies.

Buildings and Energy Efficiency

To support the greening of buildings, some states have established the goal that all new state government buildings and major renovations must be built at the level equivalent to a silver certification in the LEED system of the US Green Building Council. The city of Portland, Oregon has gone beyond the silver-level designation to require new buildings to attain LEED gold certification, and the city of San Francisco built the country's first LEED platinum municipal building. Most state governments also have an energy-efficiency standard for government buildings. In some cases the standard involves an ongoing reduction in energy consumption of 1–3 percent per year over a base-line year. The city of Austin has gone beyond energy-efficiency goals to require that all city buildings be powered by renewable energy by 2020.[18]

Generally, state and local governments don't extend their building standards policies to the private sector, because owners of commercial buildings develop powerful mobilizations against mandatory green building standards. For example, in 2009 New York's mayor, Michael Bloomberg, announced that existing buildings of 50,000 square feet or more would be required to undergo an energy audit, and the building owners would be required to pay for many of the designated changes. However, when faced with vehement opposition from building owners, the mayor backed off the plan and said he would seek only mandatory energy audits. Although New York decided not to embrace mandatory improvements from building owners, San Francisco required all new private-sector buildings and major renovations to meet LEED certification.[19]

Plans that establish mandates for new commercial and residential buildings over a long transition period are politically more palatable than immediate mandates such as those proposed by Mayor Bloomberg. One of the leading examples of a long-term mandate is the 2009 plan approved by the California Public Utilities Commission to require net zero energy for new residential homes by 2020 and for commercial buildings by 2030. The plan also provided $3 billion in funds for the state's utilities to support energy-efficiency improvements in residential and commercial buildings. The plan was the largest ever by a state for energy efficiency, and the commission claimed that it would create 15,000 to 18,000 skilled jobs to retrofit a target of 120,000 homes. At the city level, an example of a long-term mandate is the city of Austin's amendments to the building code, which required that new homes be net zero energy by 2015.[20]

Another strategy for both state and local governments is to pursue transparency measures rather than mandates. For example, in 2009 the state of Washington built on its green buildings standard for public buildings by passing the "Efficiency First Act" (SB 5854), which required nonresidential building owners to conduct audits and reveal the results to prospective buyers and lessees. The legislation also tightened long-term building codes to require buildings to be 70 percent more efficient by 2031. Among city governments, Seattle and Austin have pioneered local energy disclosure ordinances. Seattle's Energy Disclosure Ordinance requires owners of large buildings to report on energy use and disclose ratings for tenants, buyers, and lenders. Austin's Energy Conservation Audit and Disclosure Ordinance requires homeowners to have an energy audit completed before the sale of a home, and owners of commercial buildings that receive energy from Austin Energy must receive an energy rating.[21]

To support the greening of buildings in the private sector, state governments use financial incentives such as rebates, loans, and tax credits. The public benefits funds discussed above that provide support for the generation of renewable energy also support energy-efficiency programs. Where combined with assistance to low-income families and job training, the programs have become a significant source of green jobs.

In summary, the green buildings policies combine energy conservation, energy efficiency, and distributed energy to reduce net energy consumption. The programs range from very light shades of green associated with modest energy-efficiency targets and disclosure rules to the deeper shades of green associated with a long-term transition to net zero energy. Buildings that attain the net zero energy goal will be very different systems from the standard buildings of the twentieth century.

As in the case of renewable energy, for states that import their natural gas for the heating of buildings and that import coal and other energy inputs for electricity that powers buildings, energy-efficiency programs for buildings create import-substitution benefits in both the short and long term. In the short term, there are job-creation benefits, where local construction jobs replace expenditures that are going out of state for fossil fuel production. In the long term, the savings on energy expenditures amounts to a fiscal stimulus for the regional economy. Even when households and businesses spend a portion of the "stimulus" on out-of-state goods and services, some of the money will circulate in the regional economy and create local jobs.

Green Transportation and Biofuels
As in the case of energy-efficiency savings for buildings, when public transportation options are increased there are two kinds of job-creation benefits: the immediate jobs in construction (e.g., of light rail) and in running a fleet, and the long-term jobs that emerge from the fiscal stimulus of spending less money on petroleum that is imported into the economy of a state or city. In a few cases, city and state governments have linked transportation initiatives to local manufacturing. For example, New York State is a hub of rail manufacturing because of the density of passenger rail in the region, and Portland, Oregon, linked the development of a streetcar system with local manufacturing.[22]

The greening of transportation also provides direct import-substitution benefits. The use of hybrid buses is an indirect fiscal stimulus not only because of the reduced petroleum consumption but also because of the lower maintenance costs. As the number of plug-in electric vehicles increases and as regional renewable energy increases, the two technological systems will converge and shift even more out-of-state petroleum consumption to local electricity. The full convergence of the two systems is still only in the demonstration project stage. For example, in California there is a pilot project to support a bus powered by a hydrogen fuel cell that uses solar energy to produce the hydrogen.[23]

Biofuels provide another opportunity to develop local industries and jobs. Several states have supported the local biofuels industry with demand policies such as a renewable fuels standard and improvements in the availability of filling stations. Minnesota led the country in 1997 with a 10 percent minimum level for ethanol in gasoline, and the state government added a 2 percent requirement for biodiesel in 2002. In 2005 the state increased the minimum level of ethanol in gasoline to 20 percent by 2013, and in 2006 the government required the government's vehicle fleet to use biofuels. The state has also provided support for fueling stations, and it leads the country in the number of ethanol pumps. Minnesota, Michigan, and Wisconsin are among the states that have programs that help filling stations to add E85 pumps.[24]

Because of the concentration of ethanol production in the Midwest, the states in that region have the possibility of double gains from increased ethanol usage. Not only do they replace a portion of the petroleum expenditures that go to out-of-state and foreign oil suppliers with increased demand for the products of intrastate farms, but they also gain by exporting ethanol to other states. To support the goal of exporting to other states, the Midwestern states have advocated for a pipeline to reduce transportation costs. Some biodiesel has been shipped in the Southeast through existing pipelines, but Midwestern states would like to have an ethanol pipeline that would connect their production with markets on the East Coast. In response to requests from the Midwestern states, the US Department of Energy studied a proposed biofuels pipeline from North Dakota to New Jersey and found that it was feasible but required government subsidies and a higher level of ethanol blend in the national renewable fuels standard.[25]

States that shift from out-of-state petroleum to out-of-state biofuels will provide an import-substitution benefit for the country as a whole, but they will not achieve the additional benefit for their own regional economies. In other words, there is a potential tension in the greening of transportation. Biofuels may follow the pattern of coal and natural gas, in which some states become leading producers and exporters to other states. The importing states will learn that they can obtain greater local economic benefit by shifting to all-electric vehicles if the electricity is increasingly produced from intrastate renewable energy.

Summary
Demand policies at the state government level generally are fairly light shades of green; that is, they have modest standards for renewable-electricity production and the greening of buildings and fleets. Most of the latter is restricted to policies that increase the efficiency of government buildings and mandate higher levels of alternative fuels in government fleets. Goals for the private sector are still unusual and often established with a long time horizon. Furthermore, the demand policies are unevenly distributed. They are strongest in California, Oregon, and Washington and in the Northeast. Colorado, Hawaii, and some of the Midwestern states also have fairly well developed policies. The problem of explaining the unevenness will be addressed in part III; the concern here is to show what the pattern of developmentalist politics looks like at the state and local government level. Doing so requires understanding how intrastate procurement preferences, which are used to gain import substitution benefits, are connected with green energy policy.

Intrastate Procurement Preferences

As the previous section suggests, even though states cannot engage in trade protectionism, the transition to renewable energy often is linked to import-substitution benefits for the regional economy. However, the benefits of import substitution are not guaranteed, because a state's renewable energy might be purchased from out-of-state wind farms or biofuels refiners. To avoid the loss of import-substitution benefits, the policy can include provisions that require local energy sources. Such provisions are known as intrastate procurement preferences, and they show how state governments utilize a form of trade protectionism, even within the "free-trade" zone of interstate commerce, to encourage the development of local industry.

One type of procurement preference involves purchasing by state governments. In 40 states, the intrastate location of a firm can serve as a tie breaker for equivalent bids on a government contract, and in fifteen states the local firm is allowed to have a slightly higher bid than the out-of-state firm. Thirty-five states have "reciprocal" legislation, which requires the government purchasing agency to add a percentage to the bid from an out-of-state company that is equivalent to the preference percentage granted to in-state firms in that state. For example, if state Y were to give intrastate firms a preference for bids up to 10 percent of those of the competing out-of-state firm, then state X would increase bids from state Y's companies by 10 percent. Federal courts have supported the preferences, because they can be justified based on the overall tax revenues that a state retains based on local purchasing. Another type of government procurement preference is simply a guideline for state government agencies to purchase a type of product from intrastate sources. For example, in 2009 the state government of Illinois approved the Local Food, Farm, and Jobs Act (HB 3990) to guide state agencies toward the purchase of "local food or farm products" at a rate of 20 percent by 2020.[26]

State and local governments can also encourage procurement preferences among private-sector firms. One of the best-known experiments was the Homegrown Project, launched in 1982 by the mayor of St. Paul under the guidance of the Institute for Local Self-Reliance. The project emphasized small business development, included a "buy local" campaign, and set in place policies that led to the city's district heating system. Likewise, Chicago experimented with a database of goods and services available from local corporations, and the program also hosted a local purchasing fair. New York and the twin cities of Minneapolis and St. Paul also have directories of local manufacturers and programs that encourage local sourcing.[27]

What evidence is there for the intersection of such local and intrastate procurement preferences with the green energy transition? With respect to electricity generation, state governments generally don't require that the renewable electricity come from intrastate sources. However, a state's renewable-electricity standard tends to spur in-state investment in renewable-electricity generation. If there is a solar energy carve-out and support for distributed generation, then the tables are tipped even more in favor of local generation of renewable energy.

State governments can also mandate that renewable energy come from in-state sources. Those mandates tend to create conflicts with neighboring states that have ambitions of exporting their surplus renewable energy. For example, the states of Arizona and Nevada would like to sell their renewable energy to California, and the state of Maine would like to sell its wind energy to southern New England. In the latter case, Massachusetts proposed rules that would allow utilities to extend contracts only with intrastate generation sources. The proposed rules created a significant backlash. Edward Krapels, chair of a company that proposed to build a "green line" of electricity transmission from Maine to Massachusetts, argued as follows:

In New England . . . there's a real danger that the laudable environmental goals of [Deval] Patrick and other governors will be undermined by the emergence of environmental mercantilism—actions by individual states to subsidize their own renewable energy industries. State regulators and legislators are under intense pressure to help out home-grown renewable energy projects even when cheaper alternatives are available next door. (2008)

Here the term "mercantilism" is used in a pejorative sense, and the parallels between the use of the term here and in the previous chapter for China are clear. Krapels argues instead for a regional approach to New England's needs for renewable energy. Note that, like the Chinese with respect to the United States, he defends "free trade" among states against the protectionism of Massachusetts:

In history, mercantilism—the "I win, you lose" attitude—was ultimately supplanted by the better idea that cooperation and commerce would allow each region and each country to do what it does best, to the benefit of all. The same can be true in meeting New England's environmental goals: all the states can be big winners, but only if they think regionally. (ibid.)

Of course, if the pattern of successful industrialization based on protectionism and industrial policy that Ha-Joon Chang outlined for South Korea could be applied to the green energy industry of Massachusetts, then Massachusetts might find an economic justification for its protectionist policies.[28]

The resistance to intrastate energy preferences goes beyond heated rhetoric. In a lawsuit filed in 2010 in federal court against Massachusetts, TransCanada Power claimed that Section 83 of the Massachusetts Green Communities Act, which favors intrastate renewable-energy-generation facilities, discriminated against out-of-state producers and violated the Commerce Clause of the United States Constitution (which essentially creates a free-trade zone among the states). The company also claimed that the solar energy carve-out for the Massachusetts renewable-electricity standard was discriminatory because it required that a portion of the electricity be from intrastate generation. In response, the state government modified the solar carve-out, and TransCanada dropped the second claim, but the company continued to pursue its claim based on the Commerce Clause. With respect to the Cape Wind Project, in 2011 the company also joined with local opposition groups and the New England Power Generation Association to sue Massachusetts in the state's Supreme Judicial Court based on the claim that National Grid should have opened up its bidding process to other generation companies, including those located out of state. The complaint further alleged that failure to open up the bidding process resulted in unnecessary price hikes for ratepayers.[29]

Intrastate and intraregional preferences are also emerging for biofuels and biomass production. In 2006, Governor Arnold Schwarzenegger announced the target of producing by 2020 40 percent of California's biofuels within the state and 20 percent of the state's renewable electricity from biomass produced within the state. Likewise, Florida's "Farm to Fuel" initiative has the goal of producing 25 percent of the state's energy needs from the state's agricultural industry. The initiative also supports a project to convert citrus waste to ethanol, that is, to develop a form of ethanol production that would favor the state's agricultural industry and not be useful for ethanol production in most other states. The state of Illinois also requires government contracts to favor biofuels from in-state sources. The Midwestern governors' 2007 Energy Security and Climate Stewardship Platform included the goal that 50 percent of all transportation fuels in the Midwest be from regionally produced biofuels by 2025. Although the agreement was weakened after changes in party affiliation when new governors were elected in 2010, advocates claim that the policy created thousands of jobs.[30]

With respect to intrastate manufacturing preferences for green technology, the evidence is much weaker and found mostly among states that have a strong manufacturing sector. However, it is possible that other states may follow their lead once the policy models are more widely disseminated. Iowa, Michigan, Ohio, and Wisconsin have renewable-electricity standards that encourage wind energy production, and those states have also been leaders in the growth of turbine manufacturing. To some degree, the size of wind turbines favors local assembly and manufacturing of the larger components, but in the case of those states the connection between the renewable-electricity standard and local manufacturing is implicit. Michigan is one exception; the state has created an add-on for renewable-energy credits if the energy is produced on equipment manufactured within the state. Likewise, the utility company Consumers Energy buys electricity from residential solar photovoltaic systems if the equipment is manufactured or assembled in-state. In New Jersey, the state's Renewable Energy Manufacturing Incentive program supports installations of photovoltaic panels, racks, and inverters if they are manufactured in-state. Furthermore, in 2011 the state legislature considered legislation that would make it easier for solar panel installers to get renewable-energy credits if they purchase their panels from in-state manufacturers.[31]

In summary, there are some policies in support of the greening of energy that adopt explicit intrastate and local preferences. The litigation against Massachusetts also suggests that the potential for explicit policies may be limited; however, the lack of similar opposition to intrastate preferences for biomass and manufacturing also suggests that there may be less opposition to preferences in those industries. It is possible that additional court challenges may result in state governments shifting to more implicit forms of intrastate preferences, such as Florida's support for biofuels from citrus waste.

Conclusion

A traditional interpretation of demand policies for the green energy sector would view their underlying political ideology as an extension of social liberalism, in which governments intervene in the private sector in order to correct the externalities associated with fossil fuels. One might also argue that there are neoliberal inflections in some of the demand policies. For example, both renewable-electricity policy and biofuels policy have steered away from mandating a price (such as occurs in a feed-in tariff) or an overt tax (as in the carbon tax), and often renewable-electricity standards are set up to create a new market of renewable-energy or solar-energy credits.

Although the two streams of mainstream political ideology are evident in the demand policies of state governments, the policies also exhibit a strong developmentalist strand through their connection with local economic development and job-creation goals. As this chapter has shown, import substitution at a regional level allows states to capture revenues that might otherwise leave the economy, either to foreign oil producers in the case of biofuels or to out-of-state coal and natural gas producers for states that import those sources of energy. The benefits are largely implicit, but a review of policies shows that some states have begun to set goals for intrastate production and even for intrastate manufacturing. Having strong local demand for green energy can also be a selling point when economic development officials attempt to attract and retain manufacturing companies. Although demand policies in themselves are only an element of green developmentalism, they create favorable conditions for supply-side policies of green industrial development.

At the same time that state governments are using energy policy to replace out-of-state jobs and businesses with local ones, the regional economies continue to participate in the national and global economy by acquiring some of their energy sources and related manufactured goods from out-of-state sources. Out-of-state companies also monitor state government policies, and, as the case of TransCanada's lawsuit against Massachusetts indicated, they attempt to maintain open markets when confronted with policies perceived to be protectionist or mercantilist. Thus, the pattern of developmentalist liberalism involves a cat-and-mouse game in which states try to maintain both the benefits of open markets and the benefits of regional business development and job creation.

5

The Greening of Regional Industrial Clusters

Whereas the previous chapter focused on the developmentalist implications of the demand side of state and local policies, this chapter will discuss the corresponding supply side. Although regional economies reap benefits from locally produced renewable energy, they can also benefit from the other side of green industrial development: new manufacturing and biofuels refining industries that generate revenue by exporting to other states and foreign countries. The traditional policies of the economic development tool kit, such as financial incentives and tax rebates, can help to attract and retain businesses, but increasingly state governments have turned to the innovation cluster as the guiding concept for regional industrial policy. The cluster not only incubates new firms but also serves as a magnet for retaining existing firms and attracting new ones that seek the benefits of colocation.

Innovation clusters rely heavily on the business services sector to enable the regional economy to adjust to changes in global demand. Silicon Valley is often hailed as the model; the region has proved remarkably resilient when faced with changing patterns of global innovation. Once the home of manufacturing for semiconductors and personal computers, it has since developed strengths in the related industries of software and green technology. Economic development strategies based on the goal of building innovation clusters attempt to build a regional economy that can reinvent itself in response to new opportunities and changing patterns of global demand and public policy. In contrast with the older, Fordist model of the industrial cluster, in which a central factory stood at the apex of a hierarchy of supply-chain companies, in the horizontal innovation cluster the service sector—understood broadly to include venture capital, research, training programs, law firms, accounting firms, and industrial associations—has become the platform that allows old industries to fade away and new ones to emerge. The goal is to create a constant mix of social networks, venture capital, high-quality research universities, technology transfer assistance, favorable public policies, and entrepreneurial ventures. In this chapter I will begin with a discussion of the theory of industrial clusters, then I will explore how state government policies have been adapted to support green industrial clusters.

Understanding the Cluster Concept

Economists have traced the concept of an industrial cluster back to the work of Alfred Marshall, who noted in his *Principles of Economics* that firms located in the same region receive benefits such as a pool of skilled labor. Because Marshall didn't specifically address innovation, Joseph Schumpeter is often cited as another founding figure, but the more direct predecessor of work on industrial clusters today is a series of studies published during the 1980s and the early 1990s. Studies of business agglomeration in Los Angeles by the geographer Allen Scott and work on innovative, flexible manufacturing in Italy by the economist Michael Piore and the political scientist Charles Sabel drew attention to geographically based networks of transactions among businesses. Michael Porter of the Harvard Business School also studied the competitive advantage that firms derive from the tendency to become geographically concentrated. Somewhat later, the political scientist AnnaLee Saxenian's comparative study of Silicon Valley and Route 128 suggested the importance of inter-firm networks as a source of innovation, and the innovation studies scholars Henry Etzkowitz and Loet Leydesdorf drew attention to the importance of "triple helix" partnerships among industry, universities, and governments.[1]

Although the concept of an industrial cluster is widely mentioned in the dozens of policy reports written about the creation of green industries, generally there is little discussion of the extensive literature on the topic, with the exception of some of the studies by the Brookings Institution. In most of the reports for state and local governments, if a portion of the scholarly literature is cited, usually it is Michael Porter's model of the "diamond" of policy interventions. The following summary is adopted from Porter's book *The Competitive Advantage of Nations*:

• factors: stimulate education, research, technology transfer from research organizations, infrastructure needs, capital investments, supply-chain needs of industry, producer services, a qualified labor pool, and information sharing and provisioning

• demand: create government procurement policies, regulations that anticipate emerging standards, and policies that stimulate early and sophisticated demand
• related and supporting industries: align the media, trade associations, and government agencies with the economic development strategy
• firm strategy and structure: develop tax incentives, encourage inter-firm competition, and assist with start-ups.[2]

By the early 2000s, the literature on regional innovation systems and industrial innovation clusters was large enough that there were multiple review essays and handbooks available. Of most relevance for understanding green industrial policies was work dedicated to regional innovation policies. Manuel Laranja and colleagues reviewed five of the most influential theoretical frameworks in the field (neoclassical, Schumpeterian, neo-Marshallian, systemic institutional, and evolutionary) to show that they lead to different emphases on best policies. Examples of policy instruments that they discuss from the summary are subsidies, tax incentives, research parks, technological infrastructures, workforce training, extension services, and proactive brokerage. Although their "pentagon" of five theoretical strands represents a different way of conceptualizing the regional innovation policy field from Porter's diamond, the list of policies that emerges overlaps significantly with that of Porter, and the overlap suggests that from a policy standpoint the diverse theoretical strands of the regional innovation systems literature tend to converge.[3]

One of the conclusions that has emerged in studies of regional innovation policies is that industrial and regional differences are significant enough that discussion of policy strategies must take them into account. There is considerable skepticism that regional innovation policies that are successful in one circumstance can apply without substantial modification in others. Perhaps the greatest risk is to attempt to replicate the most successful regional innovation system, Silicon Valley, without first completing a diagnosis of the barriers and opportunities for the region. For example, peripheral regions may suffer from organizational thinness and require recruitment and incubation strategies, whereas old industrial regions require a focus on innovation in related industries, and fragmented metropolitan areas require efforts to integrate industries into the global economy and stronger university-industry relationships.[4]

Although research on industrial innovation clusters can be applied to clean tech industries, to date research on the topic has been limited. An exception is the work by the innovation studies scholar Philip Cooke, who finds that innovation is dependent on knowledge entrepreneurs, venture capital firms and other sources of capital, consultants, managers of research incubators, and technology transfer offices. In addition, Cooke builds on the work of the urban studies scholar Jane Jacobs to suggest that an important ingredient in regional innovation that is especially salient for the clean tech industries is the presence of industries of a "related variety," which facilitate knowledge spillovers that can lead to innovation. In the case of clean technology, he found relationships with biotechnology, information and communication technology, agro-food, and agricultural and marine engineering. Entrepreneurs who move across industrial sectors tend to be the main vehicle of innovation. Cooke also shows how some clean tech industries evolve from a locally focused industry to export-oriented manufacture, a pattern that he shows is consistent with Jacobs's work on import-substituting industrialization. From this perspective he infers three policy directions that are particularly relevant for clean tech innovation systems: public procurement (demand creation), integration of inter-industry and supply-chain relationships (to encourage knowledge spillover and entrepreneurship), and the development of "knowledge laboratories" or demonstration projects.[5]

Planning for Green Innovation Clusters

The theory and practice of developing regional innovation clusters is evident in the federal government program known as the Energy Regional Innovation Cluster (E-RIC) initiative. An important part of the E-RIC clusters is funding for commercialization and manufacturing, so that research is connected with job-creating businesses. For example, the Greater Philadelphia Innovation Cluster, which supports the building materials industry and has a goal of reducing building energy consumption by 50 percent, has participation from eleven universities, two Department of Energy laboratories, five industry partners, and various government agencies. In the Philadelphia cluster, the state government also pledged $30 million to construct a facility at the Philadelphia Navy Yard. Unlike the Department of Energy's ARPA-E projects, which are more "blue sky," the E-RIC clusters focus on bringing new technologies to market.[6]

Although federal government initiatives to support green energy industrial clusters are limited, our review of all 50 states revealed evidence for regionally focused industries. The clusters generally included a mixture of manufacturing firms, research organizations, industrial associations, and support from state and local government agencies. (See table 5.1.) The review also indicates that the development of green industrial clusters is often well beyond a planning stage; in some states there are well established networks of firms, research organizations, and government agencies.[7]

Although the most populous state, California, has green energy industrial strengths across the board, most states have specialized in one or two industries. Often the choices are determined by what Cooke called "industries of a related variety." States and metropolitan regions build on what they already have and use those industries to leverage new developments in the clean energy sector. For example, the automotive industry and its supply-chain companies have transitioned not only into production of hybrid vehicles but also into the battery and fuel cell manufacturing industries. States with a strong automotive supply chain, especially Michigan and Ohio, have also developed initiatives to use the same companies for wind manufacturing. In California, Massachusetts, and Wisconsin, the biotechnology industry has become a basis for next-generation cellulosic and algal biofuels, and in other states traditional agricultural research strengths have been valuable for the transition to the "bioeconomy," a term that includes biotechnology products in the

Table 5.1
States with prominent green energy industries (compiled from Hess et al. 2010).

Industry	States
Batteries and energy storage	Michigan, New York
Biofuels	California, Colorado, Florida, Georgia, Hawaii, Illinois, Iowa, Michigan, Texas, Washington, and Wisconsin
Building materials and control systems	Minnesota, New York, Oregon, Pennsylvania
Fuel cells	California, Connecticut, Massachusetts, Michigan, New York, Ohio, Pennsylvania, South Carolina
Smart grid	California, Washington
Solar	California, Colorado, Florida, Massachusetts, New Mexico, Ohio, Oregon
Wind	Colorado, Illinois, Iowa, South Carolina, Wisconsin

energy sector. Another related industry, the software industry of California and Washington, has supported the transition into smart-grid business development.

One of the first steps in forming a green innovation policy is to establish the planning basis for policy coordination. The planning exercises generally take the form of scenarios and roadmaps that state governments develop in order to target specific industries for development. Many cities and states have an office of sustainability or energy independence that coordinates programs and plans across different departments and agencies.

In Michigan, Governor Jennifer Granholm reorganized the state's Department of Labor and Economic Growth into the Department of Energy, Labor, and Economic Growth. Although the organizational change was short-lived (her Republican successor reversed the decision), Granholm's goal was to bring together the economic development efforts with energy policy, clean tech industry development, and green jobs training initiatives. In 2009 the new department published a report that assessed the clean tech industry and green jobs opportunities for the state and classified jobs into what it described as industrial "clusters." The report found the largest number of jobs to be in the clean transportation and clean fuels cluster (including batteries, fuel cells, and biofuels) and the energy-efficiency cluster. Using location quotients, the study also identified the transportation and fuel cluster as having a higher concentration in Michigan than average. Although the finding is not surprising for the state that is historically associated with automobile manufacturing, the report also identified the location quotient for energy efficiency as average and for renewable-energy production as below average, a finding that indicated potential for growth. The report identified wind turbine and solar manufacturing, energy efficiency, and advanced energy storage (batteries, which again overlaps with the automotive industry) as areas of likely growth, given policy initiatives and related industry strengths. Based on a survey of employers for their expectations of hiring, the report also estimated future needs for specific occupations so that training and educational programs could be connected with demand. In summary, the report is a good example of how a state government can assess its industrial strengths and weaknesses in order to develop a coordinated effort to support selected green energy industries.[8]

In New Mexico, Governor Bill Richardson developed a somewhat different strategy in 2009, when he established the Green Jobs Cabinet to produce a roadmap for the state's green energy industries. One can see in the report a good example of how a state government uses the idea of industrial clusters as part of its green energy economic development strategy:

The biggest return on investment will come through investing in clusters of related industries because these clusters maximize economic value. Industry clusters are a critical factor in the state's ability to attract sustainable investments necessary for continuous economic development. (State of New Mexico 2009: 11)

The New Mexico report noted that the state had strong natural resource endowments in solar, wind, and geothermal energy, and it was located strategically at the intersection of the country's three largest "interconnects" of the national electricity grid. Abundant renewable-energy resources, low population density, and strategic location made it possible for the state to become an exporter of renewable energy. The report also noted the potential to develop manufacturing in the solar, smart-grid, green building materials, and biofuels industries (the latter based on algae and on dry-land nonfood crops). The state's national laboratories and research universities, together with some existing manufacturing companies, created potential for innovation clusters in those four industries.

Massachusetts went beyond reports and plans to create a central clearinghouse for green energy industrial development. The Massachusetts Clean Energy Center provides training for green jobs, investments in both renewable-energy generation and green energy companies, and information on testing facilities and incubators. It also contracted with Clean Edge, Inc., to prepare a general roadmap for the state's clean energy center. The report identified the energy-efficiency, solar, and energy storage industries as three industries for which Massachusetts has relative strengths. Our research also identified wind energy, because the state has wind energy research centers as well as testing facilities and some wind energy companies. Although there is some green energy manufacturing in Massachusetts, its high density of research universities has enabled Massachusetts to focus on innovation and technology transfer.[9]

Other states have produced industry-specific roadmaps. For example, the Ohio Department of Development produced a fuel cell road map and strategy to attract new companies, support current companies, facilitate technology development, coordinate resources, develop the workforce, and assist companies with patenting and growth. The report also assessed the programs of the competing states of California, Connecticut, New York, and South Carolina. It suggested that the state government should stimulate demand for products, and it advocated a preferential procurement policy for the state government.[10]

City governments have also launched planning efforts for green economic development. Whereas the first generation of city-level sustainability plans focused on the greening of urban spaces, energy efficiency, renewable energy, bikeways, and transit-oriented development, the second generation linked urban sustainability with green jobs development. Examples of sustainability plans that include green jobs goals include the plans of Philadelphia and San José, but those plans don't target specific green energy industries for development. In a few cases, there is a planning effort that specifically assessed the city's green business strengths and potential. For example, the Minneapolis-St. Paul report outlined manufacturing and research strengths in three areas: green building, transportation, and renewable energy. Likewise, the city of Austin has focused on renewable energy, creative media, and medical technology as three areas of industrial strength.[11]

The report on Portland, Oregon, is of special interest because it shows how a green energy business cluster can be related to other industrial clusters in the region. The 2009 report began by noting that the city had lost 44,000 jobs during the preceding twelve months. As in many other cities across the world at that time, job creation had become a top priority. The report identified four "clusters" on which the city would focus its limited developmental resources: clean tech and sustainable industries, "activewear" (sports clothing) and design, software, and advanced manufacturing. The clusters in activewear and in software were built on the base of large corporations in the region, notably Nike and Intel. In defense of the highly focused strategy, the report noted the relatively small size of the city and the need to be selective in its planning for new industries that would be competitive. Citing Michael Porter's diamond model of cluster formation, the report added:

Portland's four clusters are concentrated beyond national norms and adhere to widely accepted theories regarding the emergence and evolution of clusters. In particular, the clusters have demonstrated growth beyond industry averages and have assembled the elements of tangible competitive advantage, including concentrations of talent, deepening supply chains, and a proximity to customers or product feedback loops (e.g., local outdoor recreational culture informs product development in activewear). (City of Portland 2009a: 8)

With respect to the clean tech and sustainable industries cluster, the report noted that the city had strengths in several industries, including wind, solar, and green buildings. In previous recruitment efforts the city had convinced two international companies, Vestas and Iberdrola, to locate their North American headquarters in the city. To support the cluster, the plan included various strategies and actions: mapping the regional supply chain, recruiting new firms, developing a coordinating body that links industry to the research infrastructure, and promoting demand with the Clean Energy Investment Fund. In addition, the city planned to encourage synergies among the four main industrial clusters and to promote all four clusters via international trade shows, linkages with universities, and workforce development. One of the potential areas of synergy among clean tech, information technology, and advanced manufacturing is electric vehicle manufacturing. The city is part of a corridor of 27 manufacturers of electric cars and components for them, which take advantage of the electric vehicle charging infrastructure and the skilled workforce from the information technology sector.[12]

Green Industrial Policy

As was suggested in the preceding section, at least some state and city governments have engaged in systematic planning and coordination for the creation of green industries. Although green industrial policy at the federal government level is piecemeal, at the state government level it is sometimes much more coherent. There are two main reasons why green industrial policy is largely a state government phenomenon in the United States. First, trade policy has created substantial job loss because of the transfer of manufacturing abroad, but it has also created market opportunities for American companies in the high-tech sector. Demand from voters for jobs combines with demand from new industries for support. Second, the geographical variation in factor endowments favors states in which manufacturing labor and the high-tech base of university research are strong, and conversely where fossil fuel industries don't dominate local energy politics.

This section will describe briefly the three central elements of green industrial policy at the state and city government level: networks and incubators, financial support, and training and research.

Networks and Incubators

Once a state or a city government has undertaken an analysis and planning process that leads to a decision to support one or more clean tech industries, the next step involves providing the social infrastructure for connecting the diverse elements of the regional innovation cluster. The elements include the businesses themselves, the appropriate agencies in the state and local governments, researchers in the universities and national laboratories, and the many supporting industries such as consultants and venture capitalists.

A primary strategy is to create or recruit trade associations that can accomplish the networking function. For example, the New York State Energy Research and Development Authority's (NYSERDA) formalized the networking function by creating two nonprofit trade associations. The New York Battery and Energy Storage Consortium was founded to link together universities, testing facilities, government agencies, Brookhaven National Laboratory, and businesses in the fuel cell and energy storage fields, and the New York State Smart-Grid Consortium was founded with a similar goal for smart-grid technologies. In 2009 the city of Austin recruited the leading industry association, the Clean Technology and Sustainable Industries Association, from Massachusetts. Advantages also accrue to a region that is able to establish standards for an industry. U-SNAP Alliance, a company that develops standards for smart-grid appliances, and the Electric Power Research Institute, which conducts research and development for the utility industry, are both located in California. Because the two organizations have worked together to set up a communication interface for appliances, having those organizations in-state will enhance the capacity of California to convert its strengths in electronics and software into leadership in the smart-grid industry. Likewise, the state of Michigan's economic development organization for energy, Nextenergy, helped to set up the National Biofuels Energy Laboratory at Wayne State University. The laboratory will contribute to the next stage of the renewable fuel standard, a transition from a 5 percent to a 20 percent blend.[13]

Some cities also have trade associations and industrial partnerships. Philadelphia and Boston have vibrant sustainable business associations geared primarily to the small business sector, whereas Portland, San Diego, and Oakland have organizations that support the green business sector more generally. Portland's PDX Lounge supports the city's green businesses by providing networking opportunities and promoting the city's businesses at conferences and trade shows. In 2007 the city of San Diego launched the San Diego Cleantech Initiative and issued a report on the potential for the industry in the region, and the San Diego Clean Tech Alliance was formed that year to promote the industrial sector. In the same year, Mayor Ron Dellums launched the Oakland Partnership, a public-private partnership for economic development that included representatives from government, business, education, labor, and community organizations. "Green tech" was one of the four major industry clusters that the partnership targeted. Dellums also joined with other East Bay mayors and representatives from the universities to launch the East Bay Green Corridor Partnership, which established goals for clean tech business development in the region.[14]

State and city governments have also sponsored conferences and competitions that have encouraged companies to view their region as a hub of clean energy innovation. For example, the state of Colorado sponsors an annual "New Energy Conference" that helps to showcase the state's renewable-energy industry. In partnership with a nonprofit organization in Palo Alto, the city of San José hosts the Clean Tech Open, the largest annual clean tech business competition in the country. The state of Minnesota hosts a competition for entrepreneurs called the Minnesota Cup, with a section for green businesses. There are similar conferences and competitions in several other cities, including Austin, Boston, New York, and San Francisco.

State and city governments have also encouraged networking by facilitating the colocation of green businesses. General business incubators and technology parks don't preclude clean energy businesses, but in a few cases state and local governments have developed organizations focused specifically on clean energy industries. For example, NYSERDA supported the Saratoga Technology + Energy Park, which is located close to a technology campus that houses a computer chip manufacturing plant. NYSERDA also supported the Clean Energy Center, which provides assistance to start-up companies in partnership with the Syracuse Technology Garden. Some cities have also developed plans for industrial districts or corridors. Examples include the Addison Corridor in Chicago, the Thirtieth Street Industrial Corridor in Milwaukee, the Clean-Tech Corridor in Los Angeles, and the Innovation District in Boston. The industrial districts have an expanded mission to include businesses with clean manufacturing and companies that manufacture green products.[15]

In summary, some state and city governments have amplified their role from one of planning and coordination to that of catalyst of networks. The networks not only facilitate innovation but also provide useful feedback to the state and local government to identify bottlenecks in the innovation cluster, such as the need for testing centers. Networking also connects universities with firms and helps to facilitate technology transfer.

Capital Investment and Financial Support

Another important element of green industrial policy is facilitating the finance needed to start and grow companies. For established companies, stock offerings or other equity sales can provide capital, but start-up companies need "angel" investors and venture capital. Venture capital investments in clean tech represent a relatively small portion of overall investment in the sector, but they fund the crucial early phases of innovation and business development. However, for venture capital clean tech is the most important sector, eclipsing even biotechnology and information technology. Within clean tech, the highest level of investment globally went to the solar and electric vehicle industries.[16]

One of the problems with venture capital is that firms are relatively concentrated geographically on the East Coast and the West Coast, and within those regions they are concentrated near San Francisco, New York, and Boston. Of the twenty leading venture capital firms that invest in clean technology, there are slightly more companies in California than on the East Coast. The concentration of firms and pre-existing networks of innovation favor the California start-ups, but the California firms invest globally and increasingly have opened offices both on the East Coast and in other countries.

To amplify and supplement the role of venture capital, state governments have increasingly entered the field by providing their own direct capital assistance. Some states have used a portion of public pension funds to invest in high-tech companies, and a few have included clean energy within their purview. For example, the New York State Common Retirement Fund invested about $971 million (less than 1 percent of total holdings) in its in-state private-equity program, which includes some clean tech companies. Florida also established a $1.95 billion (1.5 percent) earmark from the state pension fund for high-tech companies, and the California Public Employees Retirement System has a $480 million Clean Energy and Technology Fund and a "green initiative" for the funds' real estate investments.[17]

Another investment strategy is to set up specific government funds for investment in clean energy companies, including at the early stage. For example, the California Clean Energy Fund was launched in 2005 as a nonprofit corporation in partnership with venture capital firms with $30 million in settlements from the bankruptcy settlement of Pacific Gas and Electric Company. Many states also have general economic development programs that include clean energy as one of the targeted industries. For example, in 2005 the state of Texas designated $200 million for the Texas

Emerging Technology Fund. Although the investments have been spread over many high-tech industries, some of them have gone into clean tech businesses.[18]

Two programs have been especially important in spurring clean energy industries. In 2005, Iowa approved the Grow Iowa Values Fund for $500 million over ten years. The fund provides support for the state's Department of Economic Development for start-ups, recruitment, and retention. A portion of the fund supported biofuel and wind power companies and enabled the state to become a national leader in the two industries. In 2002, Ohio established Ohio Third Frontier to spur the state's high-tech sector and stimulate industrial clusters. The program had a budget of $1.6 billion over ten years, and some of the funding supported the state's fuel cell and solar industries. The program was considered such a success that in 2010 voters reauthorized the program through 2016 for an additional $700 million. By 2008, Ohio Third Frontier had invested $33 million in the northwestern Ohio solar energy cluster, and the resulting industry was estimated to have created 5,000 jobs. Venture capital flowed into the companies that were emerging in the area, including $40 million into Xunlight, a manufacturer of rolled thin-film photovoltaics. Toledo is historically known as a glass manufacturing center, an industrial strength that was aided by the proximity of the city to the Michigan automotive industry. The related industry provided some manufacturing knowledge that could be transferred to photovoltaics. The other leading clean energy sector is the state's fuel cell industry, which runs along a corridor from Columbus to northeastern Ohio.[19]

State governments have also used tax credits and federal grants to provide financial support for green energy businesses. For example, in 2006 Michigan's state government passed legislation that launched ten Renewable Energy Renaissance Zones, which allow companies that produce renewable energy to be exempt from most state taxes. In 2009 and 2010 the state awarded $35 million in grants to in-state clean energy manufacturers. Applicants had to show demand, local sourcing (within Michigan), proof of contribution to the state's renewable portfolio standard, recycling of waste, and compliance with the prevailing wage laws. In 2009, the state government also approved $555 million in tax credits for battery manufacturing, which could be used to match federal grants from the stimulus package. According to Governor Jennifer Granholm, the combination of state and federal support helped Michigan to become the best place in the country for battery manufacturers, and she predicted that the state would have 62,000 related new jobs within ten years. The potential job growth was especially important because of the state's heavy unemployment rate and the strong multiplier effects from new jobs in manufacturing.[20]

The states of Minnesota and Oregon have also used tax credits and exemptions to support green energy business development. In Minnesota in 2008, the Job Growth Investment Tax Credit and Small Business Investment Tax Credit were changed to have 50 percent dedicated to businesses that generate green jobs, and Governor Tim Pawlenty also extended to green businesses the tax exemption under the state's Job Opportunity Building Zone program. In Oregon, the state government aggressively recruited clean energy industries with a 50 percent tax credit for new renewable-energy facilities up to $20 million. The Business Energy Tax Credit could be applied to both production companies and clean energy manufacturing, but it was controversial because of the high levels of subsidies that were granted. As a result, in 2010 the legislature approved a reform (HB 3680) to rein in the costs.[21]

After the financial crisis that began in 2008, the capacity to provide equity investments, grants, or even tax credits declined. Likewise, the help that ARRA funding provided for the green energy economy had wound down by the end of 2011. However, one should not conclude that financial support for green energy businesses dried up completely by 2012. Rather, the form of financial support shifted to mechanisms that stretch limited funds, such as the use of revolving loan funds.

Training and Research

The third main element of the supply side of green industrial policy is to develop the local factor endowments of the workforce and research infrastructure. Green jobs training programs existed before the ARRA legislation, but during the 111th Congress they received a much higher priority from the federal government, and the federal funding motivated state governments that didn't already have programs to develop them. From 2009 to 2012, ARRA funds provided temporary support for many programs, but permanent federal government funds from the Department of Labor were also available. To make optimal use of limited funds, state and local governments drew on federal funds and turned to public-private partnerships, including support from nonprofit organizations, unions, businesses, and private foundations. Some programs were also supported with public benefits funds and, in the Northeast, regional greenhouse gas emissions funds.

Some of the earliest green jobs training programs were not linked to business development as much as the employment and training needs of the city's low-income neighborhoods. Sponsored by city governments to help persons with employment barriers, the programs addressed issues of urban poverty in the tradition of the social liberalism of the Great Society programs of the 1960s. For example, in 1994 Chicago's mayor, Richard Daly, launched the Greencorps Program, which hired about 50 people each year for a nine-month training session for jobs in landscaping and horticulture, electronics recycling, and weatherization. During the period the trainees also gained experience by assisting the community gardens program and working in a recycling center.[22]

Whereas the Chicago program is an example of one managed directly by the city government, increasingly local governments have turned to partnerships with nonprofit organizations and local educational institutions. In Oakland, the mayor's office worked with the Ella Baker Center and the Apollo Alliance to secure seed funding for a partnership with Laney College and local training organizations. In June of 2009, the Oakland Green Jobs Corps graduated its first class of 40 students, who received jobs in solar and construction companies. The Richmond Build program, another example from the East Bay region, operates with support from the city of Richmond in partnership with nonprofit organizations and local colleges. Funding has come from the federal government and from Chevron, Pacific Gas and Electric, and Home Depot. The program achieved a 90 percent placement rate with an average wage of $18.33 per hour. Part of the educational program is led by the nonprofit organization Solar Richmond, which trains students in the installation of solar energy equipment.[23]

Whereas at the city government level green jobs programs are often connected with urban constituencies that seek training and employment opportunities, at the state government level the programs are more broadly geared to the state's green industries. Some state governments have attempted to connect supply and demand by developing an inventory of programs and making the opportunities known through Web-based publications. For example, in 2009 Ohio Green Pathways produced a catalog of green jobs training programs at community colleges and in adult career centers, and in 2010 the state of New Mexico released the *Green Jobs Guidebook*.[24]

In 2009 Governor Arnold Schwarzenegger announced two green jobs training programs for California that are notable because of the different levels of funding that show the relative weighting given to the constituencies in policies. The California Green Corps, funded with $10 million of federal stimulus money and matching funds from public-private partnerships, offered 20-month training sessions for green-collar jobs for 1,500 at-risk youth. Later that year the state announced a second, much larger program: the $75 million California Clean Energy Workforce Training Program, which would train 20,000 people for green jobs though educational programs at community colleges and other sites. In effect a subsidy for the green business sector, the program absorbed training costs and provided a qualified workforce for green businesses.[25]

Although there are some success stories, the 90 percent placement rate mentioned above is not always the case for green jobs training. At the other end of the spectrum, a program in Florida that provided training in a range of green jobs skills was unable to place three-fourths of the graduates. By late 2011, $300 million of the $500 million in ARRA training funding was unspent, and programs had served only 53,000 of the targeted 125,000 workers. Although placement rates were going up, the programs had placed only 8,000 workers in comparison with the goal of 80,000. Of the 8,000 workers, just 1,336 had retained employment for more than six months.[26]

In response to widespread criticism, the Employment and Training Administration defended its record by arguing that the statistics reflected the start-up phase of the program through the end of 2010, but they didn't reflect progress in 2011. Nevertheless, the progress was far short of the original aspirations of the program, and the shortcomings provided a basis for criticisms of the president's green industrial policy initiatives from Republican opponents. To have successful placement records, green jobs training programs must be coordinated with demand policies and local needs, and one could argue that the alleged failure of green jobs training programs at a national level is closely related to the lack of political support for demand policies. Still, the programs could have been coordinated more closely with local demand. The more successful programs, such as some of the industry partnerships programs in Pennsylvania, involve region-specific coordination among local businesses, the state government, and training organizations. Where there is good coordination, precious resources are not wasted by training workers for nonexistent jobs, and businesses are even willing to provide financial support.[27]

A less controversial and arguably more successful form of factor endowment support has been for the research infrastructure. Research support does create green jobs, but they are high-end jobs for highly skilled workers, and there are relatively few jobs. Instead, the value of support for the research infrastructure is to provide a basis for developing new technologies that can be transferred to the private sector. Because the most populous states generally have several world-class universities and large companies with corporate research-and-development centers, they have the resources to develop a green energy innovation cluster. The large population also provides strong local demand for test markets, especially if the state government has put in place the demand policies discussed in the previous chapter. Finally, larger states have the budgets to support research efforts directly, much as the federal government does through the National Science Foundation, the Department of Energy, and other federal agencies that support energy research.

The most populous state is far ahead of other states in many ways. A brief review of the scope of the research programs provides a sense of what a state government can accomplish, and again this element of industrial policy is embedded in a symphony of supply and demand policies. The research infrastructure is founded on the University of California's multi-campus Energy Institute, which the state government has supported since 1980. Some of the organizations affiliated with the institute, such as the California Institute for Energy and Environment, link research in the university system with industry groups. The state has also partnered with Lawrence Berkeley National Laboratory to develop a range of solar energy, biofuels, and energy-efficiency research programs. There are institutes for transportation studies at the universities at Berkeley and Davis, and Merced hosts the California Advanced Solar Technologies Institute. California has also done well at capturing large grants (generally at $15 million to $20 million over five years) from the US Department of Energy for the Energy Frontier Research Centers.[28]

The powerful combination of the Lawrence Berkeley National Laboratory and the University of California research system would already set California apart from most other states, but the state also is home to several highly ranked private universities. Stanford University has become a world center for green energy research. Among the university's many energy-related research centers and programs, the university's Global Climate and Energy Project sponsors dozens of research projects in a network of both academic and industrial scientists. However, southern California is also a green energy research powerhouse. The incubator associated with Caltech, Entretec, has produced and supported many companies in the clean energy sector, and the E-RIC center there plus general support from the Los Angeles city government will likely result in much more innovation. In San Diego there is a cluster of academic researchers and firms that have formed the San Diego Center for Algae-Based Biofuels, which links five local research institutes and universities. In support of the biofuels cluster, in 2009 ExxonMobil announced a $600 million partnership with Synthetic Genomics, a biotechnology company founded by Craig Venter and located in La Jolla.[29]

Only the state of New York has a comparable level of support from the state government for green energy research, a similarly strong system of public and private research universities, and a national laboratory. The New York State Foundation for Science, Technology, and Innovation (NYSTAR) supports high-tech economic development through research efforts and its regional development centers. The foundation funds fifteen centers for advanced technology, which support university-industry collaboration and technology transfer. Traditionally, New York has focused its high-tech research investments on nanotechnology, advanced materials, and biotechnology; however, the state government has leveraged the existing nanotechnology strength to expand into green tech, and the state has strengths in research and manufacturing in the battery, fuel cell, and energy storage industries. Six of the NYSTAR centers focus on research directly relevant to clean energy technology. The state's environmental agency, NYSERDA, also supports both intramural and extramural research, and it planned to support several Clean Energy Advanced Research Centers, probably focused on energy storage.[30]

States that have multiple green energy industries are at an advantage, because they are likely to be able to establish an innovation culture similar to that of Silicon Valley and benefit from the flow of ideas and entrepreneurs across industries. In Colorado, the state government has actively built networks among its research universities, national laboratory, manufacturers, and industrial associations. The state government formed the Colorado Renewable Energy Collaboratory to link the National Renewable Energy Laboratory with research centers at the University of Colorado, at Colorado State University, and at the Colorado School of Mines. By also launching the Clean Tech Initiative (a consortium of research, government, and industry organizations that holds monthly meetings), the government has connected research groups with one another and with industry to encourage entrepreneurship in the industry.[31]

Other states have tended to focus on one or more industries where there is a regional advantage that can make the state a credible world center for industrial innovation. The Ohio solar energy cluster mentioned above began with investments in the University of Toledo and in nearby Bowling Green State University. Building on the success, the state's Ohio Research Scholars Program attracted scientists to the University of Toledo, and in 2009 the university created a new School of Solar and Advanced Renewable Energy. Likewise, for the state's fuel cell cluster, there were more than 87 research projects and significant research groups at universities, at Wright-Patterson Air Force Base, and at NASA's Glenn Research Center. The leaders of the state's fifteen top research universities also formed the University Clean Energy Alliance of Ohio, which organizes conferences on energy and facilitates university-industry collaboration.[32]

Michigan is another example of a state government that has targeted specific research areas as part of its focused industrial development policy. To develop Michigan's research infrastructure, in 2008 the state government developed the Centers of Energy Excellence program to encourage "the development, growth, and sustainability of alternative energy industry clusters" (Brown 2008). The program was authorized to spend up to $45 million over three years from the state's 21st Century Jobs Fund to support research and development clusters. Five of the state's leading research universities formed the Consortium for Advanced Manufacturing of Alternative and Renewable Energy Technologies to advance research collaborations. The state government also supported testing facilities that complement the research-and-development centers associated with the major automotive companies.

Other states have attempted to support research clusters and connect them with regional industries. For example, there are efforts to support research and development for the solar industry in Florida, and South Carolina has developed a network of research and industry connections in the fuel cell industry. Iowa State University has brought together its resources in the Bioeconomy Institute, which has 150 affiliated researchers and over $50 million in research funding spread across various programs. The University of Wisconsin is the lead organization for the Great Lakes Bioenergy Research Center, which includes more than 250 affiliated researchers and staff. The federal government's investment of $375 million in biofuels centers also went to Lawrence Berkeley National Laboratory's Joint BioEnergy Institute and Oak Ridge National Laboratory's BioEnergy Science Center.[33]

At the other extreme, the state government in Tennessee has not realized the potential that the state has to serve as a catalyst that connects researchers with industry. Tennessee is home to a next-generation cellulosic ethanol plant, to Nissan's Leaf factory, to a growing solar installation industry, to some solar manufacturing, and to green energy research at the state's research universities and Oak Ridge National Laboratory. In other words, all of the elements of a vibrant innovation cluster are in place. However, the crucial role of the state government as a catalyst and convener of focused green innovation networks, akin to the programs in New York and Colorado, is missing. Demand policies are also very weak, a feature that most green energy advocates in the state blame on the Tennessee Valley Authority, which has focused on building base-load generation (including plans for new nuclear generation) rather than on supporting strong energy-efficiency and renewable-energy programs. Furthermore, because Tennessee is a right-to-work state, the labor portion of green transition coalitions is much weaker than in other states. In short, the case of Tennessee suggests that even small states have the potential for diverse green industrial development, but the state government must play a leadership role in connecting the elements of incipient clusters.

Conclusions

The focus of state and local programs on developing industrial clusters, and within that strategy on green energy clusters, is relatively new. Until the 1980s, state and local governments provided general support for industries in the form of infrastructure, tax abatements, and subsidies. Attracting a large industrial manufacturing company could create a vertical cluster of supply-chain companies, and it provided an anchor for the export base of the regional economy. Neither the science nor the practice of economic development focused on industrial change, the advantages of colocation, and the role of networks in innovation. When the industrial development policies shifted from Fordist assembly-line manufacturing to the high-tech sectors designed to survive and prosper in a competitive global economy, the need was for constant innovation, and the emphasis shifted to the horizontal cluster in which new firms emerged from older firms or from universities. Industrial policy also evolved from building the material infrastructure for a regional economy (the roads, water, and sewers for a new anchor factory) to building the social and economic infrastructure. It became much more important to engage in road-mapping and planning exercises to know which industries were strong candidates for growth given the network of existing related industries, general market and policy trends, and research strengths in the region. In a liberalized global economy in which governments across the world are competing to offer recruitment packages for firms, the positive externalities of colocation in an industrial cluster help a region to attract new firms and retain existing ones. A survey of investors in the clean tech industry found that when considering where to invest, they look for a strong entrepreneurial community, favorable public policy, and a high-quality university and technology base. Once an innovation cluster is established, it can become a self-replicating machine of economic development.[34]

As the review of green energy clusters and supporting policies suggests, the model of the regional innovation system has been extended from the information technology and biotechnology industries to the clean tech industrial sector. The extension of biotechnology expertise into next-generation biofuels research and applications is one example, as is the extension of knowledge about computer chips and materials into photovoltaics, automotive expertise into wind manufacturing, and software design into smart-grid systems. Economic development offices and state and local policy makers have increasingly included clean tech as part of their planning for regional innovation systems. In this way, the idea of a green transition becomes embedded in a targeted industrial policy that selects one or more green energy industries as a priority for regional development.

In effect, state governments have been forced to embrace industrial policy and theories of cluster-oriented development in order to survive in a globalized economy that has emerged because of technological change and trade liberalization. By making the region a world center for one or more clean tech industries, state and local governments can help to nail firms to a place and entice other firms in the footloose global economy to locate in the region. The regional innovation cluster itself becomes a primary tool of recruitment and retention. The policies are anathema to the central thread of neoliberal ideology, which is to let markets replace policy, just as they are not in tune with the redistributive politics of traditional social liberalism. Instead, state and local governments are pursuing a highly interventionist and even selective approach to their economies, which have become a developmentalist's park rather than a neoliberal's wilderness or a social liberal's jungle.

6

Localist Alternatives to the Mainstream Transition

Although the innovation cluster is an important example of a developmentalist approach to the green transition, there is a second approach associated with a different type of green businesses than those in the technology sector and those in the clean tech clusters. Small independently owned businesses in sustainable agriculture, building services, community finance, and green retail often operate with different business models from those of the high-tech businesses of the regional innovation clusters.

The contrast between the two types of business is based on different financing mechanisms and associated business goals. The typical business in a green innovation cluster is a start-up venture that is on its way to becoming publicly traded or being sold to a large corporation, or it is an initiative within an established company that has identified a new market opportunity. In either case, proponents must convince their patrons that the business venture will have a high growth rate that will generate a high return on investment within a short time. Innovators tend to depend on patents that can protect their strategy of bringing a new product to market, and these new business ventures tend to be broadly in the technology sector. In contrast, many small businesses outside the sector of technology start-ups don't rely on venture capital or related forms of funding that are based on the expectation of rapid growth. Instead, the small businesses in retail, agriculture, and services are often funded with loans from family and friends, and they are privately held companies with a limited number of owners. They don't have a plan to grow rapidly with the goal of a liquidity event that rewards their investors with a high annualized rate of return. Instead, they grow much more slowly through the reinvestment of profits. Because of the higher level of autonomy from outside investors, these "independent" companies have a greater ability to pursue goals that may include community benefit, social fairness, and environmental sustainability.

Although the privately held, independent business is the primary vehicle for the alternative model of economic development, other organizational forms include the small nonprofit organization, the public benefit corporation, the cooperative, and the local public enterprise. Together with small independent businesses, this group of organizations plays an important role in the greening of the economy, and it represents a large proportion of overall jobs and job creation. However, the sector is often overlooked in discussions that focus on the bigger businesses and start-up enterprises of the green innovation clusters.

In discussing the alternative pathway in the green economic development field, it is helpful at the outset to dispel possible misinterpretations that sometimes emerge. Some advocates of small green businesses and other organizations argue that a complete transition to green energy would require that most of the economy consist of such organizations. If one includes social fairness and democracy goals in the definition of a complete and successful green energy transition, then there is some point to the argument. However, the argument is more difficult to defend if the idea of the green transition is limited to a technical goal such as shifting to a low-carbon economy. The idea that organizations with slow economic growth are environmentally more benign is problematic because a green energy transition requires rapid growth in some industries and "degrowth" in others. Thus, the high-tech model of venture capital, entrepreneurial start-ups, and the "banana" curve of rapid growth is desirable in some industries, such as solar energy, provided that they are displacing industries such as coal. Because coal has a larger ecological footprint (due to greenhouse gases and mountaintop removal) than solar, the net effect of rapid growth of solar can be a reduction in overall ecological damage.

A second misinterpretation occurs with respect to the association among ecological footprint, localization, and the small businesses of the service, retail, and food sectors. The argument appears primarily with respect to food, namely, that locally produced food has a smaller carbon footprint than nonlocal food because there is less carbon embedded in transportation of local food to markets than for distant food. Although the argument has some merit, there are many intervening variables. Food grown in a greenhouse in the winter that is heated with natural gas and has electricity powered by coal may have a larger carbon footprint than equivalent food grown under the sun in a warm climate and shipped by rail. As the debates over "food miles" indicate, everything depends on the calculation of the carbon footprints of both production and transportation.[1]

The assumptions of the chapter are that the regional innovation cluster and localist approaches to regional economic development are mostly complementary strategies and that the convergence of green energy and green economic development policies requires attention to both types of strategies. Starting with those assumptions, the chapter extends the argument that the green energy transition is becoming increasingly connected with job creation. Here, the strategy of keeping jobs and businesses in place is achieved not through the positive externalities of the regional innovation system but through the loyalties that accompany local ownership and local customers. Likewise, the relationship to the continental and global economy is less through the export of the high-tech goods of the innovation cluster and more through the import substitution of nonlocal goods and services with those produced locally.

This chapter will provide a background on localism with respect to developmentalist ideology and the green transition. After first defining localism and discussing some of the background research and concepts, it will discuss green localism and specific policies associated with it. Finally, it will consider the crucial problems associated with the lack of financing for localism and some of the organizational and policy reforms that have emerged to solve those problems.

Background

The term "localism" refers to a wide range of movements—"buy local," sustainable local foods, and community-oriented media outlets, energy, and finance—that share the goal of supporting locally owned and controlled organizations that make products or provide services mostly for local markets. The scope of "local" is itself locally defined, but for the present purposes it can be thought of from the scale of a metropolitan region to that of small American state such as Vermont. As I have argued in my previous book, localism is not inherently green. For example, in mobilizations of independent retail stores against competition from big-box stores, the bread-and-butter issue of economic survival takes precedence over concerns with regional sustainability. The goals are less green energy transition policies and more an Internet sales tax, local zoning restrictions on franchises and big-box stores, and local procurement policies. Likewise, efforts to build community financial institutions and community media are often more concerned with poverty reduction and neighborhood development than with environmental sustainability. However, some localist pathways for social change also emphasize sustainability.[2]

Within the localist movement in the United States today, there are different national-level organizations that link together diverse pathways for change, and here one can find some convergences with green transition politics. Although the American Independent Business Alliance focuses on the "buy local" theme and on anti-chain-store politics, the Business Alliance for Local Living Economies links together support from and for the locally owned independent business sector with a vision of a global economy based on small enterprises that are committed to social fairness and environmental sustainability. Again, the "Move Your Money" campaign encourages people to shift their savings and checking accounts from corporate banks to community banks and credit unions, whereas the "Slow Money" movement has a greener focus with its emphasis on a shift to investment in local farms and food organizations. Notwithstanding the differences of emphasis, the diverse forms of localism encourage an approach to regional economic development that would allow greater room for local ownership, small businesses, local nonprofit organizations, and even local public and community ownership such as municipal utilities and community-owned renewable-energy generation.

Just as the mainstream of regional developmentalist politics draws on economic theories of regional innovation systems, so localist politics can turn to a body of social science research for reflection and support. The classic study in this field is the work of the anthropologist Walter Goldschmidt, who conducted ethnographic fieldwork that compared two California towns, one dominated by agribusiness and one not. The town dominated by agribusiness had fewer social services, parks, youth facilities, and business establishments, and it had more dilapidated buildings, more concentrated political power, and greater disparities between social classes. Agribusiness attempted to suppress the study and, after it was published, pushed for curtailment of funds for the Bureau of Agricultural Economics, for which Goldschmidt worked when he conducted the study.[3]

A subsequent literature has made similar claims with quantitative documentation. Much of the evidence is reviewed in *Big-Box Swindle*, an encyclopedic work by the localist researcher and advocate Stacy

Mitchell. Quantitative studies by sociologists and economists have documented that a vibrant small-business sector is associated with several desirable metrics that serve as indicators of a higher level of overall development and quality of life (e.g., higher voter turnout, more nonprofit organizations, higher average income, and lower rates of poverty, crime, and infant mortality). A related body of literature has tracked the effects of large chain stores (generally Wal-Marts) on regional economies. The literature suggests that the construction of a new store is associated with lower levels of nonprofit organizations, reduced voter turnout, and diminished average wages for the regional economy.[4]

The localist literature sometimes criticizes mainstream economic-development strategies, especially the strategy of recruitment. Michael Shuman, author of *The Small-Mart Revolution* and research and policy director for the Business Alliance for Local Living Economies, criticized South Carolina's investment of $130 million to attract the German automaker BMW to the state. Advocates of the recruitment package estimated that the factory would create 4,300 direct jobs and 16,600 total jobs. Although the BMW deal did contribute to the growth of about 40 supply-chain firms in the region, it was a vertical cluster that involved dependency on the central manufacturer rather than a horizontal innovation cluster on the model of Silicon Valley. Shuman noted that local businesses have to make up for the subsidies granted to the showcase factories by paying higher taxes, and he asked what might have happened if the $130 million had been invested in small businesses located within the state. He argued that the strategy of recruiting a large factory is riskier than spreading the investment over many small companies.[5]

In retrospect, South Carolina's investment to attract BMW may have been a successful gamble. By 2011 the plant employed 7,000 workers and generated an estimated 23,050 direct and indirect jobs. However, in the long term the success of the state government's investment depends on the extent to which automotive suppliers in the BMW supply chain become the basis of an innovation cluster. For example, they could be integrated into the state's fuel cell and wind turbine clusters and research at Clemson and at other universities. Although in this particular case the roll of the dice may turn out to be a successful gamble, Shuman was making the general argument that in some cases more jobs, and potentially even greater innovation, could emerge if a state government were to take funds used in recruitment of flagship factories and invest them in the small-business sector. The investment could include both local technology start-up firms and established small businesses that promise to create local jobs.[6]

Shuman's concerns also raise a more general and theoretical question about the science and practice of regional economic development. Which type of small business is really crucial to the regional economy? On the one hand, high-tech start-ups will eventually sell products in national and international markets, thereby generating crucial export revenue for a regional economy. Even if they eventually locate some manufacturing overseas, they still retain high-end jobs locally, and they repatriate profits from distant branch operations. On the other hand, growth in the services, retail, and food sectors can provide import-substitution benefits by blocking vital leakages of revenue from the regional economy. In other words, both approaches shift the balance of payments for a regional economy in a positive direction, one through export revenue and the other through import substitution.

Although localist perspectives can lead to a much more diversified approach to economic development than understood by current research on regional innovation systems and the mainstream of current economic development practices, localism also provides a more fundamental challenge to thinking about economic development. The analyses of localists draw on and reinvigorate an alternative pathway in the research field of economic development studies by picking up a thread that has, for the most part, been woven out of the mainstream of developmentalist policies.

In chapter 4, I suggested that green energy policy at the state government level generated import-substitution benefits, mainly by displacing energy from out-of-state sources with that produced from in-state sources. For Michael Shuman the idea of import substitution is generalized to the whole regional economy rather than the clean energy sector. One source of Shuman's thinking is Jane Jacobs, who characterized the growth of American cities as based partly on import substitution. Large cities such as Chicago, Jacobs argued, grew by producing locally goods that were previously imported mostly from the Eastern states. As manufacturing for local markets grew, the companies sometimes innovated on products and then shifted into sales in markets outside the region. Her argument that import substitution and export-led development can be related in a cyclical manner is often missed in discussions that contrast the two approaches. Building on her work, Shuman developed a tool for "local first" organizations to calculate which industrial sectors in their regional economy are potentially the greatest candidates for import substitution.[7]

Other studies in defense of import substitution point to some counterintuitive findings. The economist Joseph Persky and colleagues note that the proportion of a local economy that produces for local consumption, especially local services, has been increasing. Even in an era of globalization, the local proportion of the economy has grown. The paradox is explained by the transition to a service economy in the United States, which is associated with localization. Persky and the sociologist Wim Wiewel also found that producer-oriented service firms, which increasingly have become recognized as contributing to the export base of a regional economy, often have a mixture of external and local revenue. In other words, it is not valid to assume that service firms exist only or mainly to support the regional export firms. Likewise, the geographers Ted Rutland and Sean O'Hagan showed that most of the growth in employment in Canadian cities could be traced to the sector that produces for local consumption, and the public policy scholar Colin Williams found that a vibrant retail sector not only prevents the leakage of consumption outside the region but also contributes to purchases from persons located outside the region.[8]

The idea of import substitution also underlies a type of multiplier study that represents an alternative to the studies used in job calculations for a new business that comes to town. In the mainstream approach, a mayor or a governor celebrates the opening of a new business, often after huge investments and concessions in order to recruit the business to the region. Part of the celebratory speech usually includes a calculation of job growth, in which direct, indirect, and sometimes even induced jobs are presented to voters. In contrast, the "buy local" campaigns led by independent business associations have created a "local multiplier effect," which shows the benefits accrued when consumers shift some of their purchases to locally owned independent businesses. For example, in San Francisco a 10 percent increase in spending at locally owned independent businesses was estimated to create 1,300 new jobs and increase revenue recirculation within the city's economy by $200 million. There are various reasons why locally owned independent businesses serve as "plugs" on leakage of revenue outside the regional economy: they retain the profits locally, they give more to local nonprofit organizations, they generally pay more taxes (because they don't have access to the subsidies and exemptions that are given to large retailers), and they tend to purchase more local goods and services.[9]

In summary, localist critiques of the approach to economic development based on the high-tech, export-oriented manufacturing base provide a complementary set of strategies that considerably widen the potential suite of regional development policies. In effect, localists question the assumptions of green industrial development policy and make possible a much more comprehensive approach. Although the mainstream and localist approaches can be construed to be in conflict, it is possible to combine an export-oriented regional innovation strategy with an import-substitution strategy into a more comprehensive and effective economic development portfolio. New synergies might emerge, too, when the retail, services, and food industries are brought into closer contact with the regional innovation networks.

Why, then, do more states and city governments not invest their economic development resources in their small-business sector of the service, food, finance, and retail industries? Although those industries provide jobs and do grow, they don't grow as rapidly as the high-tech start-ups of the innovation clusters. Furthermore, for mayors and governors the recruitment of a new factory to a region is an opportunity to show voters that the rainmaker is delivering jobs. It becomes a dramatic event that contributes to a politician's political capital. It would be possible to organize a similar event for a hundred new microbusinesses in the region, but such events tend not to grab headlines in the same way.

Localist Approaches to the Green Energy Transition

Although some advocates of green jobs would be happy to see new jobs in the small-business sector, the strong participation of labor unions in the definition of green jobs policies has generally led to a focus on green jobs among large companies, which are more likely candidates for the expansion of union membership than the small independent businesses. Likewise, many of the largest environmental organizations have partnerships with large industrial corporations and unions. Thus, green transition coalitions tend to assume that the green economy transition will occur through large corporations or through start-up businesses that will eventually be acquired by large corporations or grow into them. The main area of interest in small businesses is in retrofitting and installation services. It is hard to imagine a successful green energy transition without the involvement of large corporations, but it would also make sense to think more deeply about the role of the small-business sector, which employs half of all private-sector workers.

The concept of a "local living economy" provides a complementary perspective on what constitutes a good green job. The Business Alliance for Local Living Economies explains the concept as follows:

When enterprises are locally rooted, human-scale, owned by stakeholders, and held accountable to the rule of law by democratically elected governments, there is a natural incentive for all concerned to take human and community needs and interests into account. When income and ownership are equitably distributed, justice is served and political democracy is strong. When needs are met locally by locally owned enterprises, people have greater control over their lives, money is recycled in the community rather than leaking off into the global financial casino, jobs are more secure, economies are more stable, and there are the means and the incentives to protect the environment and to build the relationships of mutual trust and responsibility that are the foundation of community. (2009).

The vision is not one of separatism from the global economy that could be found in the post-1960s "back to the land" movement. Rather, it is closer to that of the fair-trade movement, that is, a vision of a global economy based less on large multinational corporations and more on networks of small, community-based, socially responsible businesses and nonprofit organizations. Although utopian in spirit, the movement is rooted in a large political constituency, the small-business sector and community enterprises. The constituency may be difficult to mobilize fully, but it has been quite significant politically during some periods of American history. For example, during the Progressive era of the early twentieth century, there were powerful political coalitions of trade unions, farmers, and urban small businesses.

In the mainstream of green transition coalitions, the emphasis of investing in green companies or even socially and environmentally responsible companies doesn't include screens for positive effects on the small-business sector. An investment screen might favor a retail company due to its relatively strong performance on environmental and labor issues, but the company may grow by putting independents out of business. Without naming names, it is easy to find retailers and food chains that have a strong reputation for social and environmental responsibility but have a predatory policy with respect to the small-business sector of independents. Thus, an investor who selects a "socially responsible" mutual fund may also be helping to erode the small-business sector further. Likewise, a state or a federal government policy may encourage more manufacturing of wind turbines in the state or in the country, but it doesn't take into account whether the company is locally owned, whether it is a domestic company, or whether it is a foreign multinational company. At one conference that I attended, a member of the audience asked a pointed question to the leader of an industry advocacy group about the role of foreign multinational companies in green manufacturing in the United States; the leader replied bluntly that the association tracked job growth, not ownership. In the mainstream calculus of jobs, what matters is producing good domestic jobs, not who owns the business.

The "local living economy" approach to the green energy transition seeks to shift ownership of green energy to independent businesses, state and local governments, homeowners, local nonprofit organizations and cooperatives, and other organizations outside the realm of multinational corporations. As a result, the favored form of green energy is distributed renewable energy, which favors but doesn't require local ownership. A general green energy policy that encourages the construction of rooftop solar may be relatively blind to the question of whether that solar is owned by a large company (as occurs in power-purchase agreements) or whether ownership is by city governments, independent businesses, homeowners, cooperatives, and nonprofit organizations. However, when incentives focus on homeowners or when the panels are placed on public buildings, they directly increase local ownership.

Decentralized renewable energy offers several benefits to a regional economy. A study commissioned by the San Diego County Apollo Alliance concluded that local, decentralized generation resulted in 10 times as many direct jobs as purchasing electricity from a power plant located outside the county. Furthermore, the local production of distributed solar energy creates a steady future price for electricity and captures revenues flowing out of the county in the form of electricity expenditures and future rate hikes. Here is an example of the import-substitution argument for distributed solar energy production:

The Power Link Option [nonlocal generation] will deliver imported electricity. Regardless of whether this electricity is produced renewably or with nonrenewable funds, it will continue the current *negative-electricity-purchase-cash-flow* out of the county's economy. (Bell and Honea 2007: 3)

Similar conclusions have emerged for studies of wind energy, where local ownership provides long-term economic benefits. For example, a review produced by the National Renewable Energy Laboratory compared economic impacts of community wind projects with mainstream ownership in terms of job-years:

Comparing the average of completed community wind projects studied here with the retrospective analysis of the first 1,000 MW of wind in Colorado and Iowa indicates that construction-period impacts are as much as 3.1 times higher for community wind, and operations-period impacts are as much as 1.8 times higher. (Lantz and Tegan 2009: iii)

Economic benefits derive from increased local labor, local business sourcing, profit retention, and use of local banks and credit unions. In addition, community participation and ownership increases local acceptance of wind turbines, which can be difficult to site, and distributed renewable energy provides environmental and other benefits because new transmission wires may not be needed. The distributed systems also tend to use existing rooftops and yards rather than green fields, which can provoke opposition from local residents and environmental conservation organizations.[10]

Many of the arguments for distributed renewable energy also apply to energy-efficiency improvements. At the scale of a metropolitan area, expenditures on heating and electricity for buildings generally take the form of two types of imports. Electricity is produced in power plants located outside a metropolitan area, and the source of the energy for both heating and electricity (coal, nuclear, and natural gas) is located outside the metropolitan area. By reducing expenditures on heating and electricity, the regional economy plugs not only the leaks of air flow in and out of a building but also the "leaks" of revenue flows that are going outside the local economy.

If there are so many the benefits, why have more communities not rushed to transfer more of their energy production to local distributed energy and energy efficiency? John Farrell and David Morris of the Institute for Local Self-Reliance suggest one factor: endowments of renewable-energy resources are not evenly distributed across states and regions in the United States. As a result, local production is not always the cheapest form of production. Even among the strongest supporters of localism, it makes sense to have some specialization and trade. However, Farrell and Morris add that many states could significantly increase their local production of renewable-energy resources and avoid costly and contentious investments in new transmission lines. They suggest that cost differences in production are frequently less than transportation differences:

A typical North Dakota commercial wind turbine could produce electricity at a cost close to thirty percent less than an Ohio one. But in most cases, these significant variations result in modest variations in the cost of energy to the ultimate consumer because of the cost of transporting the energy.

For example, if Ohio's electricity came from North Dakota wind farms—1,000 miles away—the cost of constructing new transmission lines to carry that power and the electricity losses during transmission would surpass the lower cost of production, resulting in an electricity cost fifteen percent higher than local generation with minimal transmission upgrades. (Farrell and Morris 2008: 2)

Although cost differences can explain some of reluctance to adopt local distributed renewable energy, there are also regulatory and financial hurdles. Net metering laws are required for building owners to gain access to the grid for their excess energy, and technical standards for installers are needed to ensure that the quality of the work is satisfactory. Some states have routinely received low grades on a report card on net metering issued by the Network for New Energy Choices. In addition to the need for strong regulatory support and standards, the financing of locally owned distributed renewable energy is limited, and often the limited funds are not spent in the most cost-effective manner. For example, rebates, low-cost home energy audits, and tax credits encourage building owners to install distributed renewable-energy systems, but the programs have been plagued by the challenge of getting building owners to "convert" their knowledge of what needs to be done into the action of implementation. Research on conversion has led to a second generation of innovative programs designed to make it easier for building owners to follow through on the intent to green a building.[11]

Community-Based Green Energy Policies

Various legal arrangements facilitate local, community-based ownership of energy production, including green energy. The oldest form of community-based energy is municipal ownership. Austin, Sacramento, Seattle, and some other cities have publicly owned electricity generation and distribution systems and also have strong renewable-energy and energy-efficiency policies. However, efforts to municipalize energy generation meet with stiff opposition from electricity utilities, which label such projects socialistic, and even successful efforts require high levels of investment from city governments. As a result, interest has grown in the alternative of community-choice legislation.

Community choice allows the local government to aggregate all customers, usually with an opt-out clause, and bid the aggregation of customers to electricity producers. State-level legislation allows communities to determine the energy mix and to negotiate a price, but without undergoing the many hurdles associated with municipalization. The energy mix can include a higher level of renewable energy. Pioneered in Massachusetts shortly after electricity restructuring went into effect, community-choice programs have been implemented in several regions, among which the best known are the Cape Light Compact (a consortium of towns on Cape Cod), the Northeast Ohio Public Energy Council, and Marin County in California. Although community-choice legislation offers tremendous benefits to customers, investor-owned utilities have resisted the changes, and sometimes vociferously so, much as they have done for proposed municipalization programs. For example, in California the investor-owned utility attempted to weaken the legislation by requiring a two-thirds referendum for cities that wish to enact community-choice programs.[12]

There are other policies that facilitate community ownership of renewable-energy generation. Minnesota has been an exemplar on this front, especially after a settlement in 1994 that allowed Xcel, the state's largest private utility, to store nuclear waste at its Prairie Island facility in exchange for mandates for wind energy generation. The state's mandates increased, and after 2004 they began to include a set-aside for small wind production. In 2005 Governor Tim Pawlenty signed into law Community-Based Energy Development legislation, and he announced the goal of 800 megawatts of community wind by 2010. Although the development of the local wind energy occurred more slowly than he had envisioned (partly due to the effects of the recession on government spending), the innovative policies have become models for other states. In addition to the state's set-aside for community wind, there is a standard purchase agreement, a standard small wind tariff, and a renewable-energy fund paid by the utility that includes some community wind investments. The state government also offers a production credit for wind producers at a small scale, a streamlined permitting process for qualified projects, and tax exemptions on turbine sales. Minnesota has also pioneered the "flip" financing model, in which a corporate partner provides up-front financing and ownership for the first ten years, then the ownership is gradually transferred to the community or other local investors.[13]

Similar legislation has also facilitated the growth of community solar projects. For example, in 2010 the Colorado state legislature passed solar garden legislation (HB 1342), which provides incentives to groups of ten or more subscribers who live nearby and jointly own solar photovoltaic installations of 2 megawatts or less. Although the subscribers can be owners, the owner can also be a company. In the state of Washington, the Community Solar Enabling Act allows similar installations (75 kilowatts or less). Ownership can be by utilities for a green pricing program or by businesses, individuals, or nonprofit organizations located in the same area as the installation. There are also incentives that reward the use of materials from in-state companies. In addition to the laws in Colorado and Washington, six other states have community net metering laws, which allow customers in the same utility area to sell power from a jointly owned solar array back to the utility.[14]

Together, public power, community choice, and community wind and solar laws facilitate local and in some cases public ownership of renewable-energy generation. The laws configure green jobs inside patterns of ownership that include local governments, nonprofit organizations, cooperatives, and community networks.

PACE Financing Laws and Related Policies

A related group of laws focuses less on enabling community and joint ownership and more on enabling residences and small businesses to own some of their energy production. When faced with a decision to take advantage of government incentives to install rooftop solar or energy-efficiency improvements, both homeowners and small business owners face several hurdles. One main problem is that the investment takes several years to pay off (longer for renewable energy and shorter for energy efficiency), and consequently the investment may be lost if the owner has to sell the home or business. A second shortcoming is that incentives often involve rebates, but they don't provide a way of financing an investment that could cost tens of thousands of dollars. Finally, there is the challenge of locating and supervising reputable contractors, and, like many home-repair projects, the task of greening a building tends to get postponed.

PACE (Property Assessed Clean Energy) bonds were a remarkable policy innovation that solved the problems of long-term liquidity and access of homeowners and small businesses to affordable loans. The basic innovation of PACE financing was that the local government provided the up-front funding for the improvement, and the payment became part of the property tax of the building, so that it could be passed on to new owners. Furthermore, because the financing of the pool of capital for PACE loans could be through local government bond issues, there was no need to increase system benefits charges for all ratepayers. As payments came back into the fund, more capital was available for future loans. Unlike government grants and tax credits, which dry up after the initial funding ends, PACE bonds provided a long-term source of government support for the greening of buildings.

The first PACE program was Berkeley's Financing Initiative for Renewable and Solar Technology (FIRST), launched in 2008 to support solar panel installations. Other California counties and cities soon followed. The Energy Independence Program of Palm Desert, financed from the city's general fund and its Redevelopment Agency, supported both solar energy and energy-efficiency improvements. Sonoma County also offered a relatively large PACE program that was financed from the general fund and a county revenue bond. In eighteen months, it funded $45 million in solar installations and energy-efficiency improvements. Loans were capped at 10 percent of property value. The ClimateSmart Program of the Colorado city of Boulder combined the support services of an auditor, who analyzes the building, and an energy concierge, who guides the owner on the decision-making process for a retrofit.[15]

One of the challenges faced by the California and Colorado programs was that interest rates were relatively high, some as high as 7 percent. The Berkeley program reached its limit of 40 subscribers within minutes of the program's launch, but because of the high interest rates only thirteen participants continued. In 2010 the program was closed down and folded into California FIRST. By aggregating programs and using other funding sources, the overhead and capital costs were reduced. The state government was planning to use funding from the ARRA, and in 2010 the governor signed legislation that approved use of the state's pension plan funds for PACE programs.[16]

Although PACE funding represented only a small percentage of the estimated $3.6 billion that utilities spent on energy-efficiency programs each year, the programs were growing at a very rapid rate. By 2010, PACE financing was approved in 22 states, and the US Department of Energy awarded hundreds of millions of dollars of ARRA funds to PACE programs as part of its Retrofit Ramp-Up Program. More than 100 cities and a dozen counties were preparing to participate in the California FIRST program. However, in May of 2010 the Federal Housing Finance Agency, which supervises Fannie Mae and Freddie Mac, objected because of the first-lien status of PACE loans. By July the agency had ended the national effort to implement residential PACE programs. Given the very challenging load of subprime mortgages that that the agency was supervising, it didn't want to enhance the losses that were already occurring from defaults.[17]

Although bipartisan federal legislation in support of PACE was rapidly introduced in both houses of Congress, it didn't win the needed votes during the following year. It is commonly assumed that PACE programs died with the Federal Housing Finance Agency decision in July 2010, but the decision didn't apply to commercial buildings. Some holders of commercial mortgages allow PACE financing, and in fact some banks see PACE financing as a financial opportunity for new, creditworthy loans. According to Pike Research, PACE financing for commercial buildings could grow rapidly to $2.5 billion annually, remove 8 million metric tons of carbon dioxide, and (no report in the era of developmentalist politics is complete without this figure) create 50,000 new jobs. By 2011, cities in California and Florida were launching the second wave of commercial PACE financing programs.[18]

There are at least three basic alternatives to PACE that retain some of the benefits. First, it is possible to use property-assessed financing but with a "junior lien" status on the mortgage. The state of Maine structured its PACE programs so that they involve a junior lien. The Efficiency Main program received $20 million in ARRA support for a revolving loan fund, and the initial interest rate was set at 5 to 7 percent. Loans covered a wide range of energy-efficiency improvements but not solar energy. A second approach is the federal government's PowerSaver Program, which the Department of Housing and Urban Development announced in 2010. The program provides a backstop for private-sector loans of up to $25,000 for solar and energy-efficiency improvements to homes. The loans have junior-lien status and were funded for single-family homes and multi-family buildings. The third approach uses on-bill financing (programs that allow borrowers to pay back a loan as a line on the utility bill) and was developed in parallel with PACE financing. The programs exist in several states, and they represent perhaps the most promising alternative to residential PACE programs, but they often require considerable negotiation with utility companies. There are two ways that the loans can be set up. If they are attached to the building owner, the owner must pay the remaining principle when the property is sold, and as a result the liquidity benefits of PACE financing are lost. If the loans are attached to the meter, then the payment shifts to the next ratepayer, and the liquidity benefits of PACE financing are retained. The programs have supported retrofitting more than rooftop solar, but they could be expanded to support distributed renewable energy.[19]

Finding Financing for Local Green Businesses

A complete approach to the funding of locally owned green energy would also include support for the incubation and growth of green small businesses. There are some general government programs to assist small businesses, but the regulatory system is structured to limit the options for small investors who wish to invest in small businesses. One set of options, microfinance and community loan funds, accept quasi-charitable donations with zero or low interest rates. Likewise, community investment options from the larger mutual fund companies, such as the Calvert Foundation Community Investment Note, provide a low rate of interest. Some community banks and credit unions also offer financial products that include investments in or donations to local environmental groups. However, interest rates are all relatively low in this set of financial instruments.[20]

Somewhat higher rates of return with correspondingly higher levels of risk can be obtained for debt investment in small businesses through Internet-based lending sites. Although in 2008 the Securities and Exchange Commission issued a cease-and-desist letter to the leading company, Prosper.com, by July of 2009 the company had successfully completed registration and was back in business. Partly in response to the perceived need to develop a better regulatory environment for new financial models, the peer-to-peer organizations formed a trade group, the Coalition for New Financial Models, in 2009. Within the peer-to-peer system, it is possible to support small businesses that meet social and environmental responsibility criteria. This approach is still a loan rather than an equity investment, but it allows investors to assume more risk and gain higher rates of return than those found in community loan funds and similar vehicles.[21]

Although the existing options for small investors are laudable, they are basically debt investments with low rates of return. Whether one goes through a loan fund, through the Calvert Foundation, through a credit union, through a community bank, or through a peer-to-peer site, non-accredited investors generally cannot make equity investments in the green small-business sector. The legal structure of investment has made it difficult to develop similar options for equity investments for non-accredited investors who might be willing to accept higher risk for the prospect of higher returns. Although there are some plans to develop the equity side of green community capital, such as regional stock markets, to date the mechanisms that could rebalance investment in locally owned independent businesses remain very restricted.

Because the retirement industry is structured to send individual investments into the stocks and bonds of publicly traded corporations, there is a gap between the need for investment in the small-business sector and the trillions of dollars of retirement savings, not to mention other invest-ments held by non-accredited investors. For persons who wish to invest in small businesses with a social and environmental responsibility mission, the options are very limited. Michael Shuman writes:

Locally owned small businesses constitute about one-half of the private economy in terms of output and jobs, but they receive almost no investment from the nation's pension funds or from mutual, hedge, venture, or any other kind of investment funds. In a well-functioning financial system, roughly one-half of the investment should go to roughly one-half of the economy. Today, every American, even the stalwart advocate of community development, is overinvesting in the Fortune 500 companies and underinvesting in local businesses key to local vital-ity. This is a colossal market failure. (2009: 81)

Shuman argues that regulations of the Securities and Exchange Commis-sion prevent small investors from investing even modest sums in small, privately held, locally owned businesses. The burdens for securing such investments are so high (he estimates them to be $50,000 to $100,000 for a private offering of stock) that the mechanism of equity investment is out of reach for most small businesses.

Shuman proposes a reform of Securities and Exchange Commission regulations to allow equity investment in small privately held companies. He argues that risk can be controlled if three conditions are met: no single investor can own more than $100 in any one company, all inves-tors must reside within the same state in which the company is located and shares are sold, and the size of the company's total stock valuation must be less than $250,000. In 2010 the Sustainable Economies Law Center sent a petition with a similar proposal to the Securities and Exchange Commission, but the government agency ignored the request and the letters of support that it received. However, during the next year the House of Representatives approved legislation (HR 2930) in support of the proposal on a bipartisan vote of 407 in favor and seventeen opposed. The law would allow small businesses to raise up to $1 million in capital and allow individuals to purchase up to 10 percent of their income in shares, and there were provisions for disclosure standards. The Securities and Exchange Commission opposed the law because of concern with securities fraud, and the companion bill in the Senate faced opposi-tion. Shuman supported the legislation in an editorial titled "Don't Occupy Wall Street, Ditch It!"[22]

One can envision many other financial products for investing in local green businesses. As I discussed in *Localist Movements in a Global Economy*, an option to have a tax-free early withdrawal from retirement funds for investment in distributed renewable energy or energy efficiency for a residence or small business could unleash billions of dollars of investment that would create green jobs primarily in the locally owned contracting sector. It would also offer people a different, "localist" option for investment: rather than investing in the future growth of the stock market, they could invest in the future savings of household expenditures.[23]

Conclusions

By studying localism and green business development, the generally unstated assumptions of mainstream approaches become clearer. The alternative pathways associated with localism have a subordinate position in most regional economic development policy fields and in the regulatory field for private-sector investment, but they need not be marginalized. Instead, localists suggest the need for a much broader view of economic development and its potential connections with the green energy transition than the focus described in the previous chapters on demand policies and regional innovation systems. Demand policies tend to restrict the scope of import-substitution benefits to intrastate energy generation, and innovation policies assume that economic development rests on the technology sector and manufacturing under a model of export-oriented production, rapid growth fueled by venture capital, and a liquidity event of an initial public offering or sale to a large corporation. Localist perspectives draw attention to the other sectors of the economy and serve as a valuable reminder that the politics of the green energy transition can provide opportunities to strengthen the small-business sector, community ownership of energy generation and transportation, and investment opportunities for the small-business sector. Localist perspectives also help to expand the understanding of "import substitution" as a counterbalancing strategy of economic development. By putting together demand policies, green industrial clusters, and localist models of economic development strategies for the green energy transition, it is possible to design policies that are much more comprehensive. Together, the approaches can create more jobs and resilience for regional economies.

Although green small businesses can play a significant role in green transition coalitions, there are also some potential differences with the view of unions about what a "good" green job is (locally owned business versus unionized) and what "fair trade" is. When unions advocate "fair trade" instead of "free trade," they generally are thinking about a global economy in which imported manufactured goods are limited to countries that have labor and environmental protections that are comparable to or better than those of the United States. In contrast, "fair trade" in the context of localism refers to consumption in the global economy from community-oriented small enterprises such as agricultural and textile cooperatives. Unions historically are divided between trade unions, which can function as small businesses and which formed coalitions with the small-business sector during the Progressive Era, and industrial unions, which are associated with factory production and share interests with the corporate sector. Likewise, while working as the co-founder of a "local first" organization I encountered some hostility to unions among the larger independent businesses (which feared unionization), whereas the owners of the mom-and-pop shops often had family or life-history connections with organized labor.

Notwithstanding the differences, there are possibilities for a common ground between how labor and localists understand a good job. Just as unions would like to see trade restrictions on goods that are made "unfairly" in factories with unorganized labor and poor environmental practices, so localist perspectives on global trade could imply a tariff or subsidy structure that favors goods imported from socially responsible, community-oriented small businesses. Likewise, just as unions favor reforms in domestic policies that would strengthen the ability of workers to organize, so localists support policies that favor investment flows that would strengthen the resources for starting locally owned independent businesses and allowing them to become successful. Both perspectives suggest alternatives to the reigning frameworks of corporate-led global-ization and neoliberal ideology. Some union leaders would like to reduce or greatly reverse trade liberalization and institute trade protection for domestic manufacturers, and some localists would like to shift more production back to locally owned independent enterprises, especially for food and energy. To the extent that unions and localists support the benefits of trade, it is on terms described as "fair": equivalent labor and environmental standards, and a leveling of the playing field to create opportunities for small businesses and cooperatives.

Thus, unions and localists represent an approach to trade liberaliza-tion that would restrict it in significant ways based on fairness issues, just as green venture capitalists and clean tech firms tend to see trade liberalization through the lens of opportunity but tempered by the need for the US government to provide equivalent subsidies and support to that of other countries. The protectionist and competitiveness strands coexist uneasily, but they can be brought together in favor of policies that support domestic businesses through fair trade, subsidies, and demand support. The elements of this uneasy green transition coalition are more likely to come together in demand-side policies such as support for distributed renewable energy and building weatherization than in supply-side policies, where the fault lines become more visible. Notwithstanding the differences, the common network of developmentalist ideas and policies suggests a departure from fundamentalist neoliberalism.

III

Processes and Explanations

7

Green Transition Coalitions and Geographical Unevenness

In the United States, some green energy policies are in the social liberal tradition of redistributive assistance to low-income populations, and others are more in the neoliberal tradition of creating new markets, but on the whole the policies cut across social liberal and neoliberal ideologies by focusing on domestic and regional industrial development in order to generate jobs. For a while, the framing of environmental policy as "green jobs" also appeared to cut across partisan divisions and make possible a broad base of support from the private sector and civil society. However, the backlash in 2010 indicated that the "environment versus jobs" frame was receiving new life. Although some of the opponents of green jobs voiced skepticism on the science of climate change, their skepticism had no traction among scientists and among scientifically minded voters and business leaders, even if they were otherwise conservative. Instead, conservatives shifted attention to the recession that began with the financial crisis of 2008, and they rewrote the national narrative of greedy banks and corporations (a narrative that is friendly to government intervention in the economy) as a story of government overspending. In this context, government investments in green energy and green jobs became an expensive luxury that governments could ill afford, much like social welfare programs. Furthermore, some of the failures of the green jobs programs, notably the Solyndra bankruptcy, served as an occasion for conservatives to remind voters of the neoliberal message that markets, not governments, should make investment decisions. If the "green jobs" frame had successfully neutralized the old conservative frame of "environment versus jobs," the new conservative frame of imprudent expenditures and unwise interference with markets would neutralize the "green jobs" frame.

Notwithstanding the backlash, a wide range of organizations and constituencies continue to support the long-term green transition in the economy. Although the green transition coalitions were not able to tip the balance of power at the federal level after the 111th Congress, they have played a more successful role in policy reforms in some state and city governments. This chapter will shift the focus of attention from the argument that developmentalist ideology has played an important role in green transition policies to the follow-up question of the role of green transition coalitions in explaining the unevenness of the policies and of the success of developmentalist politics. Beginning with a review of some of the cases that show that green jobs coalitions have achieved electoral and legislative successes, the chapter will then present a quantitative analysis that will explore the possible factors that affect success for green transition coalitions in policy fields.

Green Jobs Coalitions and Policy Change

It is not easy to demonstrate that green transition coalitions have had an effect on policy outcomes. In many cases the final signing ceremonies for new legislation provide an occasion to showcase partnerships between governors and legislators or between mayors and city councils. Green transition coalition leaders who served as catalysts for the policy changes may drop into the background, and the story of how the legislation came into being may be limited to government actors. However, through our interviews, surveys of reports, and attendance at conference events, it was possible to identify several cases in which there was a clear line of influence between the coalitions and political outcomes. The cases described below for policy fields in some of the states and cities don't represent an exhaustive set of examples of political influence, but they represent most of the better known examples where there was a clear legislative or policy victory.

California: AB 32
California is in many ways the greenest of the American states, and support for green industries and green technology has long been a part of the state's economic development policies. One of the most significant laws to be developed in the state was the Global Warming Solutions Act of 2006 (AB 32), which established a timetable for bringing greenhouse gas emissions to 1990 levels by 2020 (a reduction of 25 percent) and to a level in 2050 that would be 80 percent below 1990 levels. The legislation charged the California Air Resources Board with preparing plans for implementation, and the scoping plan released in 2010 included a

cap-and-trade system for electricity generation and large industrial facilities. With the implementation of the California policy, the two most
populous regions of the United States—California (37 million) and the
Northeastern states (48 million)—would both have cap-and-trade
regimes. Other regions were in the planning stages and appeared likely
to follow the lead of California and the Northeast until the mid-term
elections of 2010.

However, in 2010 AB 32 faced the challenge of Proposition 23, a
ballot initiative that would have suspended the law until the state's
unemployment rate was below 5.5 percent for at least a one-year period.
The central claim behind the California Jobs Initiative was that AB 32
would lead to higher energy costs that would result in job loss. The regulations would place a burden on businesses, which they could ill afford
during a period of economic weakness. Cleverly, the proposition was not
set up as a direct repeal of AB 32, but the high rate of unemployment in
the state would have triggered an indefinite delay in the process initiated
by the legislation for the foreseeable future.

In response, the California Air Resources Board released a study that
indicated that the AB 32 legislation would create jobs rather than cause
job loss. The battle over calculations of job loss or gain suggests again
how important jobs were to the legitimization of environmental reform
policies. Governor Arnold Schwarzenegger, a Republican who supported
clean tech policies, blasted the ballot initiative as the work of "greedy"
Texas oil companies. A broad political coalition that included business,
labor, environmentalist, public health, city government, ethnic, and many
other organizations formed under the banner of "stop dirty energy."
Leading organizations included the Natural Resources Defense Council,
the Union of Concerned Scientists, the BlueGreen Alliance, the Silicon
Valley Leadership Group, and the Ella Baker Center. Their spokesperson
was Steve Maviglio, the former press secretary for Governor Gray Davis
and deputy chief of staff for two of the assembly's former speakers. The
coalition raised $35 million, with about $10 million from Silicon Valley
(including venture capitalists), and it outspent the proponents of Proposition 21 by a margin of 3 to 1. The proposition failed (that is, voters
supported AB 32) by a margin of 62 percent to 38 percent.[1]

Careful polling allowed the coalition to develop a simple and disci-
plined message that framed the issue as one involving health, jobs, and
out-of-state influence, but specific messages were tailored to different constituencies. Initially, support from the labor movement was soft, because
the unions included oil and gas workers. However, the overarching goal

of the unions was a victory for gubernatorial candidate Jerry Brown, and when they learned that supporters of the coalition also voted overwhelmingly for Brown, they decided to support the "No on 26" coalition. Likewise, polling found that Latinos, Asians, and Pacific Islanders voters were opposed to Proposition 26, and their opposition increased after messaging. Here, themes of environmental justice, clean air, and job preservation were more prominent in the struggle against the "dirty energy" proposition. For workers and owners of the clean energy industries and Silicon Valley investors, there was a clear threat both to current jobs and to the stable regulatory climate needed for future investment and planning decisions. As a result, the Silicon Valley Leadership Group, which represented 335 high tech companies (including clean tech companies), opposed the ballot measure.[2]

Although the opponents of Proposition 23 used a variety of frames to support their efforts, of greatest interest for this book is the way in which the proposition was framed as an assault on California's health (via air quality) and jobs from out-of-state oil companies. In effect, the mobilization protected the state's industries and legislative process from external interference: the state's climate change legislation became a platform for protecting local jobs, air quality, and industries. Rather than sanction the flow of California dollars to out-of-state fossil fuel producers, voters opted to continue the path toward greater intrastate renewable energy and energy conservation.

Although the defeat of Proposition 23 showed the significant power that a green transition coalition could muster even against a well-funded assault, in the same election cycle voters opted to support Proposition 26, which broadened the definition of taxes to include what were currently defined as fees and services. The result was that a two-thirds vote of state and local legislatures rather than a majority vote was required for new "taxes." There was some potential for the supermajority requirement to undermine the greenhouse gas trading regime sanctioned by AB 32 and other green energy policies, most significantly system benefits charges.

California: City-Level Policies
Under Mayor Antonio Villaraigosa, Los Angeles developed a range of green transition policies that included manufacturing, transportation, and buildings, and green transition coalitions played a supporting role in several of the initiatives. The policy that most directly shows influence from the coalitions was the Green Retrofit Workforce Initiative. The Los Angeles Apollo Alliance launched the initiative in 2006, and in 2009 the

city council unanimously adopted the resolution in its support. The goal was to retrofit all city-owned buildings that met size and age guidelines to bring them to the level of LEED Silver certification. The program also required that the city hire local residents and provide them with training, and it set a goal of retrofitting 50 percent of city buildings in low-income areas of the city. In 2010 the mayor appointed Teresa Sanchez, a founding member of the Los Angeles Apollo Alliance, to implement the Green Retrofit and Workforce Development Program, which entered the pilot phase in 2011. The city government also set up an advisory council that included labor, environmental, and community organizations to provide additional recommendations. The program was initially funded with $16 million in ARRA grants.[3]

In Oakland there was no comparable landmark legislation, but there is evidence for the influence of green transition coalitions in city politics. Under Mayor Ron Dellums, Oakland developed various green jobs initiatives, and Mayor Jean Quan continued to support the initiatives. The Oakland-based Ella Baker Center for Human Rights convened a coalition of community organizations that helped to shape the city's Energy and Climate Action Plan, a ten-year plan with more than 150 action items. Part of the plan included workforce development through retrofits, solar installation, and bikeways. The Ella Baker Center also worked with the city to develop the Oakland Green Jobs Corps.[4]

In San Francisco and San Diego, the city governments developed leading programs for solar installations, but we found only limited evidence that grassroots organizations (in both cases environmental justice groups) played a major role in support of green jobs initiatives. In San Francisco, Literacy for Environmental Justice worked to close the Hunter's Point power plant and create restoration jobs in the Heron's Head Project. In San Diego, the Environmental Health Coalition worked with the city council to develop retrofit programs.[5]

In summary, at the city government level there is some evidence that green transition coalitions played a role in catalyzing and developing policy reforms. In general, the city governments were receptive to the ideas and incorporated them as part of broader green initiatives. The primary area of grassroots involvement has been programs that create jobs based on retrofitting and weatherization.

Colorado

Colorado has a reputation as a green state, but it also has large coal mining and natural gas industries. Starting in 2001 a coalition of organizations led by Environment Colorado attempted to convince the state legislature to pass a renewable-energy standard, but after several failures the coalition took the issue directly to voters in the Amendment 37 referendum process. In contrast with Proposition 23 in California, environmentalists used the ballot initiative system to develop green energy legislation. The state's investor-owned utility, Xcel, opposed the measure, but voters approved it. In 2006 the coalition launched the Energy Future Campaign to double the renewable portfolio standard to 20 percent by 2020, and by that point Xcel had shifted its position to support the measure. Because Xcel was also a union employer, the shift facilitated cooperation with unions, which played a role in the legislative reform. After passage of the Renewable Energy Act of 2007 (the year Governor Bill Ritter, a Democrat, took office), Colorado's clean energy economy took off, and labor saw explosive growth in contracting jobs. Subsequently the state government approved a wide range of energy-related laws.[6]

In 2009 the environmental community worked with Governor Ritter to develop a new initiative in preparation for the 2010 election. Ritter had supported many pro-labor laws, but on some crucial issues he had withdrawn support, and the blue-green coalition suggested that a new legislative package could improve his relations with labor. One of the issues of importance to unions was ensuring quality control through technical standards and certification. Although the environmentalists and labor differed on some issues (such as the extension of the renewable electricity standard to small electricity cooperatives), they worked together with the governor and legislature to advocate passage of one of the country's highest renewable electricity standards. In 2010 Governor Ritter signed HB 1001, which gave the state a renewable electricity standard of 30 percent by 2020. Although Ritter decided not to run for re-election, his successor, John Hickenlooper, had a strong record on environmental issues as the former mayor of Denver.[7]

Massachusetts

Massachusetts is another leader in green energy and green industrial development policies. In 2008 Massachusetts passed the Global Warming Solutions Act, which required a reduction in carbon emissions to 10 to 25 percent below 1990 levels by 2020 and 80 percent below 1990 levels by 2050. The legislature also approved the Green Communities Act, which required utilities to acquire all cost-effective energy efficiency and energy reduction measures. The law authorized the creation of the Energy Efficiency Advisory Council to guide spending priorities for funds from the Massachusetts system benefits fund, Regional Greenhouse Gas Initiative revenues, and other revenue sources.

In 2004 the Greater Boston Labor Council and community organizations formed Community Labor United, a nonprofit organization designed to address the needs of low-income and moderate-income families in the greater Boston area. In December 2008, Community Labor United formed the Green Justice Coalition, which included environmentalist and faith-based organizations as well. The goal was to seek changes in the policy guidance of the Massachusetts Energy Efficiency Advisory Council. The coalition organized members to sit in on the long meetings of the Energy Efficiency Advisory Council to demand that fairness components be introduced into the state's energy efficiency plans. Community Labor United also surveyed neighborhoods to show that the funds from the state's system benefits charges had not been spent equitably. In November of 2009 the council responded by including environmental justice concerns in its $1.4 billion energy efficiency plan, which was estimated to generate 23,300 jobs. The "high road" changes included door-to-door outreach campaigns in low-income and moderate-income neighborhoods for weatherization, up-front financing, assurances that contractors pay living wages (at least $18 per hour) and include benefits ($4 per hour) and training opportunities, and priorities for jobs to residents in the neighborhoods where the improvements are taking place.[8]

Minnesota

The BlueGreen Alliance has its national headquarters in Minneapolis and has been particularly active in the state. In 2006 the organization asked Minneapolis Mayor Raymond (R.T.) Rybak and St. Paul Mayor Christopher Coleman to host a meeting with Carl Pope, president of the Sierra Club, and Leo Gerard, president of the United Steelworkers, to explore the potential of green jobs for the Twin Cities region. The issue of job creation had become particularly salient because of the threatened loss of a Ford manufacturing plant and a paper mill that processed recycled paper. Following the meeting, the mayors launched the Green Manufacturing Initiative to support green energy manufacturing businesses in the region. The region's BlueGreen Alliance contributed to the effort by conducting benchmarking exercises to determine what could be learned from the efforts of other cities. The mayors' initiative identified energy, buildings, and transportation as industries that could be developed successfully in the region, and two other industries (green chemistry and recycling and reclamation) were later added. The cities conducted an inventory to publicize the businesses that already existed in the sectors and the special strengths within each sector. The subsequent report identified strengths in the manufacturing of windows, doors, and wind turbines, and it identified research centers at the University of Minnesota that were relevant to each of the three industries.[9]

The project then developed a directory of green manufacturing businesses in the region, and the Twin Cities shifted some of their procurement to local green businesses. Under the "Thinc.Green" initiative, the Twin Cities developed five initiatives: green procurement from local governments, green building standards, incentives for the recruitment and retention of businesses, financing for green businesses, and recognition for leadership in green manufacturing. The development of the marketing plan involved weekly meetings with a variety of stakeholders, including local union and environmental groups.[10]

In this case, the blue-green coalition served primarily as a catalyst for a process that was embraced by the two mayors. Because the mayors and their staff pursued an inclusive strategy of stakeholder participation throughout the process, the blue-green coalitions stayed involved and contributed to the evolution of the initiative.

New York

In 2009, the state government of New York approved the "Green Jobs, Green New York" law. Using $112 million in funds from the Regional Greenhouse Gas Initiative and receipts from the state's system benefits charge, the law enabled the New York State Energy Research and Development Authority (NYSERDA) to set up a revolving loan fund to provide assistance to retrofit homes and businesses, and it also authorized the state's Department of Labor to set up workforce training programs. The legislation passed the Assembly unanimously and with bipartisan support in the Senate. The goal was to retrofit a million homes (of a total of 7 million in the state), which was estimated to create 14,000 jobs and save the state's households $1 billion in heating and cooling costs. The 2011 Power NY Act included a crucial element that the first law had not included: on-bill financing to support the retrofitting projects.[11]

A blue-green coalition led by the Center for Working Families developed the proposal that led to the legislative reforms, and organizations associated with the coalition later became members of the NYSERDA advisory council for the government program. The program also funded constituency-based organizations to develop outreach for weatherization projects, recruitment for workforce training, and mobilizations to encourage landlords to undertake projects. The Green Jobs Green New York coalition worked to include hiring goals and living wage requirements for the contractors, but the language was not included in the original legislation, and the coalition lost this part of program. However, the green jobs coalition has continued to advocate for high standards from contractors.[12]

North Carolina
The passage of North Carolina's combined portfolio standard for renewable energy and energy efficiency in 2007 (S.3) is of special interest, because the Southeast has lagged behind the rest of the country for green energy legislation. The law passed with strong support from Republicans and Democrats in both houses, and the state has become a model for advocacy groups in other Southern states that wish to see demand-side policies developed in the region. So how did North Carolina become a leader in a lagging region?[13]

Because of "right-to-work" laws, Southern states tend to have a weaker labor presence, and the blue-green coalitions that are more prominent in other regions are less evident. Instead, the primary source of support was a coalition of environmental organizations and renewable-energy businesses. Before 2007 the state had only a modest green energy policy record, including a voluntary green pricing program for renewable energy and a residential credit for solar energy installations. In 2003 Environmental Defense and the North Carolina Sustainable Energy Association, the latter an organization that bridges advocacy for environmental issues and support for the state's renewable-energy industry, issued a report that included a call for a renewable portfolio standard. In 2005 the North Carolina Sustainable Energy Association drafted legislation for a study bill, but the legislature didn't approve the bill. The association then worked with the state's Environmental Review Commission of the General Assembly, which voted to study the proposal, and with the North Carolina Utility Commission, which voted to fund the study to determine the feasibility and effects of a renewable electricity standard in the state. An advisory committee consisting of a broad range of stakeholders ensured that the study was conducted by an independent consulting organization with credibility among different constituencies.[14]

After the study indicated that the program would be feasible and cost effective, the North Carolina Utilities Commission led a nearly year-long process to negotiate the contents of the bill with environmental, industry, and utility stakeholders. The process resulted in a combined standard (renewable energy and energy efficiency) of 12.5 percent by 2021 for the large investor-owned utilities and less demanding standards for the municipal and cooperative utilities. The law also improved the interconnection standard, which facilitated the generation of distributed renewable energy.[15]

The law ended up being controversial among environmentalists, because it entailed various compromises that were necessary to maintain support from powerful industrial groups. The standard has a small solar energy carve-out (0.2 percent by 2018), but it also included the much less common carve-out for energy produced from waste from swine and fowl farms. Of greater concern to many environmentalists, the law allowed utilities to pass along to customers the cost of new facilities under construction rather than wait until the plants are constructed to pass along costs. The compromise was necessary to win support from the investor-owned utilities, which wanted to improve financing to support base-load generation of coal and nuclear power. During the 1970s, many states struck down construction work-in-progress laws, and the change played an important role in ending the construction of nuclear energy power plants. The modification in the North Carolina legislation split the environmental community. The state's Sierra Club chapter expressed strong reservations about the swine waste and construction work-in-progress provisions, and the Canary Coalition, an alliance of clean air organizations, also opposed the work-in-progress provisions. Of the environmental organizations, only Environmental Defense and the North Carolina Sustainable Energy Association supported the law when it reached the final stages. In short, when one looks a little more carefully at the "model" legislative success in the South, the compromises needed to gain political support ended up becoming highly contentious.[16]

Oregon

In 2009, the city of Portland and Multnomah County launched the pilot version of the building retrofit program, Clean Energy Works Portland, and the local governments also approved the associated Community Workforce Agreement. The program and "high road" agreement have been widely hailed as a national model for energy efficiency retrofit programs. Green For All, the Apollo Alliance, and affiliated labor and community groups supported the Community Workforce Agreement and worked closely with the local governments to develop it. The agreement connects the retrofitting program with a series of other goals related to good green jobs. It requires 80 percent of the employees in the program to be hired from the local workforce, historically underrepresented and disadvantaged groups to be at least 30 percent of the workforce, and minority businesses to be at least 20 percent of the businesses involved. Employees must receive living wages, and contractors gain points for offering benefits.[17]

In the original pilot program for the city of Portland, various partners were responsible for different elements of the program. The enumeration of partners is interesting because it gives a sense of what a green transition network looks like after a policy reform has been implemented. The partners included the following: Energy Trust of Oregon, a nonprofit organization, provided guidance for homeowners and oversees the programs; ShoreBank Enterprise Cascadia, a local community bank, operated the loan program and paid contractors directly; the utilities collected payments on their bills and sent the payments to the bank; the city provided funding (mainly through federal government grants); the county coordinated the program with its low-income Weatherization Assistance Program; Worksystems, Inc. provided trained workers; Green For All provided general advice and publicized the model for other communities; and the Stakeholder Evaluation and Implementation Committee supervised the implementation of the Community Workforce Agreement. The long list of partners is an example of a full green transition coalition that goes beyond the more limited but nonetheless important labor-environmental coalitions.[18]

The success of the Portland program led to a $20 million grant from the federal government to launch Clean Energy Works Oregon. Again, Green For All played a supporting role in the program's development, and a representative sits on the governing board. The program offers financing and rebates to homeowners for energy efficiency improvements and funds an energy advocate (also known as a "concierge") to help homeowners make decisions and come up with a plan. The program also pays contractors directly and offers on-bill financing.[19]

Washington

In 2007 the Apollo Alliance, labor organizations, green business organizations, a poverty action organization, and representatives of community and technical colleges developed a green jobs proposal that was in alignment with Governor Christine Gregoire's goals to create green jobs and address global warming in the state. The resulting legislation, the Climate Action and Green Jobs Law (HB 2815), included the following goals:

labor market research and strategic planning, a "green collar job" training fund, a timetable for pollution reduction, principles for a greenhouse gas reduction program, and mandatory reporting of all major sources of global warming. Of special note is the Employment Security Department's task of analyzing the state's green industries and proposing which ones have the greatest potential for development.[20]

Green coalitions also played a role in subsequent initiatives in the state. In 2009 the governor signed into law SB 4659, which guided the investment of $14.5 million of ARRA funding with the goal of retrofitting 100,000 buildings in five years. The Sound Alliance and Spokane Alliance brought together religious, educational, labor, and other civil society organizations to support the legislation. In the following year, Mayor Mike McGinn of Seattle worked with Green For All and the Laborers International Union of America to bring together diverse stakeholders to develop the Community High Road Agreement. Like the Community Workforce Agreement in Portland, the $140 million retrofitting program provided family-supporting wages, quality standards, employment for diverse skill levels, and training opportunities with career opportunities.[21]

Factors Shaping the Policies

The case studies above indicate that green transition coalitions have played a role in general demand policies (such as California's cap-and-trade legislation and laws supporting a renewable electricity standard) and in programs to connect job creation with the retrofitting of buildings. The case of North Carolina suggests that in states where coalitions are weak, there is potential for the utilities to compromise green energy legislation. The coalitions are particularly strong in California, where historic concerns with air quality, water resources, and conservation have provided the basis for a strong clean energy industrial sector. That state has an estimated 125,000 "clean" jobs, including 17,000 solar energy jobs, in comparison with about 35,000 jobs in oil and natural gas extraction and refining. The defeat of the attack on AB 32 suggests that California may have reached a tipping point in which constituencies in favor of the green energy transition have greater political influence than those opposed to it.[22]

The case studies raise the question of what drives the overall tendency toward support for green transition policies. In California, is it the relative number of green jobs, the role of Democratic politicians, the absence of a strong coal mining industry, the presence of blue-green organizations, or some other set of factors? What about for other states? To provide a quantitative perspective on the questions, this section analyzes the relative weighting of four factors that, based on the previous qualitative analysis, might influence a state government's policy field toward green transition policies. Because there is no general index of green transition policies, an index was constructed based on a state's policies in the following areas: renewable electricity standard, public benefits fund, greenhouse gas legislation, green industrial plan, green industry support, net metering, interconnection, and climate plan. The composite index allowed states to be ranked from 1 to 100. The result corresponded generally to our qualitative research conclusions about which states were the leaders. The highest scoring states (based on policies through the end of 2010) were California, Colorado, Connecticut, Massachusetts, New Jersey, New York, and Oregon.[23]

With respect to independent variables, some patterns emerged based on the qualitative comparisons. States in the Southeast and some states in the Rocky Mountain region have a relatively undeveloped suite of green energy policies. Although we have heard the explanation that the reason for the Southeast's lagging position was due to low wind resources, the explanation could not account for the overall low score on the green energy policy index, because it included factors other than the renewable portfolio standard. One possible explanation is that states with stronger Democratic Party support tend to have stronger green policies, and the pattern appears to have hardened after President Obama elevated green jobs to national policy in 2009 and 2010. Another possible explanation is that states with a strong coal industry or oil and gas industry tend to be absent from the lists of leading green states. Third, blue-green coalitions were under-represented in the Southeastern and Rocky Mountain states. Together, those factors were possible explanations of the geographical variation in state governments' score on green energy policies.

The quantitative analysis tested four hypotheses:

1. States with stronger green energy policies will have a higher percentage of clean energy jobs. The use of a percentage controls for differences in the size of population. The reasoning behind the hypothesis is that a higher level of clean energy jobs will provide an electoral constituency in favor of green energy policy. The factor was clearly important in the defeat of Proposition 23 in California. The percent of "clean energy

economy" jobs by state in the 2009 Pew Charitable Trusts study was used.[24]

2. States with stronger green energy policies will have a lower percentage of employment in oil, natural gas, and coal mining. Here, the goal was to measure the countervailing political constituency that at a national level has tremendous influence on energy policy. The statistic for each state was compiled from the number of employees in extraction and refining of oil and natural gas, plus the number of employees in coal mining, as a percentage of overall state employment.[25]

3. States with stronger green energy policies tend to have higher levels of support for the Democratic Party. The hypothesis is based on our qualitative work, which led to the observation that Democratic governors and mayors were often strong advocates of green energy and economic development policies. Conversely, Republican governors and mayors were sometimes opposed to green energy policies or only tepid supporters of limited greening, such as energy efficiency cost saving measures and biofuels development. However, there were some exceptions, such as Governor Arnold Schwarzenegger of California. To assess this hypothesis, the vote for Senator John Kerry in the 2004 presidential election was used as a proxy variable. The reasoning behind the choice is that the 2004 election presented a clearer sense of voter sympathies for the Democratic Party versus the Republican Party than the 2008 election, because in 2008 looming economic chaos caused a strong backlash against the Republican Party. Furthermore, in 2004 there was a sharper difference between the candidates on environmental issues than in 2008.

4. States with a blue-green coalition have stronger green energy policies. This hypothesis was tested with a binary variable for the presence or absence of an Apollo Alliance or BlueGreen Alliance network in each state.[26]

Although the direction of causality for the relationship between green energy policy and three of the variables (fossil fuel employment, Democratic Party support, and green coalition presence) is intuitive, the relationship is less so for clean energy jobs and green energy policies, because policies create jobs that in turn create constituencies for policies. However, renewable electricity standards and other green energy policies change, and the cumulative changes are counted in the ranking. Thus, it is reasonable to infer that even if green energy policies helped to created green employment, green energy constituencies may have played some role in the recent changes in policy. As a result, clean energy policies are interpreted as the dependent variable, with the other four as independent variables. The results are presented as a correlation matrix in table 7.1.

A higher percentage of clean energy jobs, a higher level of support for the Democratic Party, and the presence of blue-green coalitions are positively associated with clean energy policies, whereas a higher percentage of fossil fuel jobs (with respect to all jobs in the state) is negatively associated with the policies and with Democratic Party support. The correlation coefficients for clean energy policies are moderate for three variables and strong for the Democratic Party. Fossil fuel jobs are negatively associated with all variables, although only weakly or moderately so.[27]

Taken separately, the four independent variables predict variation in the clean energy policy index at a statistically significant level. When all four independent variables are considered together in a linear regression model, they are associated with 69 percent of the variation of the mean of the clean energy policy index. However, only Democratic Party support is statistically significant in the model with all variables. The finding is consistent with our qualitative survey, which found that during the period 2000–2010 Democratic governors were often leaders of clean energy policy and green economic development initiatives. There are also occasional instances of bipartisan support for green transition policies, as a few of the case studies above indicated.[28]

To analyze the relationship between Democratic governors and green energy policies in more detail, the top states on the clean energy policy

Table 7.1
Correlation coefficients for Green Energy Policy Index. Because the sample is also the universe of 50 states, descriptive statistics that include the dependent variable may be the most insightful in this case.

	Clean energy employment	Fossil fuel employment	Democratic Party support	Green-blue coalition
Clean energy policy index	0.37	−0.39	0.79	0.48
Clean energy employment		−0.09	0.26	0.35
Fossil fuel employment			−0.47	−0.23
Democratic Party support				0.37

index (the twelve states with an index score of 70 percent or better) were examined for the number of years a Democrat was governor from 2000 to 2011. Here, the pattern was not strong: Democrats held the governor's office in only 69 of 144 possible years. However, the method of counting the number of Democratic governor years was very blunt. If one draws on our qualitative survey and looks at governors who have consistently supported landmark green energy policy reforms during this period, they are almost entirely Democrats. Examples include Chet Culver, John Corzine, Jennifer Granholm, Christine Gregoire, Deval Patrick, Ed Rendell, Ted Kulongoski, Martin O'Malley, Bill Richardson, and Bill Ritter. A few Republican governors also supported environmental and clean energy issues, including Arnold Schwarzenegger, George Pataki, and to some degree Tim Pawlenty.[29]

The Military and the Green Transition

Although 33 retired senior military officers supported the Kerry-Lieberman bill, in general the military has not played a role in green transition coalitions and policy reform at the state and local levels. However, the military's decision to pursue its own green transition has significant implications for the broader political landscape. In the past the military has played a significant role in the development of new technologies, such as the Internet, and it is possible that its shift to green technology could have similar implications for the green transition. Moreover, because the military is the largest consumer of energy in the country, a change in its demand policies could both complement efforts among state governments and partially compensate for the absence of an integrated demand policy in the federal government. As Nicole Lederer, the co-founder of Energy Entrepreneurs, stated, "When one door closed [the Kerry-Lieberman bill], a big window opened with the Department of Defense." (Eilperin 2011)[30]

The Department of Defense has a relatively aggressive greening policy when compared with those of state governments: a goal of 25 percent renewable energy by 2025, reduction of petroleum consumption by 30 percent by 2020, and all new construction at a LEED Silver or better standard. The Navy has the additional goal of cutting fossil fuel consumption in noncombat vehicles by 50 percent by 2015. In 2011 Secretary of the Navy Ray Mabus also outlined plans to have 50 percent of the energy supply of the Navy and Marines from alternative sources such as biofuels and solar energy by 2020, and the military was installing solar panels at its bases throughout the country. The Air Force also plans to use 50 percent alternative fuels for domestic flights by 2016, and both the Navy and Air Force have plans to cut overall fuel consumption on ships and planes. Military expenditures on green technology grew from $400 million in 2006 to $1.2 billion in 2009, and they were projected to reach $10 billion per year by 2030.[31]

In contrast with the civilian frame that linked environmental protection and job development, the military conceptualizes its green transition almost exclusively in security terms. By sticking to the narrow security frame, the military can avoid allegations of overreach and interference in civilian politics. However, the security frame itself is quite broad and encompasses three main elements. For the country as a whole, dependence of foreign oil is itself a security threat, because it exposes the country to supply disruptions and requires a significant military presence around the world to protect supply chains, especially from the Middle East. However, this aspect of the security frame only favors import substitution; it is neutral on the type of domestic energy used and could favor synthetic fuels and additional domestic drilling for oil. Nevertheless, the military's support for biofuels and solar energy suggests the direction that it favors: the Department of Defense is the nation's largest consumer of biofuels. Likewise, the military is also offering to host wind and solar farms on its bases, which could provide both a future revenue stream and resilience in the event of a grid disruption.[32]

The second aspect of the security frame is the security risk from the exposure of the military to price fluctuations and rising energy costs. In an era of budgetary constraints, the military's exposure to rising and fluctuating fuels creates tradeoffs between energy expenditures and other types of expenditures, such as weaponry and personnel. Undersecretary of Defense Dorothy Robyn has underscored the importance of energy efficiency measures and other ways of reducing costs.[33]

The third aspect of the security frame is the military's goal of reducing dependence on supply chains and the exposure of soldiers in combat positions due to the necessity of transporting fuel. In Afghanistan during 2010 and 2010, an average of one marine was killed in every 50 supply conveys that bring fuel to troops. By producing some energy on site, such as solar power instead of petroleum-powered generators, it is possible to reduce the amount of liquid fuel that is transported along dangerous supply lines, thereby saving the lives of soldiers. In this case the military favors distributed energy that can be produced on site, which means solar or small wind.[34]

Although the security frame is broad, it restricts the extent to which the military can affect the political field. The armed forces are unlikely to become an active member of green transition coalitions, because non-retired military personnel adopt an officially neutral stance with respect to partisan politics. However, the military's support for the green energy transition will likely have significant indirect effects. For example, research reports from the military have undermined climate change skepticism, because the science-based security risks associated with climate change and diminishing world oil supplies trump the desire not to offend anti-green political leaders. Furthermore, the military works with green businesses to encourage the conversion of research into useful technologies. Secretary of the Navy Mabus said: "We're trying to get companies past ideas and into production. The American military can be a catalyst to do this—to move from the fossil fuel economy we've got to one of alternative fuels." (Daniel 2011) One important catalyst that the military has provided is to spur domestic demand for solar energy. In 2011 the military and the unions supported the Buy American Solar Amendment to the National Defense Authorization Act (HR 1540), which required the Department of Defense to purchase only domestically manufactured solar photovoltaic systems.[35]

Conclusions

In the United States, the history of green energy and green jobs policies has been uneven not only when comparing federal policy with state and local policies but also when comparing across state and local governments. Whereas the federal government's green energy policies reached a peak in 2009 and then declined after the defeat of the Kerry-Lieberman bill in 2010, the military has stepped in with strong demand policies and research and development support. Likewise, at the state government level support for green energy policies has varied from almost no support to a full suite of supply and demand policies. Thus, the story of a simple opening and closing of political opportunities during the 111th Congress needs to be qualified by the variation across policy fields and scale of government.

The case studies discussed in this chapter show that green transition coalitions played a role in some of the green energy policies that were approved after 2000. (In none of the cases was there any evidence of military involvement.) The role of the coalitions was concentrated in programs that provided support for the retrofitting of buildings, and the coalitions successfully achieved connections between those programs and training opportunities for low-income workers. In some cases the coalitions played a more general role in green transition policies, such as the mobilization to defend AB 32 in California and to develop and increase renewable portfolio standards.

The quantitative analysis pointed to support for the Democratic Party as the most important factor in explaining the success of green transition policies, but it also pointed to the relative size of employment constituencies both in favor and against green jobs. In about half of the states, there are continuing advances toward renewable-energy generation and energy efficiency in buildings, and there is ongoing growth of clusters of green energy businesses. However, the other side of the picture is that in about half of the states there has been relatively little in the way of green energy policy development. Those states tend to have higher levels of fossil fuel industries and Republican Party leadership.

The analysis of policy reforms suggests that the green energy transition in the United States could stall for an indefinite period of time. It is possible that anti-green constituencies will triumph and lead the world into a scenario that the Tellus Institute describes as a "fortress world," which separates the haves from the have-nots. But there is also some hope that the accretion of constituencies in support of a green energy transition will reach a tipping point that overwhelms opposition. The dramatic shift of the military in favor of the green energy transition provides a strong countervailing power to the fossil fuel industry, and its demand policies will fuel growth in the number of people who view themselves as having green jobs.[36]

After 2010: Continued Unevenness in the Green Transition

By 2011 there was an intense battle of frames for defining the relationship between the global economic crisis that had begun in 2008 and the green energy transition. Whereas Democrats continued to view green jobs as a partial solution to problems of unemployment and energy costs, many Republicans had come to view green industrial policy as another example of government overspending. Renewable electricity standards, system benefits charges, and cap-and-trade programs were especially vulnerable, because opponents could depict them as taxes that businesses and households could ill afford. Green transition policies were merged with "Obamacare" to become part of a socialistic tax-and-spend conspiracy that could not be justified in an economic climate of a fragile recovery amid growing federal debt. The very financial crisis that had undermined the credibility of deregulation and other policies associated with neoliberalism was turned against green developmentalism.

The 2011 bankruptcy of Solyndra, a solar energy company that had received $500 million in federal loans, also weakened the momentum for green industrial policy. Republicans in the House held hearings on the bankruptcy of the company and used the occasion to argue against the horse-betting of green industrial policy. One Republican congressman, Fred Upton of Michigan, commented: "In this time of record debt, I question whether the government is qualified to act as a venture capitalist, picking winners and losers in speculative ventures and shelling out billions of taxpayer dollars to keep them afloat." (Wald and Savage 2011) Republicans also suggested that the administration's loan guarantees for Solyndra were linked to political campaign support, but administration officials denied any wrongdoing. A few weeks later, House Republicans approved a stopgap extension of the federal budget that provided emergency funding for flood victims but cut $1.5 billion in loan guarantees for electric vehicle manufacturing. Democrats opposed the measure, claiming that up to 50,000 jobs could be lost, and the government narrowly averted a shutdown.[1]

The solar industry pointed out that Solyndra was only one of several American solar companies that had shut down or reduced production during the preceding eighteen-month period, and it pointed the finger back at the US government's failure to establish a strong demand policy and subsidies proportional to those of China and other countries. The Coalition for American Solar Manufacturing, a group of American crystalline silicon manufacturers led by SolarWorld USA (a subsidiary of a German company), also claimed that the US government had failed to protect domestic manufacturing from predatory Chinese subsidies, which it claimed were illegal under international trade law. The coalition also asked the US government to investigate trade violations, but the request was so sensitive that the other manufacturing companies in the coalition didn't disclose their names because of fear of retaliation from China. The petition initiated a process of inquiry by the United States International Trade Commission, which determines injury, and the US Department of Commerce, which determines if imports are unfairly priced and Chinese manufacturing is at facilities with unfair subsidies. The companies also initiated similar inquiries in Europe.[2]

The call for protection of American photovoltaic manufacturing was perhaps the most visible example of the trade defensiveness side of developmentalism in 2011. Gordon Brinser, president of SolarWorld Industries USA, commented:

China's systematic campaign to dismantle the US industry has cost thousands of jobs in Arizona, California, Maryland, Massachusetts, New York and Pennsylvania. China's wrongful tactics run systematically across the board; central planning has subsidized most facets of these companies' business. China actually has no production cost advantage. Labor makes up a modest share of solar industry costs, China's labor is less productive, its raw material and equipment have come from the West, and China must pay for long-distance shipping. Yet, massive state subsidies and sponsorship have enabled Chinese manufacturers to illegally dump their products into a wide-open US market. (Cichoski 2011)

The solar industry's claims provoked a reply from China and a counter-reply from the solar industry. China promised an investigation into American subsidies of its solar, hydropower, and wind exports, and the Chinese firm SunTech turned free-trade rhetoric back on the United States:

Protectionism would not only put thousands of jobs at risk, but it would inhibit solar technology's ability to compete against traditional forms of electricity generation. A solar trade war would deal a major blow to the global economy and to our common goal of achieving a clean energy future. (Drajen and Martin 2011)[3]

The solar industry coalition responded as follows:

The Chinese government's claims that our actions are improper and protectionist, and that its illegal subsidies and massive dumping of solar product are helping the global economy and the environment, are absurd. China is one of the biggest trade protectionists in the world. In the solar industry, China is gutting manufacturing and jobs here in America and abroad while China's solar industry pollutes its own people. . . . Its policies of restricting exports of rare earth minerals, forcing companies to hand over their technology as a condition of doing business, ineffectual intellectual property enforcement, and massive industry subsidies are flat-out protectionist. Worst of all, China's manipulation of its currency severely distorts global markets. (Stanko 2011)

The conflict over Chinese subsidies and trade also threatened to divide green transition coalitions, because those with a primarily environmental orientation saw benefit in lower-priced Chinese goods, which would hasten the transition of solar energy to grid parity. Within the solar energy industry, there were divisions between installers, who benefited from lower prices, and manufacturers, who viewed the inexpensive goods as the outcome of an illegal trade strategy. Because of the division between the installation and manufacturing side of the solar industry, the Solar Energy Industry Association, which represents 5,000 companies and as many as 100,000 employees in all aspects of the solar industry, adopted a neutral stance. In a statement issued on the trade dispute, the association's president, Rhone Resch, recognized the value of global trade for the American solar industry but also recognized the need to rectify unfair trade practices where they exist:

If it appears that trade obligations are not being met, solar companies—whether foreign or domestic—have the right to request an investigation into alleged unfair trade practices. These allegations must be thoroughly examined and, if unlawful trade practices are found, action to remedy those practices should be taken.

In turn, parties accused of unfair trade practices also have the right to defend themselves in the process of these investigations.

The bottom line is that these investigations provide a legitimate, transparent mechanism for resolving trade disputes and determining what—if any—unfair practices have occurred. (Resch 2011)

President Obama replied to Republican critics by defending the administration's investments in the American solar industry, and he vowed not to surrender green tech to China. The administration also defended the broader package of $36 billion in investments from the

Department of Energy in low-carbon businesses, of which only a portion had gone to solar energy companies. The investments included about $10.6 billion for nuclear energy and $9 billion for the manufacturing of advanced vehicles, and the remainder was spread over a wide range of investments in solar, wind, geothermals, biofuels, energy storage, and energy transmission. As for venture capital in general, the portfolio of investments was risky and likely to produce failures, and it will take years before the wisdom of the investment choices will be known. However, in the case of the solar energy investments, it is possible that the administration pursued a faulty strategy in general rather than specifically for the Solyndra case. According to Dustin Mulvaney, an environmental studies scholar who is an expert on the solar industry, the funds invested in solar manufacturing favored thin-film technology rather than making American silicon-crystalline technology competitive with Chinese photovoltaics.[4]

Because of the growing backlash against green jobs and green developmentalism, President Obama distanced himself and his administration from explicit invocation of the "green jobs" frame that he had made so central in the 2008 campaign. The administration backed down from a plan to enact stricter ozone pollution standards, but perhaps the strongest indication of the shift in position on green energy policy occurred in September of 2011, when President Obama launched a campaign for a jobs bill that would serve as the opening salvo of his political campaign for reelection. Whereas green jobs had played a significant role in the presidential campaign of 2008, his opening speech on the jobs plan didn't mention clean energy or green jobs. The issue had become too partisan for him to embrace it in the upcoming presidential election.[5]

Although the president's speech avoided the topic of green jobs, the BlueGreen Alliance noted that three aspects of the plan were consistent with green jobs policies: the goal of improving school buildings, which included energy efficiency measures, investment in infrastructure, and a national infrastructure bank. Other elements of the proposed plan, such as education and innovative transportation, were also consistent with previous green jobs policies, and the plan called for closing $41 billion in loopholes for oil and gas companies. In fact, it was possible to interpret the proposed legislation as not as abandoning support for green jobs initiatives but as continuing support under the umbrella of general job creation with references to "green" excised.[6]

Even if one accepts the interpretation that the Obama administration was not doing an about-face on the green jobs issue but instead making a tactical decision to submerge green jobs programs in a general jobs-oriented campaign, one might still argue the broader point that the Republican majority in the House of Representatives in the 112th Congress had closed the brief window of political opportunity for green energy policies at the federal government level, and the political will for green energy transition policies had disappeared. Certainly the field of Republican presidential candidates in 2012 provided support for the argument of a sea change. In the presidential election campaigns for 2012, the change of tide was evident in the general lack of support for green energy policy. Whereas the Republican nominee for president in 2008, John McCain, had supported climate change legislation, in the 2012 presidential election cycle several of the presidential candidates for the Republican Party were opposed to any regulatory action, and some even denied the scientific evidence on the anthropogenic causes of greenhouse gas emissions. To win the acquiescence of green voters, President Obama needed only to pursue a moderate strategy that avoided major setbacks, such as elimination of the Environmental Protection Agency.

Against the view that green energy policy was dead in the United States after the Tea Party movement and Americans for Prosperity emerged as a political force within the Republican Party, this chapter will argue that the situation remained more complicated. Even at the federal government level, in 2011 the Obama administration announced an agreement with automakers and the state of California to increase fleet fuel efficiency standards to 54.5 miles per gallon by 2025 (from 27 miles per gallon), and the administration also developed the first efficiency standards for trucks and buses. Whereas automobile manufacturers had opposed similar agreements in the past, the $80 billion bailout that they had received from Washington and their shift into hybrid and electric technologies had softened their opposition. Supporters of the agreement also claimed that it would create 150,000 new jobs.[7]

Furthermore, when one turns attention away from Washington to the state governments, a much more complicated picture emerges than one of a straightforward end to green transition policies. Although there were examples of dramatic reversals of green energy policy goals in some states, there were also cases of continued pursuit of green jobs and green industrial development. This chapter will analyze the pattern of continued unevenness at the state government level. It will focus on states where there had been significant policy reform before 2010, as discussed in our companion policy report and in preceding chapters. Those states provide the best opportunity to assess both retrenchment and further greening. I will argue that some of the state governments have bucked the tide of anti-green sentiment by continuing to develop green energy policy reforms. The analysis is consistent with that of the previous chapter, which showed that the unevenness of policy reforms is closely related to which political party is in power. However, there were also some surprising cases of bipartisanship and even support for green policies among Republican governors. As a result, the study of state-level policies in 2011 precludes a simplistic diagnosis of the post-2010 green energy policy landscape in the United States as a lost cause. Whether it is cause for optimism that the political opportunity structure at the federal government level will reopen or whether it is a harbinger of a long-term change toward a highly polarized landscape is a question that will only be revealed in time.

Republicans and Reversals

In several cases, Republicans elected to the office of governor in 2010 initiated dramatic policy reversals on green energy issues. This section will focus on seven of the most significant shifts of green energy transition policies at the state government level—Florida, Maine, New Jersey, New Mexico, Ohio, Pennsylvania, and Wisconsin—but it will also consider some cases of more moderate and even pro-green Republican governors.

In Florida, Governor Charlie Crist, a former Republican turned independent, had established greenhouse gas reduction goals for state buildings (EO 07-126) and had approved a major legislative reform in 2008 (HB 7135) that established a mechanism for a renewable electricity standard, a cap-and-trade program, and standards for efficient buildings and renewable fuels. Crist subsequently backed away from his earlier enthusiasm for green energy issues, but environmentalists who had criticized him were even more dismayed by his Republican successor as governor, Rick Scott, whom some saw as the most anti-environmental governor in decades. Scott, a climate change denialist, was supported by groups affiliated with the Tea Party movement. In 2011 he rejected a high-speed rail line and began a review of the state's energy laws with the goal of reducing energy efficiency regulations. Arguing that electricity prices were too high, he claimed to support more cost-effective renewable energy, including solar energy, but the rhetoric indicated a shift away from any deepening of Florida's meager green transition initiatives.[8]

In Maine, Governor John Baldacci, a Democrat, had strongly supported energy efficiency measures, developed a form of property-assessed clean energy bonds, joined the Regional Greenhouse Gas Initiative, and supported renewable energy. His efforts in support of green energy earned him the Climate Champion Award from Clean Air-Cool Planet, a nonprofit environmental organization in the Northeast. His Republican successor, Paul LePage, earned national fame for ordering the removal of a mural about the state's labor history from the lobby of the building that housed the state's Department of Labor. In 2011, during his first month as governor, LePage launched 63 anti-green measures. He also proposed a voluntary program to replace the state's renewable portfolio standard (LD 1570), but his proposal didn't have support in the legislature. Instead, the Republican-dominated legislature approved the Act to Improve Maine's Energy Security (LD 553), which passed with bipartisan support but without the governor's signature. The law required the state to reduce oil consumption by 50 percent by 2050 and favored energy efficiency and renewable energy.[9]

New Jersey's Republican governor Chris Christie, elected in 2010, took a dramatically different approach to environmental politics from his Democratic predecessor, Jon Corzine. Corzine had supported the state's participation in the Regional Greenhouse Gas Initiative and the state's landmark Global Warming Response Act of 2007, which called for a long-term reduction in the state's greenhouse gas emissions and the development of an Energy Master Plan. In contrast, Christie withdrew the state from the regional accord. His proposed 2011 Energy Master Plan reduced the state's renewable-energy goal for 2021 from 30 percent to 22.5 percent, tightened restrictions for small-scale projects, reclassified natural gas as clean energy, weakened some energy efficiency programs, supported nuclear energy, and proposed the development of three natural gas plants and additional pipelines. However, the plan did continue support for offshore wind development and large-scale solar. In September of 2011, the magazine *Mother Jones* revealed that Christie's decision to withdraw from the Regional Greenhouse Gas Initiative, at considerable revenue loss for the state government, may have been influenced by David Koch.[10]

In New Mexico, Democratic governor Bill Richardson had championed efforts to boost the state's solar photovoltaic, biofuels, and smart grid industries. Republican governor Susana Martinez, a climate change skeptic who took office in 2011, worked quickly to reverse Richardson's policies. She fired the entire Environmental Improvement Board, citing its "anti-business" policies, and she appointed a climate change denier to run the state's Energy, Minerals, and Natural Resources Department. She also prevented publication of two rules in the state's register, one that required 3 percent reductions in greenhouse gas emissions and one that reduced water pollution from dairy farms' waste products. The decision created a political crisis, which the state's supreme court resolved by finding the decision unconstitutional and reinstating the regulations.[11]

In Ohio and Pennsylvania, Democratic Governors Ted Strickland and Ed Rendell had supported green industrial development programs and green energy policies. Strickland's Republican successor, John Kasich, elected in 2010, attacked the state's renewable portfolio standard during his campaign and later withdrew Ohio from the federal high-speed rail program. Likewise, Republican governor Tom Corbett of Pennsylvania pledged support for the state's fossil fuel industry, and he specifically supported hydraulic fracturing for natural gas. After he assumed office in 2011, Corbett required the state's inspectors to gain approval of top officials before issuing citations and fines to drilling companies.[12]

Scott Walker, a Republican who replaced the pro-green Democrat Jim Doyle as governor of Wisconsin in 2011, was another strongly anti-green governor. Although Walker received national attention for his ties to the Koch brothers and his standoff with Democratic legislators and labor unions, he also withdrew Wisconsin from the high-speed rail program and called for a rollback of regulations that supported wind energy development. The Wisconsin Wind Siting Rules (PSC 128), developed over two years in a stakeholder process, had been approved in 2009 by the state legislature with bipartisan support. On the day that the rules were set to go into effect, the state legislature's Joint Committee for Review of Administrative Rules suspended them in a party-line vote; a month later, two wind farm companies abandoned their plans to continue development in the state.[13]

Even where Democratic governors remained in office, they faced challenges from a new wave of anti-green Republican legislators. In New Hampshire, for example, Republicans won control of both houses and voted to repeal the state's membership in the Regional Greenhouse Gas Initiative, arguing that it represented an "income redistribution ploy" (Fahey 2011: 1). Governor John Lynch vetoed the bill, and the Senate narrowly failed to override the veto. In Ohio and Pennsylvania, Republican legislators initiated efforts intended to repeal already weak portfolio standards, and in North Carolina new Republican majorities in both houses proposed cuts of 22 percent in the environmental budget.[14]

In 2011, several Republican governors stepped forward to seek their party's nomination for president on anti-green platforms that departed from their records as governors. As governor of Minnesota, Tim Pawlenty had supported the state's renewable portfolio standard, green jobs programs, and the Midwestern Governors Greenhouse Gas Association; as a presidential candidate, however, he distanced himself from his own record and apologized for his previous support of cap-and-trade legislation. Likewise, as governor of Massachusetts Mitt Romney supported green industrial development, but his presidential campaign platform emphasized nuclear, clean coal, and more drilling for oil rather than renewable energy. Journalists identified similar inconsistencies for Jon Huntsman, the Utah governor who had supported the Western Climate Initiative. Rick Perry of Texas, a Republican elected governor of Texas in 2000, was even less consistent. As governor, he had pursued a policy of energy diversification but had also supported the state's oil, coal, and gas industries. Although he supported a renewable-energy mandate that helped Texas to become a leader in wind energy generation, he also opposed a solar energy carve-out, and he opposed the federal government's plan for greenhouse gas regulation. When he entered the presidential race in 2011, he ran as a climate change denier.[15]

Although anti-green views were becoming a litmus test for Republican presidential candidates, some newly elected Republican governors held more moderate views. Three examples of Republican governors with relatively moderate views in states that previously had green Democrats as governors are the governors of Iowa, Michigan, and Tennessee.

In Iowa, Republican governor Terry Branstad campaigned against the Iowa Power Fund, which Governor Chet Culver, a Democrat, had promoted to support the state's renewable-energy industry. As governor, Branstad supported a bill that facilitated the siting of a nuclear energy facility in the state. However, he also signed legislation (HF 672) that increased wind energy tax credits for small wind developers, and he served as vice-chair of a bipartisan coalition of state governors that sought improvements and extensions in the federal government's support for wind energy. The high level of wind energy development in Iowa may have reached a tipping point that made it difficult even for Republicans to challenge the industry.[16]

The Republican governor of Michigan, Rick Snyder, succeeded the Democrat Jennifer Granholm, who had highlighted green jobs and green industrial development. Snyder won endorsements from environmental organizations, campaigned as a Republican friendly to green innovation, and didn't openly undermine the state's manufacturing capacity in batteries, fuel cells, and wind turbines. However, he also signaled shifts in direction. His first executive order as governor was to split two environmental agencies that Governor Granholm had merged for purposes of developing synergies, and his subsequent budget proposed deep cuts in both agencies. He also renamed another department that Granholm had merged, from the Department of Energy, Labor, and Economic Growth to the Department of Licensing and Regulatory Affairs. The department's new mission was to reduce regulatory burdens on business development. Snyder subsequently irked environmentalists and supporters of renewable-energy development by supporting proposals to build coal-powered electricity plants. Environmentalists criticized the decision and argued that electricity from utility-scale wind energy was cheaper than from new coal-powered plants. Snyder also planned to reduce the tax incentives offered to businesses through the Michigan Economic Development Center and replace them with a lower overall business tax. Although the incentives are available to a wide range of businesses, the previous governor had used the incentives to support green industrial development. On some other issues, Snyder received more positive reviews from environmentalists, especially for some conservation initiatives, and he accepted federal government subsidies for high-speed rail.[17]

In Tennessee, Governor Phil Bredesen, a Democrat, had attracted clean energy manufacturing companies and had earned a reputation for the state as a leader of growth in green jobs. However, his efforts had stopped short of demand policy, such as the enactment of a renewable portfolio standard or public benefits fund, neither of which would have had much political support in the conservative state legislature. Bredesen's Republican successor, Bill Haslam, was silent on environmental and energy issues during the 2010 gubernatorial campaign, but it may have been a strategic silence that harbored a relatively sympathetic or at least neutral view toward green jobs. Haslam was once the president of a petroleum company that operated truck fueling stations, but as mayor of Knoxville he had supported solar energy and energy efficiency reforms. As governor he focused on developing jobs, and he didn't explicitly reject green jobs. For example, at the dedication of a new solar farm he praised his predecessor's record in bringing the solar industry to the state. Likewise, his Jobs4TN plan included "advanced manufacturing and energy technologies" (which included "clean energy products") as one of the state's six prioritized industrial clusters. However, environmentalists have complained that his deep budget cuts for environmental agencies limited their capacity.[18]

Finally, there is the somewhat anomalous case of relatively pro-green Republican governors elected in 2010. Bob McDonnell, governor of Virginia, had a record of work on environmental protection and support for improvement of Chesapeake Bay, and as a gubernatorial candidate he promised to conserve an additional 400,000 acres of land and to create a "Green Jobs Zone" for the state. In April of 2010, he signed several clean energy bills, which had bipartisan support and included measures for a tax credit for green jobs creation (HB803), a foundation for clean tech development (HB 928), and support for offshore wind development (HB 389). After the growth of anti-green sentiment in the Republican Party in late 2010, he didn't back down from support for the state's green tech industries. In 2011 he signed bills that supported clean energy manufacturing grants (HB 2316), net metering (HB 1983), and distributed solar energy generation (HB 1686). In 2011 he issued an executive order (No. 36) directing the state government to develop alternative fuels for its vehicles. However, as his name began to be floated as a possible vice-presidential candidate for the 2012 election, he shifted toward advocacy for fossil fuels and nuclear energy.[19]

Another pro-green-energy Republican governor elected in 2010 is Brian Sandoval of Nevada. Because of its proximity to California and its ample geothermal and solar resources, Nevada was poised to supply California with renewable energy. To that end, Sandoval developed a memorandum of understanding between the state and federal government to pursue the development of renewable energy on Nevada's extensive federal lands. He also publicly supported the recruitment and development of green energy firms in the state. Although he vetoed a bill (AB 416) to build transmission lines to California, he supported the development of transmission corridors in general. He opposed AB 416 because it was pushed through the legislature at the last minute and would have placed the estimated $1 billion cost of construction on the shoulders of ratepayers. At the National Clean Energy Summit in 2011, Sandoval reiterated his commitment to developing green energy sources for the California market. It is not clear how large that market will be, because Governor Jerry Brown cautiously replied that he also wanted his state to be an exporter.[20]

In summary, Republican governors were not uniformly hostile to green policies, but there was a sea change within the Republican Party in comparison with the election of 2008. Some of the most significant reversals involved withdrawal of support for regional greenhouse gas initiatives, but anti-green Republicans also attacked renewable-energy portfolios and other legislation. Americans for Prosperity and the American Legislative Exchange Council have helped to develop opposition to green energy laws, and well-funded primary challengers opposed moderate Republican candidates who continued to support green energy policies.

Green Democrats and Bipartisanship

In states where Democrats retained the governor's office and in states with newly elected Democratic governors, the situation is hardly one of acquiescence to the wave of anti-green sentiment. Instead, even in 2011 Democrats persevered with policies in support of green jobs and green energy industries. To begin, two of the most populous states in the country, California and New York, have continued to develop green energy policies.

In California, support for green energy and green jobs initiatives has been consistent from the administration of Republican governor Arnold Schwarzenegger to that of his successor in 2011, the Democrat Jerry Brown. Brown had pioneered green energy policies during his gubernatorial administration from 1975 to 1983, and he continued his support after his return to the governor's office. Unlike President Obama, Governor Brown maintained an explicit linkage between green jobs and green energy legislation in 2011. Brown's centerpiece legislative initiative in 2011 was SB 1X-2, the law to advance the renewable-energy standard to 33 percent by 2020. Republican legislators claimed that the standard would raise electricity rates significantly, and although the bill won approval in the legislature, the vote was sharply partisan. In contrast, the legislature approved unanimously, and the governor signed, AB X1 15, an apparently minor change that extended a tax exemption for solar energy to lease-back arrangements. Although less significant than some of the other green energy legislation in the state, it paved the way for SunEdison, a leader of solar power services and installations, to move its headquarters to California. The move would facilitate private financing for rooftop solar energy in the state, a pathway to financing that remained open after the collapse of residential PACE programs.[21]

Brown also backed renewal of the state's system benefits charge, which was set to expire in 2011, under the title of the Clean Energy, Jobs, and Investment Act of 2011 (SB X1 28). In response to California's relatively high unemployment rate that year (12 percent when the national average was 9 percent), the proposed legislation would inject about $500 million into the state's economy for clean energy and energy efficiency projects. Brown's office defended the initiative because of its "proven job-creation potential and role in galvanizing California's innovative clean-tech economy" (Lifsher 2011: B1). The Howard Jarvis Tax Association and a manufacturing organization opposed the bill, and it failed to obtain the necessary level of support in the state legislature in 2011.[22]

New York is another large state that has had relatively consistent support of clean energy and green industries under both a Republican governor (George Pataki) and the subsequent Democratic governors (Elliot Spitzer, David Patterson, and Andrew Cuomo). In 2011 the state legislature approved and Governor Cuomo signed the Power New York Act. The bill facilitated the permitting of power plants by returning to rules that were in effect before 2003. Some cities opposed the measure, because they feared that air pollution could increase under the old rules. However, the compromise worked out in the act addressed the environmental concerns of the cities and also provided incentives for renewable energy generation and reduced emissions in power plants. The act was significant for green jobs advocates such as the Center for Working Families, because it provided for on-bill financing for weatherization projects. The state also approved remote net metering legislation (AB 6270), which removed the requirement that net metering for electricity must be connected to the site.[23]

In Hawaii, there was also a relatively high level of bipartisan support for green energy policies across governors. In the 2010 gubernatorial election, the Democrat, Neil Abercrombie, and the Republican, James Aiona, clashed on strategy issues but agreed in their underlying support for the state's ambitious clean energy initiative, which had been launched in 2008 under Governor Linda Lingle, a Republican. Based on an agreement signed between the state government and the federal Department of Energy, the goal of the initiative was to achieve 70 percent of the state's energy needs by 2030 from a combination of renewable energy and energy efficiency. Abercrombie, who was elected governor, campaigned on a broad platform in support of green jobs, on-bill financing, local energy production, and renewable energy. Although his ambitious program didn't become law during his first year of office, the state legislature did approve HB 1520. The law directed the state's public utilities commission to study on-bill financing for renewable electricity installations, a program that would open opportunities for green jobs similar to those in Oregon and New York.[24]

Vermont is another state in which there has been relatively consistent support for green energy across the political divide. Although in 2007 Republican governor James Douglas vetoed H 520, a strong renewable-energy bill, he promised to implement the general strategy of 25 percent renewable energy by 2025, and he also acted on many of the other proposals in the bill. His Democratic successor, Peter Shumlin, founded the Council on Environment and Energy, renewed the state's support for the Regional Greenhouse Gas Initiative, made improvements to the state's Clean Energy Fund, and developed a new Comprehensive Energy Plan. He also worked to close the aging Vermont Yankee nuclear plant and argued that small, community-based renewable energy is preferable to imported power from Quebec. In 2011, the state government approved the Vermont Energy Act (H 56) to facilitate permitting of small solar facilities (less than 5 kilowatts), improve net metering, and facilitate financing for renewable energy.[25]

Several newly elected Democratic governors in states that were already leaders continued to support green energy legislation, some of which was significant. In 2011, Colorado's state legislature approved unanimously, and Governor John Hickenlooper signed into law, HB 1083, which authorized the construction of an $800 million pumped hydroelectric facility. The state government also approved the Fair Permit Act (HB 1199), which reduced the costs of solar installations. In Connecticut, Republican governor Jodi Rell had vetoed a sweeping clean energy reform bill at the end of the spring 2010 legislative session, but in 2011 the newly elected governor, Democrat Dannell Malloy, signed SB 1243, a comprehensive clean energy bill that included provisions for renewable-energy credits, energy efficiency for buildings and appliances, a residential solar rebate program, and municipal financing programs for building retrofits. In Minnesota, Governor Mark Dayton issued an executive order (11-12) in support of energy efficiency measures in state government buildings, vetoed a bill that would have reduced goals for carbon dioxide emissions from utilities (SF 86), and mitigated cuts to environmental programs in the state legislature's Omnibus Environmental Finance Bill (SS-2). In Oregon, Governor John Kitzhaber supported green energy bills for energy efficiency improvements in schools (HB 2203, 2194, and 2888) and inaugurated a ten-year planning process for green energy. Kitzhaber also proposed that the states of California, Oregon, and Washington form a green energy coalition. "These three states," he said, "have a unique opportunity to change the national narrative and demonstrate the value of clean economic policies." (Esteve 2011)[26]

Other states with Democrats as incumbent governors continued to support green energy legislation even after the 2010 election season. In Maryland, Governor O'Mally, a Democrat elected in 2007, continued to push green energy in 2011 by proposing legislative initiatives to support electric vehicles (including an Electric Vehicle Infrastructure Council), renewable-energy credits for solar water heating, and the development of offshore wind energy. The states of Massachusetts and Washington were leaders in green energy policy reform under Governors Deval Patrick and Christine Gregoire, and the governors continued to develop their programs in 2011. For example, Gregoire signed legislation (SB 5709) to close two of the state's coal-burning electricity plants and smooth the transition away from coal-based electricity.[27]

In summary, Democratic leaders continued to push for policy reforms and achieved some successes even after the emergence of the anti-green Republican groups. Moreover, in some cases the legislation achieved bipartisan support.

General Patterns

The previous section indicated that there were some instances of bipartisanship in state legislatures, even after 2010. What areas of green energy policy provide the greatest political opportunities for bipartisanship? To answer this question, we compiled data on political party affiliation and votes on clean energy legislation in selected state governments between 2007 and 2011. We focused on states that had significant legislative activity on the topic, and we included states from different regions of the country. Some states didn't have information available as part of the public record; they were dropped from the analysis.

The first question that we examined is the extent to which bipartisanship ended after the 2010 elections, when anti-green candidates, many of them associated with the Tea Party movement, rode a wave of electoral success. In response to that question, we found some examples of bipartisan support for laws in 2011; however, the 2011 laws for which bipartisan support was strongest generally involved limited issues that were not easily framed as a tax increase or financial burden on voters. Examples include more efficient permitting and enabling legislation for on-bill financing (New York A08510), reduction of electricity demand (North Carolina SB 75), tax credits for solar and wind (Iowa SF 516), cost reductions for solar permits (Colorado HB 1199), and an exemption on solar energy leases described above (California AB X1–15). A possible exception is the nearly unanimous bipartisan support in Connecticut for a comprehensive energy bill (SB 1243), which supported PACE-like programs and provided energy efficiency guidelines. However, the law didn't increase the renewable portfolio standard. In contrast, the 2011 increase in the renewable portfolio standard (SB X1-2) in California triggered a partisan chasm.

The second question was as follows: If one looks within a state government's record for green energy laws during this period, are some kinds of laws more likely to earn bipartisan support than others? In a few cases, a single state enacted enough green energy laws of moderate or high significance over the period 2007–2011 to review a selection of laws for a possible pattern. For example, the California legislature approved several laws during the period that also received a range of party support (data are in the appendix). AB 532 (the 2007 law that supported solar energy for state government buildings) and SB X1-2 (the 2011 law that increased the renewable electricity standard) had no more than 25 percent support from Republicans. Likewise, the Green Collar Jobs Act (AB 3018, 2008) had only 7 percent support from Republicans in the Senate and 28 percent in the House. In contrast, PACE enabling laws had higher levels of support from Republicans, ranging from a high of 100 percent in the Senate for SB 77 in 2010 to a low of 48 percent in the House for AB 811 in 2008. Republicans and Democrats also unanimously supported the 2011 law (AB X1-15) that provided for an exemption on solar leases. Likewise, in the Senate in 2007 both Republicans and Democrats voted unanimously in favor of a law to facilitate utilities' recovery of expenses from solar energy (SB 1036).

The case of California suggests that laws that increase regulatory efficiency (such as permitting laws) and laws that authorize voluntary programs (such as PACE laws) are likely to receive greater bipartisan support than laws that appear to create a cost burden, such as an increase in the renewable portfolio standard. Does the pattern hold up for other states? The appendix provides a record of voting patterns by party for California and four other states selected because there was available information and a consistent level of legislative activity during the period.

In Colorado, the first increase in the renewable portfolio standard (in 2007) received bipartisan support in the legislature's lower chamber, but the second increase (in 2010) had strong Republican opposition. There was bipartisan support for energy efficiency standards, renewable fuels, the first PACE law (2008), net metering, and two laws that made regulatory changes in 2011. The second PACE law, passed in 2010, had stronger Republican Party opposition, but the law also authorized $800 million in financing for renewable energy and for improved energy efficiency. So again, there appears to be a pattern that bipartisan support can be obtained on a range of issues, but perceptions of increased taxpayer burdens (a renewable portfolio standard or authorization for financing) tend to trigger partisan divisions.

In the states of Maryland and Washington, there was a similar pattern of low Republican support for legislation that is either comprehensive or potentially perceived as raising taxes and cost burdens. For example, there were low levels of Republican Party support for laws that established a timetable for carbon emissions, reduced per capita electricity consumption, increased the renewable portfolio standard, and increased the solar carve-out in the renewable portfolio standard. However, net metering expansion, green standards for buildings (which save money in the long term), and a plan for low-emission vehicles drew relatively higher levels of support from Republicans. In the state of Washington, the comprehensive job training and greenhouse gas reduction law drew relatively little Republican support, and a subsequent law that authorized a green jobs plan and training was supported by no more than a third of Republicans in either house. Limits on carbon emissions from electricity generation, which can be perceived as an implicit carbon tax, was supported by a majority of the Republicans in the House but not in the Senate.

In Oregon, the pattern held up only partially. As one would expect from the other states, there were partisan divides over the increase in the renewable portfolio standard, timetable for carbon regulation, and green jobs training. However, there was a higher level of bipartisan support for the solar feed-in tariff and financing for energy efficiency and renewable-energy projects. Because both measures could be viewed as cost burdens, the relatively high level of bipartisan support is anomalous.

Although the pattern of voting doesn't lend itself to easy generalizations, a few general comments can be made. First, even in 2011, that is, even after the emergence of the Tea Party movement, there were still some cases of bipartisan support for green energy legislation in the state legislatures. Second, an increase in the renewable portfolio standard, a proposal to regulate carbon, green jobs training programs, and other plans that involve even short-term financial burdens for taxpayers or spending increases for governments tend to trigger higher levels of partisan divisions. There are lower levels of partisan division for laws that modify regulations to facilitate green energy development, such as net metering, PACE-like legislation, and to some degree energy-efficient building standards for public buildings. We didn't review the voting record on all PACE laws, but a review by the organization PACENow concluded that states that passed PACE laws (all between 2008 and 2011) included eight states with a Republican majority in the legislature and seventeen states with a Democratic majority. The second Colorado law may be an exception to the generalization that PACE legislation and variants are a strong candidate for attracting bipartisan support, but the opposition to that law may fit the broader pattern because it entailed an increase in expenditures.[28]

If it is correct that a renewable portfolio standard is controversial because it is perceived as increasing costs for consumers, then one would expect that attempts to institute or increase electricity standards would be met with highly partisan responses. One might also expect that an original standard would have a better chance of receiving bipartisan support than an increase to an existing standard, because an original standard might be viewed as simply playing catch-up to the demand policies of other states. To answer the question about the political support for and opposition to renewable portfolio standard laws, we reviewed party votes for new or expanded legislation for all states with available information for the years 2007–2011. (See table 8.1.) The data suggest that whereas a first-time renewable portfolio standard tends to get bipartisan support, an expansion of the renewable portfolio standard is likely to provoke a partisan split, as occurred in California, Colorado, Maryland, Oregon, and Vermont. Each of those states had a legislature controlled by Democrats at the time of the legislative reform. In the one state with a Republican-controlled legislative body that passed an expanded renewable portfolio standard, Pennsylvania, the law (HB 2200 of 2008) was mostly directed at energy efficiency, and it only slightly expanded the scope of the renewable electricity standard. Thus, it appears that, whereas it may be possible to find bipartisan consensus for the creation of the first renewable electricity standard, the expansion of such standards may be more likely to create partisan divides and is politically feasible only in legislatures controlled by Democrats.

Conclusion

The survey of state government policies after 2011 shows a pattern of increased partisanship on the green energy transition, but it also makes

Table 8.1
Party votes on renewable portfolio standards. See appendix for sources of data. Data for the table were assembled by Jonathan Coley. Although there was more activity if one includes regulatory decisions for public utility commissions (as in figure 4.1), the analysis here focused on the smaller set of votes in state legislatures.

		Legislature controlled by Republicans		Legislature controlled by Democrats	
		House	Senate	House	Senate
New RPS	Republican support	90%	84%	85%	95%
	Democrat support	92%	94%	97%	97%
Expand RPS	Republican support	96%	90%	54%	43%
	Democrat support	100%	100%	99%	98%

possible two conclusions that are less obvious. First, there was no blanket rejection of green energy policies across the country; instead, green energy and green industrial policies continued to be developed in many states where Democrats were in power. Second, even within the Republican Party there were some governors with a relatively moderate position on support for green industries.

The rise of anti-green sentiment in the Republican Party is a complicated development that can be explained by three main factors. Among Republican Party leaders, the policy shift is part of a general strategy to reframe developmentalism as social liberalism in order to discredit Democratic Party opponents. Republicans often argue that green energy demand policies are in effect taxes, even regressive taxes, and that businesses and households can ill afford to pay more taxes during a period of high unemployment. Thus, green jobs could be connected with the perceived high cost of "Obamacare" and the federal government's debt, which are the result of spendthrift Democrats.

The strategy of blaming the recession on tax-and-spend social liberalism may explain the failure to compromise that occurred in the 2010 debate about the cap-and-trade bill and the form that the Republicans' alternative proposal took, but it doesn't explain the more virulent forms of anti-green sentiment that have emerged within the Republican Party. One must also take into account the rise of the Tea Party movement and the support that it has received from conservatives in the media. Although the overall concern is with government debt and the need to reduce government spending, a survey of persons who identify themselves with the Tea Party movement in 2011 indicated that they held dramatically different views on several environmental issues than self-identified Republicans, Democrats, or independents. Whereas the majority of the latter believe that global warming is happening, support a 20 percent renewable electricity standard, agree with the proposal for an international treaty to restrict carbon dioxide emissions, and don't support the new construction of a nuclear reactor in their region, the majority of those who support the Tea Party movement held the opposite views. They also opposed even relatively innocuous changes such as the federal mandate to shift to compact fluorescent light bulbs and other forms of energy efficient lighting.[29]

In turn, the tremendous success of the Tea Party movement cannot be explained only as a grassroots phenomenon based on the capacity of movement leaders to mobilize resources, frame issues in an appealing way, build coalitions with similar organizations, and take advantages of political opportunities. Rather, a third factor is needed to explain the strong anti-green sentiment that is found both among the Republican leaders and in the Tea Party movement. Numerous accounts have described the financial support from the network of organizations supported by David and Charles Koch. The Koch brothers have made the repeal of greenhouse gas emissions initiatives a top priority, and the network of industrialists who join in their annual meetings includes leaders of diverse fossil fuel companies. Although climate change skepticism and denialism has a much longer history of support by conservative foundations that predated the mobilization of Tea Party activists and anti-green Republican candidates, since 2010 opposition to the scientific consensus on the anthropogenic causes of contemporary climate change has been translated into a significant political force through Americans for Prosperity, which has strident anti-green positions on a wide range of issues. Increasingly, the battles have also moved from Congress to state legislatures and even local governments.[30]

In summary, the anti-green sentiment that became widespread in the Republican Party after 2009 can be explained as the effects of the party's strategy to counter the success of the green jobs frame, the results of a grassroots movement that has been encouraged by conservative media outlets, and the financial support from the network of anti-green donors associated with the Koch brothers. The lessons of 2011 indicate that the primary targets of conservative political leaders within the field of green energy policy have been policies that can be easily labeled as taxes, such as greenhouse gas emissions regulations, renewable electricity standards, and system benefits charges. The politics activate the old political polarities of American ideology in a battle between market-oriented neoliberalism and a more interventionist social liberalism. If the former triumphs, then green energy policy will increasingly be limited to laws that reduce government regulations, such as relatively incremental changes in favor of laws that block solar permitting or enable distributed energy generators to connect more easily to the grid.

Furthermore, the politics of developmentalism may also be reconfigured. In 2011 Republicans used the Solyndra case to develop a broad attack on green industrial policy. However, other forms of support for industrial development may pass through a neoliberal filter. Governor Rick Snyder's focus on streamlining licensing and permitting for all businesses, including green ones, to the point of reorganizing a government department to address the issues, suggests that the conservative approach to green economic development may be to remove regulatory barriers. The high level of competition among states and with foreign governments for economic development projects also suggests that subsidies from state governments will not disappear. Furthermore, the skepticism in the Tea Party movement over foreign trade suggests that protectionist policies may have continued bipartisan political support in the federal government, and it may be possible to align the sentiment with the needs of green energy manufacturers.

The transition to a post-carbon economy is already of such magnitude that it will take decades to achieve, and even the most rapid transition will involve a period of continued fossil fuel use with unpredictable long-term effects on the global climate. Furthermore, opposition to the green energy transition also has spill-over effects on many other types of green transition policies, so that broader ecological degradation continues unchecked. Anyone with knowledge of basic climate science and the broader problem of ecological carrying capacity for the planet can only look on with deep sadness as one of the world's largest emitters of greenhouse gases steps back from global leadership.

Conclusion

To reduce the level of greenhouse gases and other environmental burdens, it would be necessary to make substantial shifts in the generation and production of electricity, the ways in which buildings conserve and use energy, and the structure and energy sources of transportation. The transition would take place over many decades at different scales, and it would require the integration of technological innovation, different consumer practices, and new government regulations. In this book I have expanded on the theory of large-scale technological transitions by drawing attention to the importance of contested policy fields that result in uneven, incremental, and often failed reforms. Instead of viewing long-term, macrosocial change as an exogenous landscape, I have shown how the policy fields where the reforms of the green energy transition are contested are also sites for the construction of the political landscape. Specifically, I have argued that the green energy transition in the United States of the twenty-first century involves an uneven shift toward developmentalist ideology and policies. Slow changes in the political landscape such as underlying shifts in political ideology are both a response to the contestations over the greening of the economy and a shaping framework that structures those changes.

Because I conceived this as a work of historical social science rather than of normative policy evaluation, I used a broad definition for "green energy." Although I distinguished different shades of green energy technology and their relationships to political constituencies, the goal was not to impose, *a priori*, a normative definition of green energy on the politics but instead to explore how the definitions of green energy are themselves at stake in the policy fields. This descriptive and empirical approach results in several general conclusions about the green energy transition in the United States. The results may generalize to other countries, but comparative work must be left to another project. The six central conclusions are as follows:

1. Because energy policy has become increasingly connected with business development and job creation, energy policy fields have become a primary site where articulations of developmentalist ideology can be found. However, like other policies, green energy policies are compromise formations. In some cases green energy policies show evidence of social liberalism by sanctioning government intervention in the economy for environmental purposes, drawing attention to distributive issues such as environmental justice issues, and tilting job creation toward low-income populations. Likewise, some green energy policies have a neoliberal strand, which configures policies to strengthen and benefit markets dominated by large corporations. There are also areas of green energy policy that involve public ownership and support for transfers of ownership to households and small businesses.

2. The focus on job creation and business development has linked trade and industrial policy as two central elements of developmentalism. Of special note is concern with the decline of manufacturing jobs that accompanied trade liberalization. Federal government policies show evidence of increasing trade disputes and protectionism, and state governments also pursue import substitution for energy and local procurement preferences. However, because green energy manufacturing can also benefit from global sales, there is a countervailing current that focuses more on competitiveness policies, such as investments into green energy research, subsidies, tax credits, and green jobs training programs. Together, the protectionist and competitiveness approaches to green business development involve a new pragmatism with respect to trade. Although the new pragmatism represents a shift away from a strident belief in the benefits on ongoing trade liberalization, it doesn't completely return to the protectionist, import-substituting policies of the United States during the nineteenth century.

3. The patchwork of policies in support of green jobs at the federal, state, and local level add up to an uneven green industrial policy. In some states, green industrial policy is explicitly formulated through industrial development roadmaps and targeted industries, whereas in other states the support is more general or even absent. Green industrial policy for the federal government has been much more problematic because of sectional differences between regions that are still tied to the fossil fuel economy and regions that are largely importers of fossil fuels. An excep-

tion is biofuels policy, which tends to escape from the pattern of sectional and partisan rivalries that has often been the downfall of industrial policies in the United States.

4. In a global economy in which companies in both highly industrialized and newly industrialized countries compete for a market share of green energy industries, industrial policy has increasingly turned to the synergies of colocation and the advantages of place. State and local governments have sought to build the innovation economy and place-based clusters of firms, research organizations, and government organizations, and the federal government has also sanctioned the idea of green industrial clusters with its E-RIC program. The new emphasis in economic policy is accompanied by new areas of social science inquiry. Whereas Keynesian economics and supply-side economics were associated respectively with social liberal and neoliberal political ideologies, developmentalism is associated more with research on regional innovation systems.

5. Significant political constituencies beyond the base in labor-environmentalist organizations and the renewable-energy industry have emerged in support of the green energy transition. The green transition coalitions also include large corporations that have adopted sustainability goals and metrics, green venture capital and investment organizations, community-oriented small businesses, "new economy" progressives, and anti-poverty and faith-based organizations. The military is also playing a background role by spurring demand policy and encouraging innovation. When mobilized in support of specific political issues, the resulting green transition coalitions are able to achieve political successes under some circumstances. At the federal government level, green energy policies since 2008 have become increasingly associated with the Democratic Party and increasingly opposed by conservative Republicans.

6. The politics and economics of the green energy transition have also become embedded in reform movements among the small-business sector that have combined calls for local ownership and import substitution as strategies for local economic development and job creation. They offer an alternative pathway in the policy fields of green industrial development by drawing attention to the role of small companies in the retail, services, and food industries and by focusing on import-substituting industrialization. Some policy reforms facilitate shifts to increased local ownership, such as in policies that lead to enhanced distributed generation, community ownership, and public power.

In summary, green industrial policies are an important site for the renegotiation of the shifting position of the United States in the global economy and the underlying political ideologies that guide the thinking and policy that negotiate the change. On the one hand, trade complaints, tariffs, "buy American" rules, in-state procurement preferences, continued energy independence rhetoric, and public opinion polls about free trade suggest growing protectionist sentiment. Even if most of the protectionist sentiment is articulated within the framework of World Trade Organization rules, it results in skepticism toward increased trade liberalization, and there is potential for trade conflicts to escalate into a fundamental restructuring of the global trade regime. On the other hand, the ability for some American firms to stay at the peak of green-tech innovation (e.g., smart-grid technologies, biotechnology-based biofuels, and fuel cells) suggests the ongoing value of an export-oriented industrial economy for some industries. The global intellectual property regime supports those companies and allows them to sell the new products on global markets for healthy profits. The philosophical polarities that marked the political landscape during the era of American hegemony—redistributive policies versus cuts in welfare programs, an interventionist philosophy of government versus a more laissez-faire attitude—do not disappear, but they are transected by the developmentalist politics of job creation, business development, and trade defensiveness.

The Green Energy Transition and Global Economic Change

Having achieved the pinnacle of the global economy after World War II and become the world's strongest advocate of trade liberalization, the United States in the twenty-first century finds itself in a position of relative decline with respect to emerging industrial countries such as China. A significant risk for the United States is that it could continue to lose manufacturing industries, including high-tech green energy manufacturing. During the early phases of the liberalization of the global economy, the loss of the lower-end, labor-intensive manufacturing to other countries did not present an economic threat to the innovation economy. However, the loss of manufacturing companies in electronics, materials, metals, capital goods, and other industries that are part of the supply chain of high-tech manufactured products could lead to a collapse of the benefits of place. When manufacturing leaves, the designers and engineers follow, and behind them the world-class researchers may leave as well. Without a fully integrated system of innovation that includes at least some manufacturing, a regional innovation cluster is likely to suffer over the long term. The policy strategy that Ha-Joon Chang referred to as "kicking away the ladder" (that is, using protectionist policies until the economy achieves a leading position in the world system, then trying to force trade liberalization on other countries in order to open their markets to exports from the leading country) is no longer as effective today as it was during the years after World War II, when the United States was the world's creditor and its leading manufacturer. The export capacities of other countries have shifted up the value chain into high-tech manufacturing and even into research and development.[1]

Because of growing competitive pressure in technology and manufacturing, the country is forced to develop an industrial policy that identifies some American industries as necessary for the country's economic health and self-preservation. Support for green energy technology is one example of an invigorated industrial policy that the country has pursued, but the policy must undergo continual adjustments to keep up with the vigorous support that other countries are giving to their green-tech industries. Thus, the developmentalist policies of other countries, especially newly industrializing countries such as China, provide a spur to the United States to adopt similar policies. Even when the federal government doesn't adopt the policies, state and local governments often fill in the gap.

The confluence of two major historical changes in the twenty-first century—the green energy transition and the relative decline of the US economy with respect to the global economy—created three major dynamic processes that result in an interaction between changes in the domestic energy regime and global political economy: green job creation and political support for the green transition, the decline of the dollar as reserve currency and the value of domestic energy sources, and the decline of the dollar and the capacity for and direction of investment in green energy technology.

In the first dynamic process, the liberalization of the global economy has created anxiety about jobs among those who are not part of the export or tradable sector. The anxiety translates into support for job-creation and business-development policies, which green transition coalitions then translate into support for green energy policies. When successful, the coalitions create more green jobs that in turn increase the political strength of the coalitions, which in turn have a stronger basis for successful policy reform. Growth of coalitions is not only in the number of people who identify themselves as having a green job and benefiting from green transition policies but also in the breadth of organizations and jobs that are included. At some point the growing pro-green constituencies will reach a tipping point in which their lobbying expenditures and their voter-mobilization capacity exceed that of the coalition of fossil fuel industries and conservatives. As was noted in the case studies I have described in this book, there is some evidence that a tipping point may have been reached in some states. Generally, those states have relatively weak fossil fuel industries and strong green energy industries and tend to have Democrats in control of the state legislature and governor's office.[2]

Although the creation of green jobs is itself a political event in the specific policy fields associated with green energy, it also has general implications. Because of the close relationship between green jobs and the Democratic Party, the growth of green jobs is likely to increase the number of Democratic Party voters. Furthermore, because green jobs (other than manufacturing) tend to be service jobs that are difficult to outsource, and because the labor unions have taken up the banner of "good" green jobs, there is some potential for the creation of green jobs to be associated with growth of unionized labor. In other words, the greening of the economy has political implications for the long-term balance of power between political parties, and it could even be associated with a reinvigoration of the unionized political left. If one assumes that the cost of creating a green job is $50,000 and that a trillion-dollar investment over a decade or two would create 20 million jobs, then one can see the reasons why Republicans might fear the greening of the economy as potentially leading to long-term political realignment. Thus, there is a dynamic process between the creation of green jobs and the balance of power in the political field in support of green energy policies.

The second dynamic process involves the fate of the dollar as the world's reserve currency and the choices of energy sources. Although the dollar is no longer backed by gold, sales of much of the world's oil are cleared in dollars, and the United States has jealously guarded the privilege. For example, Saddam Hussein tried to sell Iraqi oil in euros, but after Americans invaded the country, the sale of oil was returned to dollars. Notwithstanding American opposition to the erosion of the dollar-oil regime, there is a general trend for the sale of oil and other commodities to shift away from dollars. Both Venezuela and Iran have shifted away from dollars, and Russia sells oil to China through a currency swap that doesn't clear in dollars. China has also set up bilateral contracts with other countries, including the oil exporter Angola, and more generally it has pursued bilateral contracts for commodities throughout the world. In 2011 the president of China, Hu Jintao, said that the global currency system with the dollar as the world's reserve currency was a "product of the past" (Browne 2011).[3]

The bilateral currency swap for fossil fuels is one mechanism by which the political economy of energy affects the need for the dollar as the reserve currency, but another mechanism is the effect of the green transition itself on the demand for dollars. Globally, the greening of transportation fleets and other means of reducing petroleum consumption will enable some countries to reduce their dependency on foreign petroleum. Although the change is more long-term than the effects of currency swaps, it will also contribute to declining demand for the dollar due to the lower need for reserves related to energy purchases.

To the extent that the decline of the dollar as the reserve currency is associated with the decline in its value, the price of oil in the United States will increase, a change that will favor domestic energy broadly. As the price of imported energy goes up, the profitability of domestic renewable energy and domestic fossil fuels will increase. The decline of the dollar as the reserve currency creates opportunities for domestic energy, which in turn could lead to increased production of domestic renewable energy.

However, the relationship between the decline of the dollar and domestic renewable energy is historically contingent. Political coalitions are currently attempting to tilt the increasing relative value of domestic energy toward fossil fuels. Furthermore, as the dollar declines in value, American fossil fuels such as coal will become less expensive to other countries. China is already importing some coal from the United States, and were the renminbi to increase dramatically with respect to the dollar or even become the new global reserve currency, the United States probably would be tempted to export more coal to China in order to gain valuable foreign reserves. Natural gas from the hydraulic fracturing technologies could also be liquefied and exported, and American biofuels might also be exported as well. In 2011 the United States also became a net exporter of petroleum products, even though it remained dependent on foreign crude oil. Even if the United States winds down its use of domestic fossil fuels, foreign demand will cause ongoing environmental conflicts within the United States with respect to mountaintop removal, natural gas and oil extraction, and food versus biofuels. To the extent that coal, natural gas, and biofuels become export industries, the debates about their future will be recast in light of the country's needs for export earnings. The need for export earnings to improve the trade balance could increase when the demand for treasuries declines, thereby setting up economic motivations for the country to become an exporter of fossil fuels even as it undergoes greening of its own energy infrastructure.[4]

The third dynamic process involves the effect of the downward pressure on the dollar and declining appetite for treasuries on the finances of the US government and the country's capacity and motivation to deepen the green transition. To maintain the global appetite for treasuries, the US government probably will have to curtail government spending, and the focus on deficit reduction will reduce the availability of resources for investment in green business development. Opposition to green industrial policy on economic grounds is already evident. However, the effects of government austerity on employment and the general concern with fiscal austerity will also have effects on the form that the green energy transition takes in the United States. Not only is the Republican Party's distaste for types of green policy that look like financial burdens on businesses and taxpayers a harbinger of future green politics, but it also suggests the ways in which the green transition will move forward. Austerity pressures will focus attention on the economic benefits of green energy policies, and issues such as speed of return on investment will favor energy-efficiency policies. This doesn't mean that renewable energy will be forgotten; rather, the tilt within green energy transition policies will increasingly favor conservation and energy-efficiency measures with short-term returns on investment.[5]

To the extent that an austerity mentality shapes the green jobs frame and that green energy policies tilt toward energy-efficiency programs, new programs will likely emerge as compromise measures between developmentalist and social liberal goals. In other words, energy-efficiency policies will be set up to encourage integration from demand interventions to industrial manufacturing (such as for energy-efficient appliances, vehicles, and building materials that are manufactured domestically). But the developmentalist side of the policies will likely also be coupled with support for demand programs geared toward the needs of low-income households. The coupling will help to maintain broad political support from a wide range of green transition constituencies. In turn, those programs will contribute to the first dynamic process by enrolling people in the green transition because of the employment or energy benefits that they see from the policies.

In summary, some feedback loops from the declining relative economic position of the United States will serve potentially as spurs to the green energy transition (such as the potential increases in the cost of imported fossil fuels relative to domestic fuels), but other feedback loops (such as austerity measures and higher interest rates that will be needed to maintain currency stability as the dollar erodes) will reduce the capital available for speeding up the transition and channel the green transition toward energy-efficiency programs. The green energy transition will deepen and develop, but it will likely advance at a very slow pace in comparison with what is needed from a global ecosystems perspective to stabilize the global climate and other aspects of environmental degradation. It seems unlikely that the United States will generate the policy reforms needed to shift away rapidly from dependence on coal and natural gas. Safe and effective carbon sequestration may lead to dramatic reductions in carbon emissions, but it would not solve the ecosystem destruction and contamination that is occurring in extraction. A next-generation solar energy technology that is well below the cost of fossil fuels is arguably the only solution that would make it possible for countries to avoid the temptation of using cheap fossil fuels. A rapid transition to that technology would require an order of magnitude of investment much greater than the levels currently provided by the US government, but an increase in the investment in disruptive green technologies is becoming difficult due to the declining position of the United States in the global economy and the mobilization of anti-green constituencies. The slow growth of the green constituencies may not occur rapidly enough to counteract the austerity conditions that are likely to prevail as the US economy undergoes further relative decline.

Sustainability and Resilience

The web of feedback relationships between the green energy transition and global economic changes may seem complex enough, but a complete analysis in the tradition of ecological economics and environmental sociology would also require connecting those changes with the changing relations between human and natural systems. The task is particularly difficult because the level of unknowns is so high. One can assume generally that there will be increasing ecosystem instability or even collapse because of the slow pace of the green transition, not only in the United States but in many other countries. Some types of collapse will be driven by weather instability, and other types will be the result of the collapse of crucial food and water resources due to population and land-use factors as much as to climate change. Here the multi-level analysis of transition theory must be modified to disaggregate the relationship within the landscape between macrosocial structures and ecosystems. As climate change and other forms of environmental destruction proceed, governments will be forced to spend limited resources on emergency responses to disasters caused by floods, droughts, blizzards, and food shortages. Societies are then forced into a second, long-term transition: an adaptation transition.

Whereas the green transition has been focused on energy and on climate-change mitigation, the adaptation transition will be focused on water and disaster responses. Whereas the sustainability of sociotechnical systems is the primary point of reference for the green transition, the resilience of those systems becomes the main focus of the adaptation transition. Although the relationship between the sustainability and adaptation transitions is not necessarily zero-sum, it will emerge in some cases as a choice between types of investments in society-ecosystem relationships. As resilience issues become more salient, developmentalist politics and policies will become permeated by questions that explore the responsiveness of regional economies to environmental and economic perturbations.[6]

When I attended a conference on sustainable cities that involved mayors in the Hudson Valley region of New York, the leading concern was neither the greening of energy nor the reduction of a town's carbon footprint but the management of water in the event of droughts and floods. Although the mayors recognized the connection between carbon emissions and water management issues, they were concerned with the more pressing challenge of adaptation to climate change. Given such concerns, resilient technologies such as improved storm sewerage systems, rain gardens, porous pavement, rooftop gardens, swales, rechanneled creeks, cisterns, and rain barrels may take priority over programs that support rooftop solar or building insulation. To address concerns such as those of the mayors, green transition policies will increasingly have to be formulated in ways that go beyond carbon reduction and pollution abatement to include resilience in the face of natural disasters. To some degree the resilience goals of water- and infrastructure-management programs and the sustainability goals of green transition programs have a zero-sum relationship, and it is important to recognize the potential conflicts between resilience and sustainability as two competing policy goals. For example, consider the tradeoffs in four areas:

1. Electricity generation and storage. A sustainability perspective would focus on the least carbon-intensive source of electricity generation, such as renewable energy, and on the most efficient manner of storing energy, such as through smart-grid technologies and grid-based storage. In contrast, a resilience perspective would seek a broad mixture of electricity generation sources (under the assumption that system diversity increases resilience) and multiple forms of energy storage, including hydrogen tanks and batteries located in buildings. Although pumped water is an inefficient way to store energy from intermittent sources such as solar photovoltaics or wind turbines, it may have "dual use" advantages for water control in times of flooding and droughts.

2. Transportation. A sustainability perspective would seek ways to reduce the use of carbon-based transportation (through fuel efficiency, electric vehicles, public transportation, or human-powered transportation), whereas a resilience perspective would seek multiple sources of energy and types of vehicles. As in the case of electricity generation, resilience considerations could seek to have a percentage of the transportation system in fossil fuels as a way to increase system diversity. As a result, there is a point where alignments between sustainability and resilience perspectives could break down. At the minimum, a resilience perspective would suggest the value of distributed solar energy for charging vehicles and advantages of fleets that used a mixture of batteries, biofuels, and hydrogen to power vehicles.

3. Buildings and energy generation. A sustainability perspective would seek ways to increase the energy efficiency of buildings and to decrease overall energy consumption (through smaller buildings, compact design, and so on). A resilience perspective would seek to increase the diversity of energy supply sources and diverse ways of storing energy. Having a mixture of energy produced on-site and from the grid increases resilience, just as having on-site storage (such as battery packs) provides resilience in the event of grid failure. Ideally a building could shift between being completely on grid or completely off grid depending on the availability of energy sources. Likewise, building energy systems that are separate

(one for heating, electricity, and hot water) are more resilient than having one interconnected but efficient system.

4. Food. Whereas a sustainability perspective would seek ways to decrease the toxicity of the food (through organic production methods) and its carbon content (through increased localization, ceteris paribus, and the reduction of meat in the diet), a resilience perspective would seek diversity in food sources and types. Resilience considerations could run into conflict with sustainability goals at high levels of localization, because a highly localized food economy could reduce adaptability in the event of a regional disaster. Apart from the controversy over food miles, carbon, and transportation for food, a resilience perspective might seek an optimal mixture of local and nonlocal food sources. Likewise, including meat in the diet would increase the diversity of the food supply and might potentially increase resilience. More generally, the capacity to shift among local and nonlocal food sources would increase resilience.

As the examples suggest, the greatest zone of potential conflict between resilience and sustainability goals is with green technologies that are highly efficient but brittle, for example, an off-grid house powered entirely by solar energy. However, sustainability and resilience considerations can be made compatible. The greatest opportunity for compatibility is with the reduction of consumption, because reduction eliminates the need for resources in the event of a challenge to system resilience. Likewise, systems that facilitate rapid shifts across energy sources and different sites of energy storage can increase resilience while also increasing the levels of energy efficiency, conservation, and low-carbon energy sources.

In summary, it is possible that the growing recognition that more resources will be required to adapt infrastructure may reduce the political will for deepening the green transition, but it is possible to find points of convergence between the two goals of adaptation and mitigation. Thus, there are opportunities for a broadening of green coalitions to include groups that are concerned with adaptation and disasters, but there are also dangers that can come with a lifeboat mentality that avoids policies oriented toward a long-term green transition and instead focuses on short-term protective measures. Finding a balance between the opportunities and dangers will require careful thinking about how to design sociotechnical systems that meet both sets of goals.

The return of the economy-versus-environment tradeoff in the form of resilience-versus-sustainability politics may provide a resource for anti-green policy makers to mobilize adaptation concerns to weaken the case for green transition policies. I have argued that the "green jobs" frame served as an alternative to the "jobs versus environment" frame that anti-green constituencies had used. Although the latter has not disappeared, increasingly the anti-green constituencies have utilized a frame of government deficits and fiscal crisis to claim that green policies are too expensive. However, a third alternative for anti-green constituencies is the related idea that precious government funds should be invested first in adaptation and disaster response. Thus, even if green developmentalism were to triumph and gradually displace neoliberal ideology with a focus on job creation, trade pragmatism, and industrial policy, new frames for continued opposition are in formation. Field analysis for the study of transitions provides the tools to perceive an ongoing swirl of change rather than a succession of technological and ideological regimes. The changes in the underlying ideologies of the political field immediately generate an opposing position in addition to the legacy positions of social liberalism and neoliberalism. The lifeboat mentality of the emergent politics of resilience and adaptation promises to provide a new countervailing force to green transition coalitions in the policy fields where they mobilize for change. Just as the "green jobs" frame helped to supersede the old "environment versus economy" divide, so a new frame of resilient, sustainable design will be needed to overcome this emerging challenge.

The Green Energy Transition and Political Ideology

Although the outcomes of the battles between advocates and opponents of green energy transition policies cannot be predicted, the coalitions are participating in the construction of a form of liberalism in American politics that is increasingly at odds with the ideologies of social liberalism and neoliberalism that dominate the mainstream of American politics. Central to the post-World War II doxa of social liberalism and neoliberalism was the belief in deepening trade liberalization, but for the United States free-trade ideology was adapted to a particular historical period that has drawn to a close. Free-trade ideology was suited to a country that was the world's leading creditor and manufacturer, but as other countries have become creditors and manufacturers the ideology no longer matches the country's relative decline (or their relative rise) in the global economy.

Hourly and salaried workers who have seen companies closed and jobs outsourced have personal experience with the effects of free trade. Although organized labor has long voiced opposition to free trade without fair trade (that is, by arguing that trading partners should have fair wages and strong labor standards), in the twenty-first century chronic unemployment and underemployment have created general dissatisfaction with continued trade liberalization. As the opinion polls suggest, the dissatisfaction spans the political spectrum, from unions on the left to the Tea Party movement on the right. They watch with chagrin as their country's leaders do nothing to stop the hemorrhaging of good jobs, especially manufacturing jobs, to foreign countries. Their approach leads to a defensive or protectionist form of developmentalism.[7]

However, for the underlying structure of relationships among political ideologies in a political field to undergo a change, the elites who dominate the political and economic fields must also be convinced that it is in their interest to shift their way of thinking. The smaller, domestically based manufacturers in the United States have voiced protectionist sentiment, but business elites associated with large multinational corporations tend to think more in terms of competitiveness and innovation than protectionism. For the globally oriented elites, the goal is to avoid a collapse of the liberalized global economy into autonomous trading zones and instead to find ways to make American businesses as competitive as possible by focusing on high-technology goods, investment, and services. From this perspective, the country needs higher levels of investment in its innovation systems and education. When those investments are focused on specific industries, either for reasons of strategic importance or budgetary constraints, the outcome is an invigorated industrial policy and the enforcement of trade violations rather than the type of protectionism found in "buy American" programs. This approach leads to a liberal (in the sense of support for free trade) approach to developmentalism.

From either the defensive perspective or the competitiveness perspective, the changing position of the United States in the global economy shows cracks in the neoliberal ideology that has been so prominent in the country since the 1980s. From the protectionist position, the goal is to include more industries behind a wall of trade protection. Examples of protected industries are manufacturing industries that are crucial to defense (electronics, vehicles, weapons) and the underlying supply-chain manufacturers (including vehicle and parts manufacturers), but, as I have shown, domestic renewable energy and related green energy manufacturing have also become candidates for protection. From the competitiveness perspective, the goal is to identify potential new industries with which the United States may be able to compete globally, and clean tech has become a part of the list in many regions of the country. This approach requires higher government investment in the private sector in the form of an industrial policy, but even when combined with support for existing trade agreements, the horse-betting of industrial policy is anathema to a neoliberal's insistence on market-based selection of industrial success.

To the extent that one accepts the argument that the changing position of the United States in the global economy is leading to an underlying ideological shift in the pattern of its politics, one doesn't have to agree that the shift will be toward developmentalism. Conservatives may argue that the decline of the United States in the global economy will require an even deeper commitment to neoliberalism by sanctioning additional trade liberalization, privatization of government services, austerity programs, and devaluation of the currency that will re-power exports. Their proposed list of reforms would coincide with the absence of industrial policy, and instead policy decisions over the future direction of the economy would be left up to the wisdom of markets. In contrast, progressives hope that the demise of neoliberalism might lead to a reinvigorated social liberalism that was the hallmark of the New Deal and the Great Society. The growing gap between rich and poor, or workers in the tradable and nontradable sectors, within the United States will eventually provoke a revolt against the rich, and a new era of redistributive populism will be born.

My view is that neither the future path of deepened neoliberalism nor a return to social liberalism seems likely. With respect to neoliberalism, when confronted with aggressive developmentalist policies from trading partners, especially China, deference to the wisdom of markets amounts to unilateral disarmament in trade and industrial policy. The long-term result could be a transition of the global division of labor in which the export industries of the United States are increasingly dominated by natural-resource extraction and agriculture. The United States would suffer a fate like that of Argentina during the twentieth century, and it would lack an industrial base for military defense. Likewise, the wistful return to the happy days of the redistributive politics of social liberalism is in conflict with an era of austerity caused by declining ecosystem resources, growing global demand for commodities, rising competition from trading partners, and dimming prospects for the dollar's status as the leading reserve currency. In an era of austerity, the focus will be less on entitlements than on job creation and less on regulating businesses than on keeping them alive.

The underlying politics in the United States of the twenty-first century are likely to be different from the polarities of social liberalism and neoliberalism that characterized much of the twentieth century. Instead, a pragmatic developmentalism will target some industries and jobs for support, and it will work to widen the zone of protected domestic industries by adopting a more defensive approach to trade relations. If I am correct about the shift among mainstream ideologies toward developmentalism, the United States may also move away from the internationalist aspirations of the World War II era and the Cold War era, in which the country portrayed itself as the world's leader on a path to a global future based on political freedom, market-based economies, and trade liberalization in opposition to the alternatives of fascism, communism, and nationalism. Instead, the US in the twenty-first century will be less like the outward-oriented country of the twentieth century and more like the inward-looking, import-substituting country of the nineteenth century. A more inward-looking US may not be a bad development for the rest of the world, particularly if the country can find the cost-effective alternative technology that allows it to avoid the temptation of removing more fossil fuels from the ground and the global military presence that dependence on oil requires. In a multi-polar global economic and political system, the US could become a more constructive agent in world politics.

It should be clear that I am offering a prediction of what appears to be a likely course of action, not a prescription for what would be a good course of action. The co-constitution of the green energy transition and a political ideology of developmentalism implies a continued and deepening separation of green energy policy from the green progressive political tradition, which would have linked the transition of sociotechnical systems to opportunities to shift more energy ownership to communities, households, and small businesses and might have made possible a rapid transition to renewable-energy technologies supported by a strong carbon tax, other demand policies, and substantial government investment. It is possible that the twenty-first century will surprise us by yielding such profound systemic crises that a deep form of the green transition emerges, that is, in which economic and political institutions are profoundly modified to make possible a more socially just, democratically functional, and technologically green society than we have today. But the potential for linking the green energy transition to what some have called a great transition is, in my view, highly unlikely, and perhaps even less likely today than it was in the 1970s, when such visions were first articulated.[8]

On the basis of current trends, it seems much more likely that the politics of the green transition, at least in the United States, will be focused on job creation and business development rather than on broader distributive issues and an imaginative rethinking of the built environment. This green transition will not be great and deep green; instead it will be incremental and light green—that is, it will be modest and slow, so much so that many of the worst effects of climate change, ecosystem destruction, and pervasive toxics in the biosphere will not be averted. The feedback loops from ecosystem change will entail a second, forced, adaptation transition that will recolor the green transition with the politics of resilience. Although there are glimmers of hope in some of the green transition policies of American cities and states, as well as in the green policies of some governments throughout the world, the achievements to date are far too modest to allow us to ponder the world that we are leaving our grandchildren without a sense of shame and failure.

Appendix: State Government Votes for Green Energy Laws

David Hess and Jonathan Coley

We reviewed legislative votes in a selection of states for which it was possible to compile the information and for which there were multiple, significant laws passed between 2007 and 2011. The tables describe the date that the bill was signed into law. The header "% Repub" is the number of Republicans voting "yes" for the bill divided by number of Republicans voting overall multiplied by 100; "% Dem" is the number of Democrats voting "yes" divided by number of Democrats voting overall multiplied by 100; and Dem/Total is the number of Democrats total divided by total number of senators from both parties (or, in the House votes, representatives from both parties). The Dem/Total column shows which party controls the legislative body.

Table A.1 shows legislative votes for new or expanded renewable portfolio standards in all states for which data were available from 2007 to 2011. The tables that follow show a range of laws in selected states. Our preliminary survey included four western states (California, Colorado, Oregon, and Washington), three northeastern states (Connecticut, Maryland, and New York), two midwestern states (Iowa, Michigan, Ohio), and three southern states (Florida, North Carolina, Texas). Only states with the highest legislative activity (California, Colorado, Maryland, Oregon, and Washington) are presented here. States that didn't have a record of individual votes by party were Hawaii, Indiana, Kentucky, Massachusetts, and Minnesota.

PACE stands for property-assessed clean energy, RPS for renewable portfolio standard, and RFS for renewable fuels standard. For the five states presented here, we reviewed major laws signed from 2007 through 2011. California's AB 32, which was signed in 2006, is the sole exception, because the law is so important and is discussed in the book.

These tables were assembled by Jonathan Coley under David Hess's supervision.

Table A.1
Votes on renewable portfolio standards.

State	Law	Description	Date signed by governor	Senate or House	% Repub	% Dem	Dem / Total
CA	SB X1–2	Expand RPS	2011	Senate	25%	92%	0.63
				House	18%	98%	0.67
CO	HB 1281	Expand RPS	2007	Senate	43%	100%	0.6
				House	76%	100%	0.68
	HB 1001	Expand RPS	2010	Senate	0%	100%	0.6
				House	0%	97%	0.55
CT	HB 7432	Expand RPS	2007	Senate	80%	96%	0.72
				House	82%	100%	0.71
	SB 1243	Expand RPS	2011	Senate	100%	100%	0.67
				House	87%	100%	0.61
FL	HB 7135	New RPS	2008	Senate	100%	100%	0.35
				House	100%	100%	0.36
KS	HB2369	New RPS	2009	Senate	96.67%	87.5%	0.23
				House	98.7%	61.36%	0.37
MD	HB 375	Expand RPS	2008	Senate	8%	97%	0.70
				House	31%	98%	0.73
MI	PA 295	New RPS	2008	Senate	47.37%	100%	0.45
				House	52%	100%	0.53
MN	SF 4	New RPS	2007	Senate	90.91%	97.73%	0.67
				House	79.17%	100%	0.64
MO	SB 795	Expand RPS	2010	Senate	78.26%	81.82%	0.32
				House	100%	100%	0.45

Table A.1
(continued)

State	Law	Description	Date signed by governor	Senate or House	% Repub	% Dem	Dem / Total
NH	HB 873	New RPS	2007	Senate	100%	100%	0.58
				House	N/A	N/A	N/A
NC	SB 3	New RPS	2007	Senate	100%	97%	0.62
				House	90%	94%	0.57
OH	SB 221	New RPS	2008	Senate	100%	100%	0.38
				House	98%	100%	0.47
OR	SB 838	Expand RPS	2007	Senate	33%	100%	0.63
				House	41%	97%	0.5
PA	HB 2200	Expand RPS	2008	Senate	90%	100%	0.42
				House	96%	100%	0.50
VT	SB 209	Expand RPS	2008	Senate	57%	100%	0.77
				House	98%	100%	0.62
WV	24-2F-1	New RPS	2009	Senate	N/A	N/A	N/A
				House	30%	97%	0.72

The 2008 Florida legislation is classified as a new RPS, although there was previous legislative authorization in 2006 (Section 366.92, F.S.) and an executive order by Governor Crist in 2007 (07-127). In 2009 the rules did not win approval in the Florida House of Representatives, so the state remained without an RPS. The split Pennsylvania House is classified as Republican because the Speaker was Republican.

Table A.2
California votes for significant green energy legislation by party.

Law	Law Description	Date signed by governor	Senate or House	% Repub	% Dem	Dem / Total
Global Warming Solutions Act (AB 32)	Establishes timetable for carbon regulation	9/26/2006	Senate	0%	100%	0.63
			House	3%	96%	0.61
AB 1109	Lighting and appliance standards; phase out incandescent bulbs	10/12/2007	Senate	7%	92%	0.63
			House	10%	100%	0.59
AB 532	Solar for state buildings	10/13/2007	Senate	15%	100%	0.63
			House	6%	100%	0.6
SB 1036	Allows utilities to use SBCs for above-market prices	10/14/2007	Senate	100%	100%	0.6
			House	38%	100%	0.59
AB 811	PACE	7/21/2008	Senate	72%	95%	0.63
			House	48%	100%	0.6
Green Collar Jobs Act (AB 3018)	Training and workforce development	9/26/2008	Senate	7%	100%	0.63
			House	28%	100%	0.61
AB 920	Corrects solar market irregularities	11/11/2009	Senate	0%	88%	0.63
			House	21%	98%	0.65
SB 32	Adjusts feed-in tariffs	11/11/2009	Senate	100%	100%	0.63
			House	41%	100%	0.65
SB 77	PACE	4/21/2010	Senate	100%	100%	0.64
			House	57%	100%	0.65
SB X1–2	RPS increase	4/12/2011	Senate	25%	92%	0.63
			House	18%	98%	0.67
AB X1–15	Exemption on solar leases	6/28/2011	Senate	100%	100%	0.63
			House	100%	100%	0.66

Table A.3
Colorado votes for significant green energy legislation by party.

Law	Description	Date signed by governor	Senate or House	% Repub	% Dem	Dem / Total
Renewable Energy Act (HB 1281)	RPS increase	3/27/2007	Senate	43%	100%	0.6
			House	76%	100%	0.68
SB 51	Green standards for state buildings	4/16/2007	Senate	92%	100%	0.6
			House	95%	98%	0.68
HB 1150	Clean Energy Dev. Authority	5/23/2007	Senate	93%	100%	0.6
			House	100%	100%	0.68
HB 1228	Renewable fuels standard	6/1/2007	Senate	77%	100%	0.6
			House	95%	100%	0.68
HB 1160	Net metering expansion	3/26/2008	Senate	77%	100%	0.63
			House	95%	100%	0.66
HB 1350	PACE and bond authority	5/27/2008	Senate	N/A	N/A	N/A
			House	95%	100%	0.69
HB 1001	RPS increase	3/22/2010	Senate	0%	100%	0.6
			House	0%	97%	0.55
Clean Air, Clean Jobs Act (HB 1365)	Coverts coal to natural gas in three power plants	4/19/2010	Senate	23%	85%	0.6
			House	65%	95%	0.59
HB 1342	Creation of community solar gardens	6/5/2010	Senate	7%	100%	0.6
			House	72%	100%	0.58
New Energy Jobs Creation Act (HB 1328)	PACE	6/11/2010	Senate	7%	100%	0.6
			House	0%	97%	0.59
HB 1083	Expanding hydro-electricity	3/29/2011	Senate	100%	100%	0.6
			House	100%	100%	0.48
Fair Permit Act (HB 1199)	Reduces costs for solar permits	6/10/2011	Senate	93%	95%	0.6
			House	100%	97%	0.48

Table A.4
Maryland votes for significant green energy legislation by party.

Law	Description	Date signed by governor	Senate or House	% Repub	% Dem	Dem / Total
Maryland Clean Cars Act (SB 103)	Low emission vehicles	4/24/2007	Senate	36%	100%	0.70
			House	63%	97%	0.73
SB 595	Net metering expansion	4/24/2007	Senate	29%	76%	0.70
			House	84%	100%	0.73
SB 268	Plan to invest RGGI funds	4/24/2008	Senate	100%	100%	0.70
			House	100%	100%	0.73
SB 208	Green standards for state buildings	4/24/2008	Senate	64%	100%	0.70
			House	84%	100%	0.73
HB 375	RPS increase	4/24/2008	Senate	8%	97%	0.70
			House	31%	98%	0.73
SB 309	Establishes timetable for carbon regulation	2008 (No vote in House—was not signed by governor)	Senate	0%	94%	0.70
HB 374	15% reduction in per capita electricity consumption	4/24/2008	Senate	8%	97%	0.70
			House	19%	96%	0.73
SB 277	Solar carve-out increase	5/20/2010	Senate	0%	94%	0.70
			House	27%	96%	0.73

Table A.5
Oregon votes for significant green energy legislation by party.

Law	Description	Date signed by governor	Senate or House	% Repub	% Dem	Dem / Total
Oregon Renewable Energy Act (SB 838)	RPS increase	6/6/2007	Senate	33%	100%	0.63
			House	41%	97%	0.5
HB 3543	Establishes timetable for carbon regulation	8/7/2007	Senate	30%	5%	0.63
			House	38%	100%	0.5
Energy Efficiency and Su-stainable Technologies Act (HB 2626)	Financing for energy efficiency and renewable-energy projects	7/22/2009	Senate	75%	100%	0.6
			House	100%	100%	0.6
HB 3039	Solar feed-in tariff	7/22/2009	Senate	75%	50%	0.6
			House	50%	80%	0.6
HB 3300	Green jobs plan and training	8/4/2009	Senate	30%	100%	0.6
			House	33%	100%	0.6

For HB 3039, the relatively low vote by Democrats in the Senate reflected a campaign to stop the law in favor of stronger legislation.

Table A.6
Washington (State) Votes by Party for Significant Green Energy.

Law	Description	Date signed by governor	Senate or House	% Repub	% Dem	Dem / Total
SB 6001	CO$_2$ Limits on Electricity Generation	5/3/2007 (partially vetoed)	Senate	38%	100%	0.67
			House	62%	100%	0.62
HB 1303	Greening public fleets – 100% by 2015	5/7/2007 (partially vetoed)	Senate	73%	100%	0.67
			House	49%	100%	0.62
Climate Action and Green Jobs Law (HB 2815)	Job training and greenhouse gas reduction	3/13/2008	Senate	0%	94%	0.65
			House	27%	93%	0.61
HB 5921	Creation of Clean Energy Leadership Initiative	5/4/2009	Senate	23%	100%	0.63
			House	18%	97%	0.61
HB 5854	Energy efficiency for homes, buildings	5/8/2009	Senate	0%	96%	0.63
			House	24%	98%	0.61
HB 5769	Closing coal-burning plant	4/29/2011	Senate	33%	100%	0.55
			House	78%	100%	0.59

The partial vetoes were for relatively technical reasons such as redundancy rather than more controversial reasons.

Notes

Introduction

1. The description is based on my notes from the 2009 meeting.

2. The fact that China subsequently faced some problems with its high-speed trains could strengthen the unions' argument that construction work requires well-qualified labor.

3. There was some improvement in the number of manufacturing jobs beginning in 2010. That improvement was due in part to some recovery in the automotive industry.

4. On industrial policy, see Cohen 2006; Nester 1998; Rodrik 2004, 2009, 2011. My analysis also builds on work by Block (2008), who argues that partisan politics lead to the "hidden developmental state." I include trade and state-level industrial policy, which tend to be less hidden.

5. For the approach to politics as a contentious field characterized by dominant and subordinate positions, see Bourdieu 2005.

6. Two influential approaches to the study of neoliberalism are those of Foucault and Harvey. Foucault (2010) emphasizes cultural dimensions such as entrepreneurialism and marketization; Harvey (2005) emphasizes class conflict. For an introduction to neoliberal ideology and environmental policy, see Driesen 2010.

7. Chang 2011.

8. On the tradable and nontradable sectors, see Spence and Hlatshwayo 2011. On the stagnation of income for working people, see Labor Research Organization 2004; US Bureau of Labor Statistics 2009.

9. Bernstein and Shapiro 2006; Federal Reserve 2010; Foster and Magdoff 2009; Labor Research Organization 2004; Mooney 2008; US Census Bureau 2007; US Bureau of Labor Statistics 2009.

10. On the poll, see Harwood 2010. On the comparison of Canada and China, see Pew Research Center for the People and the Press 2010.

11. I thank Keith Pezzoli for encouraging me to emphasize this distinction between short-term and long-term transitions.

12. Heckscher 1935; Ekelund and Tollison 1997; Furtado 1968.

13. Chang 2008.

14. Chang 2008, 2011; Chernow 2004; Hamilton 1913; Nester 1998, Smith 1904.

15. Jefferson 1787, 1793, 1816; Hudson 1975; Randall 1993; Thornton and Ekelund 2004. Jefferson's views changed after the War of 1812 and became closer to those of Hamilton, but the extent of subsequent import restrictions incensed other Southern leaders. On the profession of economics, see Hudson 2005.

16. Chang 2008; Hudson 2005.

17. Chang 2008; Portes 1994; Portes and Roberts 2005.

18. Hughes 1987.

19. Ibid.

20. On energy transitions, see Podobnik 2006 and Smil 2010.

21. See Geels 2002, 2005, 2007, 2011; Kemp et al. 1998; Rotmans et al. 2001; Van der Brugge et al. 2005. On evolutionary theory and technological regimes, see Nelson and Winter 1982, the critique developed by Rip and Kemp (1998), and the review and extension by Smith et al. (2010).

22. On the transitions and Dutch policy, see Kemp and Rotmans 2009. On the political sociology of science and technology, see Frickel and Moore 2005.

23. Smith and Raven 2010. See also Verbong and Geels 2006, 2010.

24. On different types of regime change for electricity, see Verbong and Geels 2006, 2010.

25. Kemp and van Lente 2011; Brown et al. 2011; Hielscher et al. 2011. For an additional perspective on power and transition studies, see Flor and Rotmans 2009.

26. Jørgensen 2012; Jørgensen and Sorensen 1999.

27. Bourdieu 2001. On a subsequent development of field sociology that uses social movement theory to account for change, see Fligstein and McAdam 2011. The approach taken here is part of a broader perspective in the sociology of technology known as the new political sociology of science and technology. See Frickel and Moore 2005; Moore et al. 2011; Kinchy et al. 2008.

28. The study of the long-term, underlying shifts in ideology has parallels with the work of Foucault on underlying shifts in epistemes and regimes (e.g., Foucault 1970, 2010) and to a lesser degree with the tradition in American cultural anthropology of the study of cultural systems (e.g., Geertz 1973). However, field sociology compensates for the emphasis of structuralism and culturalism by including social structure and agency.

29. In Bourdieu's work, the closest to this approach is in the study of cross-field homologies. See Bourdieu 1981.

30. Fligstein and McAdam (2011) also develop a model of how fields change because of challenges from below. On the incorporation and transformation process, see Hess 2007a.

31. I have been arguing for some time in favor of the relevance of social movement studies for science and technology studies (e.g., Hess 2005, 2007). There

are some indications that transition studies is also seeing the relevance of social movement studies (e.g., Elzin et al. 2011; Haxeltine et al. 2011). My approach here emphasizes political opportunity theory and coalition theory from social movement studies.

32. Gould et al. 2008; Mayer 2008; Nugent 2011; Obach 2004; Rose 2000. For a criticism of the "class culture" approach, see Norton 2003. On social movements and coalitions in general, see Van Dyke and McCammon 2010.

33. See the extension of this argument in Hess and Lamprou 2012. For background, see Mol 1995; Mol and Spaargaren 2000, 2005; Pellow et al. 2000; Scheinberg 2003; York and Rosa 2003.

34. Meadows et al. 2004.

35. For example, on the problems associated with nuclear energy, see Sovacool 2011.

36. Daly 1990, 1996; Schnaiberg and Gould 1994.

37. World Commission on Environment and Development 1987. On local achievement of sustainability at the expense of global nonsustainability, see York and Rosa 2003.

38. Victor 2008.

39. For the practitioner-oriented research report that we prepared, see Hess et al. 2010.

Chapter 1

1. Galpern 2009; Hudson 2005. Although Britain retained the right to denominate oil sales in pounds within the sterling area, the relationship was short-lived. In 1958 pounds became formally convertible to dollars for non-sterling-area residents.

2. Galpern 2009; Stagliano 2001; Tomain 2010.

3. Clark 2005; Hudson 2003, 2005.

4. Hudson 2005.

5. Benjamin 1999; Berry et al. 1999; McGowan and Vaughan 1988. In 1964 President Johnson also imposed a tax of 25 percent on light trucks in response to the importing of Volkswagen vans from Germany.

6. Friedman 1987.

7. Cobb 1982. By the 1920s there was organized activity in support of economic development at the national level, with meetings organized by the US Chamber of Commerce that led to the founding of the American Industrial Council in 1930. (See Denn and Webb 2000.) In addition, the governments of some states (Alabama, Florida, North Carolina, Maine) had established economic development bureaus. (See Eisinger 1986.)

8. Cassell 2000; Cobb 1982; Hudson and Edwards 2000. In rollback neoliberalism (generally associated with the policies of the 1980s), political leaders curtailed regulatory and welfare programs. See Peck and Tickell 2002.

9. Cassell 2000; Cobb 1982; Eisinger 1986; Hudson and Edwards 2000.

10. Massachusetts Technology Collaborative 2009.

11. Ibid.

12. Eisinger 1986, 1995, 2002.

13. Eisinger 1986. On the new intellectual property regimes, see Berman 2012.

14. Glasmeier 2000. See also Bradshaw and Blakely 1999; Brooks 1986; Gibson 1988. In the early 1990s Eisinger surveyed state economic development officials and found that there was still a strong emphasis on recruitment (Eisinger 1995).

15. Blum 2008.

16. Block 2008; Eisinger 1986; Nester 1998.

17. Stagliano 2001.

18. Tomain 2010. On the history of solar energy policy and research before the 1970s, see Laird 2001.

19. On Neiman, see Sullivan 2010. For background on California's renewable-energy policy, see Righter 1996 and Taylor 2008.

20. Stagliano 2001.

21. On the connections between restructuring and neoliberalism in electricity policy, see Hess 2011.

22. Holt and Glover 2006; Union of Concerned Scientists 2006; US Department of Energy 2011d, 2011e. The programs in the 2007 law included grants for the creation of plug-in electric vehicles, loan guarantees for manufacturers of fuel-efficient automobile parts and advanced battery systems, green jobs training for building retrofits, assistance to small businesses for energy-efficiency projects, and direct loans for advanced technology vehicle manufacturing.

23. Hirsh 1999.

Chapter 2

1. Hirsh 1999, Reece 1979.

2. Dreiling and Robinson 1998; Gottlieb 1993, 2001; Obach 2004.

3. On the idea of a bridge technology, see Delborne et al. 2011.

4. Dodge 2009; Independent Petroleum Producers Association 2009. The report of the Independent Petroleum Producers Association contains a chart, titled Total Employment and US Petroleum Employment, which shows that about half of the 1.8 million employees are in gasoline stations. The estimate corresponds with employment codes 44719 and 44711 (about 846,000 jobs) for gasoline stations and convenience stores with gasoline stations in IBISWorld 2011. The estimate of 9 million direct, indirect, and induced jobs is from a report commissioned by the American Petroleum Institute, which estimated direct jobs in the oil and gas industry to be 2.1 million (including 1.1 million gasoline station workers, fuel dealers, and merchant wholesalers). (See PriceWaterhouseCoopers 2009.) When

one removes the 1.1 million workers in filling stations (who would find jobs selling biofuels or some other renewable-energy alternative), the study corresponds to my estimate of about a million employees in oil and gas. The industry self-estimate for the subset of natural gas employment is 622,000 direct jobs in 2008. See IHS Global Insight 2009.

5. For the industries' self-estimates, see American Wind Energy Association 2011; Resch 2011; Solar Energy Industries Association 2011a; Solar Foundation 2010; Urbanchuk 2011a. The energy-efficiency estimate is from Goldman et al. 2008. The energy-efficiency estimates are for 2008, the solar and wind estimates are for 2011, and the ethanol estimate is for 2010. It is hard to get the estimates for the other renewable-energy industries, but various sources that I consulted led me to the broad estimate of 50,000 direct jobs, which may be high. Biodiesel is said to "support" 12,000 jobs in 2010, but the estimate is not clarified as direct or indirect jobs. See Urbanchuk 2011b. There is an estimate of 4,500 direct jobs for geothermal in 2004 in Geothermal Energy Association 2011. For hydropower I used the electric power generation estimate of 10,000 in table 2.1. The estimate seemed more accurate than some very high estimates that have appeared in industry reports.

6. On the comparison with coal jobs, see O'Carroll 2009; Woody 2009b. The estimate of 76,000 coal mining jobs is from IBISWorld 2011.

7. On lobbying and the Koch brothers, see Anderson 2011; Fang 2010; Open Secrets 2011. The total for lobbying contributions on the Open Secrets Web site for "alternative energy" is $38 million, but it includes water-related organizations and some other organizations that would not be classified as renewable energy and energy efficiency. The total for the latter category may be $20 million, including the $10 million estimate for the ten largest donors. On general spending and climate-change skepticism, see Dunlap and McRight 2011. On New Hampshire, see McDermott 2011.

8. My presentation of Gerard's characterization is based on my notes from his comments at Good Jobs, Green Jobs meetings.

9. Another program, the AFL-CIO Center for Green Jobs, was launched in 2009 to assist unions in training and job development.

10. Apollo Alliance 2008b, 2011a.

11. On the statistics for the loss of green energy manufacturing jobs, see Mayrl et al. 2010.

12. Calvert Investments 2011; Domini Social Investments 2011; Winslow 2011. Among the other similar funds are Guinness Atkinson Alternative Energy, New Alternative Fund, and Pax World Global Green Fund.

13. Doerr 2007; Doerr and Immelt 2009; Khosla 2006.

14. National Venture Capital Association 2008.

15. American Energy Innovation Council 2010.

16. Apollo Alliance 2009; Partnership for Communities 2009.

17. New Economy Network 2011. The paragraph is also based on my conversations with members of the network.

18. Sadowski 2009.

19. See also Pinderhughes 2007.

20. This paragraph is based on numerous conversations that I have had with people who work on the ground in the implementation of the programs.

21. These comments are based on attending conference presentations and talking with policy makers and advocacy leaders who work on energy-retrofit policy.

22. Feldman 2009; Galbraith 2010; Home Performance Resource Center 2010b. The study didn't break out how much was final assembly and the percentage of parts that were manufactured abroad.

23. Pinderhughes 2007; Renner et al. 2008.

24. On the multiplier for the automotive supply chain, see Center for Automotive Research 2010.

25. On the United States Conference of Mayors, see Global Insight 2009. On the California community colleges, see Centers of Excellence 2008. On the California jobs, see Next10 2009.

26. California Employment Development Department 2010; Next10 2009. The estimates for the biotech and software industry are from the Next10 study.

27. Next10 2009; Pew Charitable Trusts 2009.

28. Muro et al. 2011.

29. Ibid.

30. On the mayors' report statistic, see Global Insight 2009.

31. On venture capital and job costs, see Burtis et al. 2006. On the estimate of $50,000 per job (direct, indirect, and induced), see Pollin et al. 2008. The study estimates that a $100 million investment would create 2 million green jobs.

32. Mazmanian and Kraft 1999.

Chapter 3

1. See also Roberts 2010.

2. Hawkins 2005.

3. On the subcategories of imports and exports, see US International Trade Commission 2010.

4. The phrase "unilateral disarmament" is widely used. See Brown 2011; Rees 2005.

5. Earlier he had worried about protectionist sentiment. (See Samuelson 2007.) On the 2.8 million lost jobs, see Scott 2011.

6. Back and Ho 2009; Mufson 2010; Prasso 2010.

7. On Chinese factories in the United States, see Prasso 2010. On the ENN Group, see Lian and Kwok 2011.

8. Office of the United States Trade Representative 2011; United Steelworkers 2010a,b, 2011.

9. United Steelworkers 2010a.

10. On the benefits of low prices, see Comfort and Weiss 2009 and Biggs 2010b.

11. *Beijing Review* 2010; Hall 2010.

12. On the trade data, see Solar Energy Industries Association 2011b.

13. Bradsher 2010.

14. Comfort and Weiss 2009. On the trade complaint, see Drajen and McQuillen 2011.

15. Bradsher 2011; Evans-Pritchard 2010; Stewart et al. 2011.

16. On the investment statistics, see Pew Charitable Trusts 2010a,b. The numbers are for "overall clean energy finance and investment," including investments in the generation of renewable energy (about $18 billion of China's $35 billion and $12 billion of the $18.6 billion for the United States), initial public stock offerings, and private equity, but they don't include research and development.

17. For a summary of the legislation and the "Make It in America" campaign, see Pelosi 2011. The campaign claimed effectiveness, because manufacturing jobs had increased slightly after 2008. For manufacturing employment statistics, see US Bureau of Labor Statistics 2011. On the 2011 senate bill, see Steinhauer and Landler 2011.

18. Apollo Alliance 2010; Benjamin 1999; Berry et al. 1999.

19. Goldstein 2010; Mattera 2009; Sanger 2009.

20. US Chamber of Commerce 2009a, 2009b. For the Peterson study, see Hufbauer and Schott 2009. For background, see King and Miller 2009.

21. Alliance for American Manufacturing 2010; Stewart and Drake 2009.

22. American Wind Energy Association 2010a; Choma 2010; Maryle et al. 2010.

23. American Wind Energy Association 2009; Bode 2010. On the general repatriation of manufacturing, see Sirkin et al. 2011.

24. Prasso 2010.

25. See also Pew Charitable Trusts 2010b.

26. Bolton 2010.

27. Lugar 2011.

28. Thrush 2009; Weiss et al. 2010.

29. A public opinion poll at that time showed that 71 percent of Americans favored the regulation of greenhouse gases. See *Washington Post* 2010.

30. Gold et al. 2011; Mader 2010. The smaller Better Buildings Program instead provided federal government funding to test innovative building-improvement programs. See US Department of Energy 2011a.

31. Beatty 2010; Wheeland 2009. The Energy Independence and Security Act of 2007 had set a target for all new and renovated federal government buildings to be carbon neutral by 2030.

32. On the desirability of the increase in the ethanol blend, see Renewable Fuels Association 2010a,b. On Governor Culver, see State of Iowa 2009. On the

Environmental Protection Agency ruling, see Wald 2011. On the increase in jobs with a 5 percent increase in the blend, see Hodur et al. 2009.

33. On industry analysts, see Styles 2010. On the costs of solar panels, see Mehta 2011. On the tax holidays, see Engardio 2009.

34. On funding from 2002 through 2008, see Environmental Law Institute 2009. On budget proposals, see Dubois 2008; US Department of Energy 2011b,c. The figures are budget requests, not final allocations, but they are useful to give a sense of the different priorities of the two administrations and the continuity in the relative emphasis on fossil fuels and nuclear energy. The statistics for renewable energy reflect expenditures for the Office of Energy Efficiency and Renewable Energy, which supports innovation and development of new technologies.

35. Muro 2010; Pew Center on Global Climate Change 2009.

36. Balducci et al. 2009; US Department of Labor 2010a–c; US Environmental Protection Agency 2010.

37. US Department of Energy 2011c. The budget of $5 billion in 2010 was separate from that of the Office of Energy Efficiency and Renewable Energy.

38. Childs 2007; Sanders 2007; State of Kentucky 2009; University of South Carolina 2009.

Chapter 4

1. The statistics for systems benefits charges and renewable-electricity standards are based on tallying individual state government records in the Database of State Incentives for Renewables and Efficiency 2011b.

2. On the soil survey and industry response, see Lafleur 2010; Orcutt 2011.

3. Kinchy and Perry 2011; Sovacool 2011.

4. Database of State Incentives for Renewables and Energy Efficiency 2011b.

5. In the US, a renewable portfolio standard is a goal established by a state government for the percentage of electricity to come from renewable energy within a time period, such as 25 percent renewable energy by 2025. Usually the goal is for large utilities, and they are allowed to pass on additional costs to customers.

6. When the public is included in the siting process and when there is local ownership of the turbines, opposition tends to decline, but in general siting is more successful in less sensitive areas, such as agricultural regions and military bases. See Devine-Wright 2005; Firestone and Kempton 2007; Pasqualetti 2002; Toke et al. 2008; Woolsink 2006.

7. Streater 2010; Woody 2009a.

8. Mulvaney 2011a, 2011b; Silicon Valley Toxics Coalition 2009. On the environment issues associated with nanosolar, see Hess and Lamprou 2012.

9. On the rebound effect, see Herring 2009.

10. Electronic Privacy Information Center 2010; Krebs 2009; Lee and Brewer 2009; National Institute of Standards 2009; Province of Ontario 2009; Quinn 2009. On how some of the issues were deleted from the National Institutes of Standards Report, see Harold 2009. On Marin County and Santa Cruz County, see Baker 2011.

11. On the equity issues, see Bullard et al. 2004; Hess 2007b.

12. On the comparison of the efficiency of electric vehicles and hydrogen-powered vehicles, see Mazza and Hammerschlag 2004.

13. On the meta-analysis, see Farrell et al. 2006. On the growth of cropland for corn to 50 percent, see Runge 2010.

14. On water consumption for algae-based biofuels, see Clarens et al. 2010. The Algal Biomass Organization responded by arguing that the data were based on outdated assumptions, and it is likely that the controversy will continue through additional studies. See Algal Biomass Association 2010; Bhanoo 2010; Howell 2010.

15. Database of State Incentives for Renewables and Efficiency 2011b.

16. Regional Greenhouse Gas Initiative 2011.

17. McGowan 2010; Simon 2010; Zito 2008. On the argument that a carbon tax would be more effective than a cap-and-trade regime, see Hansen 2009.

18. City of Austin 2007.

19. City of New York 2009; City of San Francisco 2008.

20. California Public Utilities Commission 2008, 2009; Austin Energy 2010a,b.

21. On the state of Washington, see Gregg 2009; Washington State Legislature 2010. On Austin and Seattle, see Austin Energy 2010c; Muro and Rahman 2009.

22. Lowe et al. 2010; Wheeler 2009.

23. AC Transit 2010.

24. Pawlenty 2006; Way 2008; Williams 2009.

25. Galbraith 2009; US Department of Energy 2010.

26. New Rules Project 2011; State of Illinois 2009.

27. Imbroscio 1977; Persky et al. 1993; Sandro 1994.

28. Chang 2008.

29. Ailworth 2010; Garrett 2011; Holmes 2010a,b.

30. California Energy Commission 2006; Midwestern Governors' Association 2007. On Florida, see Bevill 2008. For Illinois, the reference is to Statute 30 ILCS 500/45–60.

31. On Michigan, see Database of State Incentives for Renewables and Energy Efficiency 2011a, 2011b. On New Jersey, see Johnson 2011; New Jersey's Clean Energy Program 2011. The definition requires that at least 50 percent of the product cost is from facilities located in-state. The New Jersey program was planned for phase-out at the end of 2011 and replacement by the Edison Innovation Clean Energy Manufacturing Incentive.

Chapter 5

1. Etzkowitz and Leydesdorf 1997; Marshall 1890; Piore and Sabel 1984; Porter 1990; Saxenian 1996; Schumpeter 1942; Scott 1988a, 1988b. By 2008 the field had become so large that a handbook was published. See Karlsson 2008.

2. See also Porter 2000, 2003. For policy reports that make reference to the literature, see Cortright 2006; Mills et al. 2008; Muro and Katz 2010. For a review of the criticisms of Porter's approach, see Motoyama 2008. For an application of Porter's diamond to clean technology, see Allen and Potiowsky 2008. For qualifications of Porter's arguments, see Cortright 2002 and Simmie 2008. On the distinction between clusters and regional innovation systems, see Asheim and Coenen 2005.

3. Laranja et al. 2008.

4. For an overview, see Fritsch and Stephan 2005. For typologies of regions and associated policies, see Asheim and Coenen 2005 and Tödtling and Trippl 2005.

5. Cooke 2005, 2008a, 2008b, 2009; Jacobs 1969, 1984. A manufacturing base in a related industry appears to be an important factor, and Fitzgerald's 2010 comparison of the solar industries in Austin and Toledo suggests a similar conclusion.

6. On the Philadelphia cluster, see Pool 2010. The other innovation hubs were centered at California Institute of Technology for fuels from sunlight and Oak Ridge National Laboratory for nuclear energy modeling. For background, see Mills et al. 2008 and Muro and Katz 2010.

7. For references in reports to building clean tech clusters as an economic development strategy, see Burtis et al. 2004, 2006; New York State Energy Research and Development Authority 2009; Puget Sound Regional Council 2009; State of Ohio 2009; State of Washington 2009.

8. State of Michigan 2009.

9. Clean Edge 2010; Hess et al. 2010.

10. State of Ohio 2009.

11. City of Philadelphia 2009; City of St. Paul 2009; City of San José 2010; Leffingwell 2010.

12. City of Portland 2009a; Lapowsky 2011.

13. Fowler 2009; National Biofuels Energy Lab 2011; New York Battery and Energy Storage Consortium 2010; New York State SmartGrid Consortium 2009; U-SNAP Alliance 2009.

14. PDX Lounge 2011; GlobalConnect 2007; Redman 2009.

15. Ailworth 2011; Fitzgerald 2009; Graven 2009; New York State Energy Research and Development Authority 2009.

16. Ernst and Young 2011; Pew Charitable Trusts 2009.

17. Biggs 2010a; DiNapoli 2008, 2010, 2011; Kleindienst 2008; Nearing 2009; State of California 2005.

18. State of Texas 2011.

19. Calzonetti 2008; Fitzgerald 2010; Ohio Third Frontier 2008; State of Iowa 2010. Because of the increasingly difficult picture for solar manufacturing in the United States, the long-term prospects for Ohio's solar industry are uncertain. In 2011 Xunlight had to lay off workers due to a delayed payment from an Italian customer. See Harrison 2011.

20. Meghan Brown 2009; Foshay 2010; Luke 2009; US Department of Energy 2009. In 2009 the state received more money than any other state from the federal government's $2.4 billion Electric Drive and Vehicle Component Manufacturing Initiative.

21. Esteve 2010; Knutson 2009; State of Minnesota 2008; State of Oregon 2011.

22. Chicago Jobs Council 2007; City of Chicago 2009.

23. City of Richmond 2009; Ella Baker Center 2010; Fitzgerald 2009.

24. Ohio Green Pathways 2009; State of New Mexico 2010.

25. State of California 2009a,b; Willon 2009.

26. Fletcher 2010; US Department of Labor 2011.

27. US Department of Labor 2011. On Pennsylvania, see Herzenberg 2010.

28. University of California Merced 2009; US Department of Energy 2009.

29. Bigelow 2009; Blumenstyk 2003; Howell 2009.

30. New York State Foundation for Science, Technology, and Innovation 2009; New York State Energy Research and Development Authority 2009; Syracuse Center of Excellence in Environmental and Quality Systems 2009.

31. Renewable Energy Institute 2009.

32. Calzonetti 2008; Ohio Third Frontier 2008; Ramsey 2009; State of Ohio 2009.

33. On South Carolina, see Berkey and Powers 2005 and University of South Carolina 2009. On Florida, see Institute for Economic Competitiveness 2009 and University of Central Florida 2009. On bioeconomy initiatives, see Bioeconomy Institute 2009 and Content and Gallagher 2007.

34. Burtis et al. 2004, 2006.

Chapter 6

1. For a more complete discussion of the food miles controversy, see Hess 2009.

2. Hess 2009.

3. Goldschmidt 1978.

4. Goetz and Swaminathan 2006; Goetz and Rapasignha 2006; Tolbert et al. 2002; Tolbert 2005.

5. Shuman 2006.

6. On the 2011 figures for BMW, see Newkirk and Bass 2011.

7. Jacobs 1969, 1984; Shuman 2006. For other defenses of import substitution as a regional or local economic development strategy, see Bellows and Hamm 2001; Cortright 2002; Power 1996.

8. Persky et al.1993; Perksy and Wiewel 1994; Rutland and O'Hagan 2007. See also Williams 1994, 1997.

9. Civic Economics 2011; Hess 2009.

10. Farrell and Morris 2008; Lantz and Tegan 2009; Weinrub 2011.

11. Rose 2010.

12. Hess 2009.

13. Bolinger 2004; Mazza 2008; Minnesota Project 2009; Shoemaker and Brekka 2006; Windustry 2011.

14. Farrell 2010a.

15. Colorado Green Building Post 2010; Home Performance Resource Center 2010a; Farrell 2010c; Van Nostrand 2011.

16. Institute for Building Efficiency 2010.

17. Farrell 2010b, 2010c.

18. Institute for Building Efficiency 2010; PACENow 2011a; Pike Research 2010.

19. Balchunas 2010; Matthew Brown 2009; Efficiency Maine 2010; Flanigan 2011.

20. Examples of green financial products in community banks and credit unions include offerings from the Community Bank of the Bay, the Green Bank of Houston, Shorebank Pacific, and VanCity.

21. Prosper 2009; Stone 2008.

22. Shuman 2006, 2011; Mitchell 2011.

23. Hess 2009.

Chapter 7

1. California Air Resources Board 2010; Nothoff et al. 2011.

2. Hull 2010; Nothoff et al. 2011; Roosevelt 2010; Silicon Valley Leadership Group 2010.

3. Apollo Alliance 2011b; Hess et al. 2010; Los Angeles Apollo Alliance 2009, 2011.

4. Hess et al. 2010.

5. Ibid.

6. Kiely 2007; Montgomery et al. 2011.

7. Bartels 2010; Montgomery et al. 2011.

8. Community Labor United 2011; Dean 2010; Foshay and Connelly 2010; Massachusetts Community Labor United 2009.

9. City of St. Paul 2009; K. Mitchell 2009.

10. BlueGreen Alliance 2010; City of St. Paul 2009; Dybvig et al. 2011.

11. Gelman 2009; New York State Energy Research and Development Authority 2010.

12. Gelman 2011.

13. On our tally of the votes, see table A.1 in the appendix.

14. Environmental Defense and North Carolina Sustainable Energy Association 2003; La Capra Associates et al. 2006; North Carolina Sustainable Energy Association 2008; Quinlan 2010.

15. North Carolina Sustainable Energy Association 2009.

16. Meehan 2007; Quinlan 2010, 2011. On opposition to the provisions, see Friedman 2007; Sierra Club 2007. On construction work-in-progress laws and the anti-nuclear movement, see Moyer et al. 2001.

17. Green For All 2010.

18. Ibid.

19. City of Portland 2009b; Energy Trust of Oregon 2010; Green For All 2010; Hess et al. 2010; Home Performance Resource Center 2010a. The authorizing legislation for on-bill financing was the Energy Efficiency and Sustainable Technologies Act of 2009 (HB 2626).

20. Neville 2008; White and Walsh 2008.

21. Green For All 2009, 2011; Simmons 2010.

22. For the total "clean energy jobs," see Pew Charitable Trusts 2009; for the solar jobs, see Solar Foundation 2010; for the oil and gas jobs, see Independent Petroleum Association of America 2010. Comparing across studies can result in distortions due to different counting methods and inclusion criteria, but the figures give a rough size of the constituencies in California.

23. States with a renewable electricity standard were assigned a score from 0.5 to 3 as a measure of the strength of the standard, with 0.5 assigned to states with a voluntary standard and 0 assigned to states with no standard. Net metering and interconnection policies were scored based on a report card from Network for New Energy Choices 2010. A grade of A received one point, B a score of 0.6, C a score of 0.3, and D or F a score of 0. Climate Action Plans were scored based on a report by the Pew Center on Global Climate Change 2011. Other policies were scored 1 or 0 based on presence or absence of the policy. Thus, the total points could be 10, or 100 on a scale of 0 to 100.

24. Pew Charitable Trusts 2009. It is difficult to get state-by-state estimates of green jobs, and the Pew Center study provided one of the most carefully constructed measures. The number is imperfect because it includes a wide range of jobs, but state-by-state estimates were not available for general renewable-energy jobs. I did locate state-by-state statistics for solar energy employment, but they were skewed in a predictable way to states with high levels of sunshine. As a result, I used the broader statistics from Pew.

25. Independent Petroleum Association of America 2010; United States Energy Information Administration 2010. The most recent statistics available were used. The figures don't capture total employment in the industries, but they provide a good measure of the relative strength of the industries by state.

26. The assessment was based on the state-by-state listings of the two organizations on their websites. The classification was verified by the extensive reading, interviews, and participation at conferences, which gave a general sense of where the blue-green coalitions were active.

27. The correlation coefficient for the ratio of clean energy jobs to fossil fuel jobs and the clean energy index was 0.37.

28. In individual models of ordinary least-squares linear regression with one independent variable regressed on green energy policies, the p values were all less than 0.01. In the least-squares linear regression model with all four independent variables, the betas and p values (t, two-tailed) were as follows: clean energy jobs, 0.13, not significant (NS); fossil fuel jobs, –0.01, NS; Democratic Party support, 0.69, $p < 0.00$; and blue-green coalition presence, 0.18, $p < 0.07$ ($R^2 = 0.69$, $F < 0.0000$). The results are roughly consistent with those of Huang et al. 2007, who found that political party affected the adoption of renewable portfolio standards. Chandler (2009) found a similar relationship with a variable for ideology that is probably closely associated with political party. Likewise, Vachon and Mentz (2006) found a statistically significant relationship between green policy outcomes and political interests (defined as the voting record of a state's federal representatives on environmental issues), which again is probably closely related to political party. We are exploring additional variables and interactions in ongoing research with a more extensive data set of 6,000 votes for PACE laws and renewable portfolio standards laws in state legislatures. Preliminary results confirm the general pattern outlined here.

29. Pawlenty shifted more toward environmental skepticism when he decided to become a presidential candidate. The twelve states with a score above 70 were California, Colorado, Connecticut, Hawaii, Illinois, Iowa, Massachusetts, Minnesota, New Jersey, New York, Ohio, and Oregon.

30. On the 33 officers, see Romm 2010.

31. Daniel 2011; Eilperin 2011; Pew Charitable Trusts 2011; Robyn 2011.

32. Daniel 2011.

33. Ibid.

34. Ibid.

35. Udall 2011.

36. Tellus Institute 2011.

Chapter 8

1. Welna 2011.

2. The scope of the inquiry into unfair trade practices was restricted to crystalline silicon, not thin-film technologies, which was what Solyndra manufactured. The

claim that China had loaned more than $40 billion to its solar companies in 2010 and 2011 may be overstated, because the figure is based on loan credits available, often at high interest rates, rather than the much smaller figure of loans actually taken. However, China had subsidized its solar industry heavily. See Wesoff 2011.

3. Cichoski 2011.

4. See Mulvaney 2011c. See also US Department of Energy 2011f. The figure of $36 billion included programs known as 1703, 1705, and Advanced Technology Vehicles Manufacturing. On not surrendering to China, see Condon 2011.

5. Kaufman 2011b.

6. Blue-Green Blog 2011; Marchetti 2011.

7. Kaufman 2011b; Vlasic 2011.

8. Kaufman 2011a; Klas 2011.

9. Baxandall 2011; Gallucci 2011.

10. Friedman 2011; Navarro 2011a,b; Rao 2011.

11. Barringer 2011.

12. Koshmri 2011; Lustgarten 2011.

13. Reopelle 2011.

14. Kaufman 2011a; Powers 2011; Provance 2011.

15. Davenport 2011; Galbraith 2011; Kucinich 2011; Matthews 2011.

16. Boshart 2011; Koshmri 2011; Seldon 2011.

17. Dulzo 2011; Michigan League of Conservation Voters 2011; Michigan Policy Network 2011.

18. Little 2011; Southern Alliance for Clean Energy 2011.

19. Caldwell 2011; Commonwealth of Virginia 2011; McDonnell 2011; Thornley 2011. In a speech in late 2011, McDonnell advocated an "all of the above" approach to energy, including clean energy, but he focused on fossil fuels and nuclear energy.

20. Demirjian 2011; Kinner 2011; Schwartz 2011.

21. McGreevy 2011; Silverfarb 2011.

22. Lifsher 2011. After a request from the governor, the state's Public Utilities Commission extended the charge for 2012.

23. McGeehan 2011.

24. Abercrombie 2010; Fawcett 2010.

25. Etnier 2008.

26. Campbell 2011; Morse 2011; Sustainable Business 2011a, 2011b.

27. State of Maryland 2011; State of Washington 2011.

28. PACENow 2011b.

29. Leiserowitz 2011.

30. On the Koch brothers, see Carrk 2011; Fang 2010; Greenpeace 2011; Mayer 2010. On the broader issue of support for climate change denialism, see Dunlap and McRight 2011; Jacques et al. 2008. On environmental issues, see Americans for Prosperity 2011.

Conclusion

1. Gomery and Baumol 2009; Chang 2008.

2. On the tradable sector, see Spence and Hlatshwayo 2011.

3. Clark 2005; Downs 2007; Miller 2007; T. Mitchell 2009; Stroupe 2006; Vail 2006.

4. On the export of petroleum products, see Pleven and Gold 2011.

5. The business press has already recognized the favorable scenario for energy-efficiency technologies in comparison with renewable-energy technologies. See Morales and Downing 2011. On the decline of the dollar as reserve currency and its connection with austerity measures, see Eichengreen 2011.

6. The potential for positive-sum relationships is also discussed in Hess 2012. On households and different types of resilience, see Hess 2010.

7. Harwood 2010.

8. The point is not to argue against the desirability of future scenarios such as that of the "Great Transition," which points to the potential for a more just and sustainable future. See Tellus Institute 2011. My argument here is descriptive and predictive; in other words, the future direction appears to be headed in other ways (and unfortunately so).

References

Abercrombie, Neil. 2011. Energy Policy. www.neilabercrombie.com.

AC Transit. 2010. Linde Hydrogen Technology to Fuel AC Transit Buses. 511contracosta.org.

Ailworth, Erin. 2010. State Sets Aside Key Rule on Energy. *Boston Globe*, June 10.

Ailworth, Erin. 2011. A Showcase for Building Green: Fraunhofer Center for Sustainable Energy Systems Arrives in Innovation District with a Mission. *Boston Globe*, May 16.

Algal Biomass Organization. 2010. Algal Biomass Organization Questions Accuracy of University of Virginia Algae Life Cycle Study. www.algalbiomass.org.

Allen, Jennifer, and Thomas Potiowsky. 2008. Portland's Green Building Cluster. *Economic Development Quarterly* 22 (4): 303–315.

Alliance for American Manufacturing. 2010. Buy America Works: Longstanding United States Policy Enhances the Job Creating Effect of Government Spending. www.americanmanufacturing.org.

American Energy Innovation Council. 2010. A Business Plan for America's Energy Future. www.americanenergyinnovation.org.

Americans for Prosperity. 2011. Energy and Environmental Protection Regulations, September. www.americansforprosperityfoundation.com.

American Wind Energy Association. 2009. Annual Wind Industry Report. www.awea.org.

American Wind Energy Association. 2010a. AWEA Statement on Senators Schumer, Casey, Brown, and Tester Urging Administration to Suspend Stimulus Program. archive.awea.org.

American Wind Energy Association. 2010b. AWEA Wind Power Value Chain. www.awea.org.

American Wind Energy Association. 2011. Resources: How Many People Work in the U.S. Wind Industry? archive.awea.org.

Anderson, David. 2011. Koch-Funded Group Mounts Cut-and-Paste Attack on Regional Climate Initiatives. *Grist*, March 16. www.grist.org.

Apollo Alliance. 2008a. Green Collar Jobs in America's Cities: Building Pathways Out of Poverty and Careers in the Clean Energy Economy. apolloalliance.org.

Apollo Alliance. 2008b. The New Apollo Program: An Economic Strategy for American Prosperity. apolloalliance.org.

Apollo Alliance. 2009. Imagining Newark's Green Future: A Year Building the Green Economy. apolloalliance.org.

Apollo Alliance. 2010. Buy America: Transportation Manufacturing and Domestic Content Requirements. apolloalliance.org.

Apollo Alliance. 2011a. Achievements. apolloalliance.org.

Apollo Alliance. 2011b. Los Angeles. apolloalliance.org.

Asheim, Bjørn, and Lars Coenen. 2005. Knowledge Bases and Regional Innovation Systems: Comparing Nordic Clusters. *Research Policy* 34 (8): 1173–1190.

Austin Energy. 2010a. About the Energy Conservation Audit and Disclosure (ECAD) Ordinance. www.austinenergy.com.

Austin Energy. 2010b. City Council Adopts new Energy Code Amendments; Action Moves Austin Closer to "Zero-Energy" Homes. www.austinenergy.com.

Austin Energy. 2010c. Energy Efficiency. www.austinenergy.com.

Back, Aaron, and Patricia Ho. 2009. Beijing Slams U.S. Tariffs in Growing Clash. *Wall Street Journal*, November 9.

Baker, David. 2011. Marin Supes Push Delay on Installing SmartMeters. *San Francisco Chronicle*, January 5.

Balchunas, Michael. 2010. Federally Backed "PowerSaver" Loans May Help Pay for Solar. *Solar Home and Business Journal*, November 18. www.Solarhbj.com.

Balducci, Delight, Stephanie Haas, Cullen Howe, Kara Murphy, Giselle Vigneron, and Jason Wiener. 2009. Green Jobs Position Paper. Lawyers for Green Jobs. lawyers4greenjobs.

Barringer, Felicity. 2011. Court Reverses New Mexico Governor on Environmental Rules. Green: A Blog about Energy and the Environment. green.blogs.nytimes.com.

Bartels, Lynn. 2010. Ritter Signs Clean Energy Bill. *Denver Post*, March 23.

Bartholemew, Carolyn. 2010. The Great Industrial Wall of China. *American Prospect* 21 (1): A13–A16.

Baxandall, Phineas. 2011. In the Public Interest: Maine Approves Historic Law to Reduce Oil Use (Really!) *Huffington Post*, July 5. www.huffingtonpost.com.

Beatty, MaryAnne. 2010. GSA Moves to LEED Gold for All New Federal Buildings and Renovations. United States General Services Administration. www.gsa.gov.

Beijing Review. 2010. An Energetic Solution. November 15. www.bjreview.com.cn.

Bell, Jim, and Heather Honea. 2007. Electricity Supply and Price Security in San Diego County. San Diego Regional Apollo Alliance. www.jimbell.com.

Bellows, Anne, and Michael Hamm. 2001. Local Autonomy and Sustainable Development: Testing Import Substitution in Localizing Food Systems. *Agriculture and Human Values* 18 (3): 271–284.

Benjamin, Daniel. 1999. Voluntary Export Restraints on Automobiles. *PERC Reports* 17 (3). www.perc.org.

Berkey, Edgar, and Garry Powers. 2005. The South Carolina Hydrogen Economy: Capitalizing on the States R&D Assets. Concurrent Technologies Corporation. www.ctcbrownfields.com.

Berman, Beth. 2012. *Creating the Market University: How Academic Science Became an Economic Engine.* Princeton University Press.

Bernstein, Jarred, and Isaac Shapiro. 2006. Nine Years of Neglect: Federal Minimum Wage Remains Unchanged for Ninth Straight Year. Center on Budget and Policy Priorities. www.cbpp.org.

Berry, Steven, James Levinsohn, and Ariel Pakes. 1999. Voluntary Export Restraints on Automobiles: Evaluating a Trade Policy. *American Economic Review* 89 (3): 400–430.

Bevill, Kris. 2008. Florida Ag Department Announces Grant Recipients. *Ethanol Producer Magazine,* January 24. www.ethanolproducer.com.

Bhanoo, Sindya. 2010. Biofuels Companies Attack Algal Study. Green: A Blog about Energy and the Environment. green.blogs.nytimes.com.

Bigelow, Bruce. 2009. San Diego Algae Biofuels Industry Gains Steam with R&D Consortium. www.xconomy.com.

Biggs, Stuart. 2010a. Calpers's Mandate Drives Capital Dynamics $800 Million Green Fund Target. www.bloomberg.com.

Biggs, Stuart. 2010b. Rutgers' Solar Panels Show Clean-Energy Shift. www.bloomberg.com.

Bioeconomy Institute. 2008. Annual Report. www.biorenew.iastate.edu.

Block, Fred. 2008. "Swimming Against the Current: The Rise of the Hidden Developmental State in the U.S." *Politics and Society* 36 (2): 169–206.

BlueGreen Alliance. 2010. Mayors Rybak and Coleman to Launch Thinc. GreenMSP. www.bluegreenalliance.org.

BlueGreen Alliance. 2011. Trade. www.bluegreenalliance.org.

BlueGreen Blog. 2011. Pass It (and More) Now. blog.bluegreenalliance.org.

Blum, Ulrich. 2008. Institutions and Clusters. In *Handbook of Research on Innovation and Clusters: Cases and Policies,* ed. C. Karlsson. Edward Elgar.

Blumenstyk, Goldie. 2003. Greening the World or "Greenwashing" a Reputation? *Chronicle of Higher Education,* January 10.

Bode, Denise. 2010. Plenary Remarks, Green Jobs, Good Jobs Conference, Washington.

Bolinger, Mark. 2004. A Survey of State Support for Community Wind Power Development. Lawrence Berkeley National Laboratory. eetd.lbl.gov.

Bolton, Alexander. 2010. Liberal Activists Say Good Riddance to Kerry-Lieberman Climate Legislation. *The Hill*, July 24. thehill.com.

Boshart, Rob. 2011. Branstad Pushes for Legislative Passage of Nuclear Bill. easterniowagovernment.com.

Bourdieu, Pierre. 1981. *The Political Ontology of Martin Heidegger*. Stanford University Press.

Bourdieu, Pierre. 2001. *Science of Science and Reflexivity*. University of Chicago Press.

Bourdieu, Pierre. 2005. *The Social Structures of the Economy*. Polity.

Bradshaw, Ted, and Edward Blakely. 1999. What Are Third-Wave State Economic Development Efforts? From Incentives to Industrial Policy. *Economic Development Quarterly* 13 (3): 229–244.

Bradsher, Keith. 2010. Beijing Turbine: China Sets Rules and Wins Wind Turbine Game. *New York Times*, December 15.

Bradsher, Keith. 2011. China Consolidates Grip on Rare Earths. *New York Times*, September 16.

Brooks, Oliver, Jr. 1986. Economic Development through Entrepreneurship: Incubators and the Incubation Process. *Economic Development Review* 4 (2): 24–29.

Brown, Halina, Philip Vergragt, and Maurie Cohen. 2011. Socio-technical Transitions, Social Practices, and the New Economics: Meeting the Challenges of a Constrained World. Presented at annual meeting of Sustainable Consumption Research and Action Initiative, Princeton.

Brown, Matthew. 2009. Paying for Energy Upgrades Through Utility Bills. Brief 3, Alliance to Save Energy. ase.org.

Brown, Megan. 2009. Granholm, Cherry Hail 12 Michigan Projects Awarded Federal Advanced Battery Grants. Office of the Governor, Michigan. www.michigan.gov.

Brown, Sherrod. 2010. Sen. Brown Statement on 37,000 New Ohio Jobs in April. brown.senate.gov.

Brown, Sherrod. 2011. Senate Passes Brown-Led Bill Cracking Down on Illegal Chinese Currency Manipulation. brown.senate.gov.

Browne, Andrew. 2011. China's President Lays Groundwork for Obama Talks. *Wall Street Journal*, January 18.

Bullard, Robert, Glenn Johnson, and Angel Torres, eds. 2004. *Highway Robbery: Transportation Racism and New Routes to Equity*. South End.

Burtis, Patrick, Bob Epstein, and Roland Hwang. 2004. Creating the California Clean Tech Cluster: How Innovation and Investment Can Promote Job Growth and a Healthy Environment. Natural Resources Defense Council and Environmental Entrepreneurs. www.nrdc.org.

Burtis, Patrick, Bob Epstein, and Nicholas Parker. 2006. Creating Cleantech Clusters: 2006 Update. www.e2.org/jsp/generic.jsp.

Business Alliance for Local Living Economies. 2009. A Local Living Economy. www.livingeconomies.org.

Caldwell, Jeff. 2011. Governor McDonnell Signs Legislation to Promote Clean and Renewable Energy in Virginia. Commonwealth of Virginia Department of Natural Resources. www.naturalresources.virginia.gov.

California Air Resources Board. 2010. AB 32 Scoping Plan. www.arb.ca.gov/homepage.htm.

California Employment Development Department. 2010. State Survey Identifies Over 300,000 Jobs in California with Major Emphasis on Green Practices. www.edd.ca.gov.

California Energy Commission. 2006. A Roadmap for the Development of Biomass in California. PIER Collaborative Report CEC-500-2006-095-D. biomass.ucdavis.edu.

California Public Utilities Commission. 2008. California's Long-Term Energy Efficiency Strategic Plan. www.cpuc.ca.gov.

California Public Utilities Commission. 2009. CPUC Makes Largest Commitment Ever by a State to Energy Efficiency. docs.cpuc.ca.gov.

Calvert Investments. 2011. Sustainable and Responsible Investing Signature Criteria. www.calvert.com.

Calzonetti, Frank. 2008. The Role of an Antecedent Cluster, Academic R&D and Entrepreneurship in the Development of Toledo's Solar Energy Cluster. In *Globalising Worlds and New Economic Configurations*, ed. C. Tamásy and M. Taylor. Ashgate Publishing.

Campbell, Ricky. 2011. Energy Bill Receives Praise from State Organizations. Office of the Governor, Connecticut. www.ct.gov.

Carbon Tax Center. 2010. FAQs. www.carbontax.org.

Carrk, Tony. 2011. The Koch Brothers: What You Need to Know about the Financiers of the Radical Right. Center for American Progress. www.americanprogressaction.org.

Cassell, Robert. 2000. The Changing Nature of Economic Development Practice. *Economic Development Review* 17 (2): 32–35.

Center for Automotive Research. 2010. Contribution of the Automotive Industry to the Economies of All Fifty States and the United States. www.cargroup.org.

Centers of Excellence. 2008. Green Industries and Jobs in California. www.coeccc.net.

Chan, Sewell, and Keith Bradsher. 2010. U.S. to Investigate China's Clean-Energy Aid. *New York Times*, October 15.

Chandler, Jess. 2009. Why Do States Adopt Sustainable Energy Portfolio Standards? *Energy Policy* 37 (8): 3274–3281.

Chang, Ha-Joon. 2008. *Bad Samaritans: The Myth of Free Trade and the Secret History of Capitalism*. Bloomsbury.

Chang, Ha-Joon. 2011. The 2008 World Financial Crisis and the Future of World Development. In *Aftermath: A New Global Economic Order?* ed. C. Calhoun and G. Derluguian. New York University Press.

Chernow, Ron. 2004. *Alexander Hamilton.* Penguin.

Chicago Jobs Council. 2007. The Greening Industry: GreenCorps Chicago. cjc.net.

Choma, Russ. 2010. Renewable Energy Money Still Going Abroad, Despite Criticism from Congress. Presented at Investigative Reporting Workshop, American University School of Communication. investigativereportingworkshop .org.

Cichoski, Devon. 2011. SolarWorld and a Coalition of U.S. Solar Manufacturers Petition to Stop Unfair Trade by China's State-Sponsored Industries. www .solarworld-usa.com.

City of Austin. 2007. Climate Protection Plan. www.ci.austin.tx.us.

City of Chicago. 2009. Job Training. Department of the Environment. egov .cityofchicago.org.

City of New York. 2009. PlaNYC Progress Report 2009. www.nyc.gov.

City of Philadelphia. 2009. 2009 Greenworks Plan. www.phila.gov.

City of Portland. 2009a. City of Portland Economic Development Strategy: A Five-Year Plan for Promoting Economic Growth and Job Creation. www .portlandonline.com.

City of Portland. 2009b. Portland City Council Approves Community Workforce Agreement to Support Equity and Workforce Goals for Clean Energy Portland. www.portlandonline.com.

City of Richmond. 2009. Richmond BUILD. www.ci.richmond.ca.us.

City of San Francisco. 2010. Green Building Ordinance. www.sfdbi.org.

City of San José. 2010. Green Vision 2009 Annual Report. www.sanjoseca.gov.

City of St. Paul. 2009. Making It Green in Minneapolis and St. Paul. www.stpaul .gov.

Civic Economics. 2011. Retail Economics. www.civiceconomics.com.

Clarens, Andres, Eleazer Resurreccion, Mark White, and Lisa Colosi. 2010. Environmental Life Cycle Comparison of Algae to Other Bioenergy Feedstocks. *Environmental Science & Technology* 44 (5): 1813–1819.

Clark, William R. 2005. *Petrodollar Warfare: Oil, Iraq, and the Future of the Dollar.* New Society.

Clean Edge. 2010. A Future of Innovation and Growth: Advancing Massachusetts' Clean-Energy Leadership. www.masscec.com.

Cleantech Group. 2009. Cleantech Definition. www.cleantech.com.

Cobb, James. 1982. *The Selling of the South: The Southern Crusade of Industrial Development, 1936–1980.* Louisiana State University Press.

Cohen, Elie. 2006. Theoretical Foundations of Industrial Policy. *EIB Papers* 11 (1): 84–106.

Colorado, Green Building Post. 2010. Lights Out for Boulder REAP Program. www.usweatherizing.com.

Comfort, Nicholas, and Richard Weiss. 2009. Conergy, SolarWorld Seek Protection from Chinese Price Dumping. www.bloomberg.com.

Commonwealth of Virginia. 2011. Executive Orders. Office of the Governor. www.governor.virginia.gov.

Community Labor United. 2011. Past Victories. www.massclu.org/ achievements.

Condon, Stephanie. 2011. Obama on Solyndra: I Won't "Surrender" to China on Green Tech. *CBS News*, October 6. www.cbsnews.com.

Content, Thomas, and Kathleen Gallagher. 2007. UW Wins Biofuel Grant. *Milwaukee Journal Sentinel*, June 27. www.jsonline.com.

Contorno, Steve. 2011. McDonnell Blasts Obama at Energy Summit. *Washington Examiner*, October 4. www.washingtonexaminer.com.

Cooke, Philip. 2005. Regionally Asymmetric Knowledge Capabilities and Open Innovation. Exploring "Globalisation 2"—A New Model of Industry Organisation. *Research Policy* 34 (8): 1128–1149.

Cooke, Philip. 2008a. Cleantech and an Analysis of the Platform Nature of the Life Sciences: Further Reflections on Platform Policies. *European Planning Studies* 16 (3): 375–393.

Cooke, Philip. 2008b. Regional Innovation Systems, Clean Technology, and Jacobian Cluster-Platform Policies. *Regional Science, Policy, and Practice* 1 (1): 23–45.

Cooke, Philip. 2009. Regional Innovation Systems, Collective Entrepreneurship, and Green Clusters. In *Entrepreneurship and Growth in Local, Regional, and National Economies*, ed. D. Smallbone, H. Landström, and D. Jones-Evans. Edward Elgar.

Cortright, Joseph. 2002. The Economic Importance of Being Different: Regional Variations in Tastes, Increasing Returns, and the Dynamics of Development. *Economic Development Quarterly* 16 (1): 3–16.

Cortright, Joseph. 2006. Making Sense of Clusters: Regional Competitiveness and Economic Development. Brookings Institution, Metropolitan Policy Program. www.brookings.edu.

Daly, Herman. 1990. Toward Some Operational Principles of Sustainable Development. *Ecological Economics* 2 (1): 1–6.

Daly, Herman. 1996. *Beyond Growth: The Economics of Sustainable Development*. Beacon.

Daniel, Lisa. 2011. Mabus: Energy Initiatives Make Us Better War Fighters. Department of Defense. www.defense.gov.

Daniels, Mitch. 2009. Day 2: Governor Talks Jobs, Energy, and Health Care in China. Governor's Office, Indiana. www.in.gov.

Database of State Incentives for Renewables and Energy Efficiency. 2011a. Michigan. Consumers Energy: Experimental Advanced Renewable Program. www .dsireusa.org.

Database of State Incentives for Renewables and Energy Efficiency. 2011b. Rules, Regulations, and Policies for Renewable Energy. www.dsireusa.org.

Davenport, Coral. 2011. Pawlenty: Running from His Past Moves on Environmental Policy. *National Journal*, June: 23. www.nationaljournal.com.

Davis, Mike. 2006. *Planet of Slums*. Verso.

Dean, Amy. 2010. Doing Green Jobs Right. *The Nation*, September 13: 20–22.

Delborne, Jason, Aubrey Wigner, and Abby Kinchy. 2011. Hope for Sustainability, Hype for Natural Gas. Presented at Conference on the Political Sociology of Science and Technology, Rensselaer Polytechnic Institute.

Demirjian, Karoun. 2011. Competition Brewing Among States Over Renewable Energy Exports. *Las Vegas Sun*, August 30. www.lasvegassun.com.

Denn, J. Huber, and Michael Webb. 2000. A History of the Economic Development Council, 1926–1960. *Economic Development Review* 17 (2): 18–25.

Devine-Wright, Patrick. 2005. Local Aspects of U.K. Rural Energy Development: Exploring Public Beliefs and Policy Implications. *Local Environment* 10 (1): 57–69.

DiNapoli, Thomas. 2008. Green Strategic Investment Program: Fact Sheet. www .osc.state.ny.us.

DiNapoli, Thomas. 2010. Green Initiative. www.osc.state.ny.us.

DiNapoli, Thomas. 2011. NYS Pension Fund Invests $3.2 Million in Biomaxx Wood Pellet Company. Office of the New York State Controller. www.osc.state .ny.us.

Dodge, Robert. 2009. API Issues Statement on Senate Climate Hearing. American Petroleum Institute. www.api.org.

Doerr, John. 2007. John Doerr Sees Salvation and Profit in Greentech. TED Conference Presentation. www.ted.com.

Doerr, John, and Jeffrey Immelt. 2009. Falling Behind on Green Tech. *Washington Post*, August 3.

Domini Social Investments. 2011. Global Investment Standards. www.domini. com.

Doring, Mike. 2010. Obama: Venture Capitalist-in-Chief. *Bloomberg Businessweek*, August 9–15: 28–31.

Downs, Erica. 2007. China's Quest for Overseas Oil. *Far Eastern Economic Review*, September: 52–56.

Drajem, Mark, and William McQuillen. 2011. Solar Panel Imports from China Said to Face U.S. Trade Complaint. www.blomberg.com.

Drajem, Mark, and Eric Martin. 2011. U.S. Solar Manufacturers Request Duties on Solar Imports. www.Bloomberg.com.

Dreiling, Michael, and Ian Robinson. 1998. Union Responses to NAFTA in the U.S. and Canada: Exploring Intra- and International Variation. *Mobilization* 3 (2): 163–184.

Driesen, David, ed. 2010. *Economic Thought and U.S. Climate Change Policy*. MIT Press.

DuBois, Denis. 2008. FY 2009 Budget Means Big Cuts for Efficiency, Renewables. www.energypriorities.com.

Dulzo, Jim. 2011. Is Snyder Readying a New Coal Rush? Michigan Land Use Institute. www.mlui.org.

Dunlap, Riley, and Aaron McRight. 2011. Climate Change Denial: Sources, Actors, and Strategies. In *Routledge Handbook of Climate Change and Society*, ed. C. Lever-Tracy. Routledge.

Dybvig, John, Shawn Hesse, Anne Hunt, and Cathy Polasky. 2011. Making It Green: Three Case Studies of Planning to Create Green Jobs. Panel presentation at annual Good Jobs, Green Jobs conference, Washington.

Efficiency Maine. 2010. Background on Maine's Home Energy Savings Loan Program and PACE Law. www.efficiencymaine.com.

Eichengreen, Barry. 2011. *Exorbitant Privilege: The Rise and Fall of the Dollar and the Future of the International Monetary System*. Oxford University Press.

Eilperin, Juliet. 2011. Building a Green Military Machine. *Washington Post*, September 26.

Einhorn, Bruce, and Tara Patel. 2011. A European Shadow on China's Solar Industry. *Bloomberg Businessweek*, February 7–13: 44–45.

Eisinger, Peter. 1986. *The Rise of the Entrepreneurial State: State and Local Economic Development Policy in the United States*. University of Wisconsin Press.

Eisinger, Peter. 1995. State Economic Development in the 1990s. *Economic Development Quarterly* 9 (2): 146–158.

Eisinger, Peter. 2002. Financing Economic Development: A Survey of Techniques. *Government Finance Review,* June: 20–23.

Ekelund, Robert, Jr., and Robert Tollison. 1997. *Politicized Economies: Monarchy, Monopoly, and Mercantilism*. Texas A&M Press.

Electronic Privacy Information Center. 2010. The Smart Grid and Privacy. epic.org.

Ella Baker Center. 2010. Green Collar Jobs Campaign FAQs. www.ellabakercenter.org.

Elzin, Boelie, Frank Geels, Cees Leeuwis, and Barbara van Mierlo. 2011. Normative Contestation in Transitions "in the Making": Animal Welfare Concerns and System Innovation in Pig Husbandry. *Research Policy* 40 (2): 263–275.

Energy Trust of Oregon. 2010. Clean Energy Works Portland Attracts $20 Million Federal Grants; Spawns New Statewide Nonprofit. energytrust.org.

Engardio, Peter. 2009. Can the Future be Built in America? *Business Week*, September 21: 46ff.

Environmental Defense and North Carolina Sustainable Energy Association. 2003. Charting North Carolina's Clean Energy Future. apps.edf.org/documents/2720_NCcleanEnergyFuture.pdf.

Environmental Law Institute. 2009. Estimating U.S. Government Subsidies to Energy Sources: 2002–2008. www.elistore.org.

Ernst and Young. 2011. U.S. Venture Capital Investment in Cleantech Grows to Nearly $4 Billion in 2010, an 8% Increase from 2009. www.prnewswire.com.

Esteve, Harry. 2010. Oregon Governor Signs New Limits on Business Energy Tax Credit. *The Oregonian*, March 18.

Esteve, Harry. 2011. Kitzhaber Says It's Time for a 10-Year Clean Energy Plan in Oregon. *The Oregonian*, April 13.

Etnier, Carl. 2008. Douglas Has Made Some Progress on Energy Initiative. www.vtpeakoil.net.

Etzkowitz, Henry, and Loet Leydesdorff, eds. 1997. *Universities in the Global Economy: A Triple Helix of University-Industry-Government Relations*. Pinter.

Evans-Pritchard, Ambrose. 2010. Hot Political Summer as China Throttles Rare Metal Supply and Claims South China Sea. *Daily Telegraph*, August 1. www.telegraph.co.uk.

Evans-Pritchard, Ambrose. 2011. Protectionism Beckons as Leaders Push World into Depression. *Daily Telegraph*, October 2. www.telegraph.co.uk.

Fahey, Tom. 2011. Senate Upholds Lynch Veto Blocking RGGI Appeal. *Union Leader*, September 7. www.unionleader.com.

Fang, Lee. 2010. Memo: Health Insurance, Banking, Oil Industries Met with Koch, Chamber, Glenn Beck to Plot 2010 Election. thinkprogress.org.

Farrell, Alexander, Richard Plevin, Brian Turner, Andrew Jones, Michael O'Hare, and Daniel Kammen. 2006. Ethanol Can Contribute to Energy and Environmental Goals? *Science* 311 (5760): 506–508.

Farrell, John. 2010a. Community Solar: Obstacles and Opportunities. www.energyselfreliantstates.org.

Farrell, John. 2010b. Municipal Energy Financing. Presented at Southwest Renewable Energy Conference. www.swrec.org.

Farrell, John. 2010c. Municipal Energy Financing: Lesson Learned. www.newrules.org.

Farrell, John, and David Morris. 2008. Energy Self-Reliant States: Homegrown Renewable Power. Policy brief, New Rules Project. www.newrules.org.

Fawcett, Denby. 2010. Abercrombie, Aiona Differ on Energy Goals. KITV News, September 28. www.kitv.com.

Federal Reserve. 2010. Credit Market Debt Outstanding. www.federalreserve.go.

Feldman, Jonathan Michael. 2009. From Mass Transit to New Manufacturing. *American Prospect* 20 (3): A12–A16.

Firestone, Jeremy, and Willett Kempton. 2007. Public Opinion about Large Offshore Wind Power: Underlying Factors. *Energy Policy* 35 (3): 1584–1598.

Fitzgerald, Garrett. 2009. Green Jobs Corps Helps Businesses and Residents. In *Oakland: Building Green Business*, special supplement to *San Francisco Business Times*, February 27–March 5.

Fitzgerald, Joan. 2010. *Emerald Cities: Urban Sustainability and Economic Development*. Oxford University Press.

Flanigan, Ted. 2011. PACE Perspectives. EcoMotion.

Fletcher, Michael. 2010. Retrained for Green Jobs, But Still Waiting Work. *Washington Post*, November 23.

Fligstein, Neil, and Doug McAdam. 2011. Toward a General Theory of Strategic Action Fields. *Sociological Theory* 29 (1): 1–26.

Flor, Avelino, and Jan Rotmans. 2009. Power in Transition: An Interdisciplinary Framework to Study Power in Relation to Structural Change. *European Journal of Sociology* 12 (4): 543–569.

Foshay, Elena. 2010. How States Are Using the Recovery Act to Scale Up Clean-Energy Manufacturing. Presentation at annual Good Jobs, Green Jobs conference, Washington.

Foshay, Elena, and Mary Jo Connelly. 2010. An Industry at the Crossroads: Energy Efficiency Employment in Massachusetts. Apollo Alliance and Community Labor United. massclu.org.

Foster, John, and Fred Magdoff. 2009. *The Great Financial Crisis: Causes and Consequences*. Monthly Review Press.

Foucault, Michel. 1970. *The Order of Things*. Vintage.

Foucault, Michel. 2010. *The Birth of Biopolitics*. Palgrave.

Fowler, Tom. 2009. Texas to be Home for Clean Technology Group. *Houston Chronicle*, June 9.

Frickel, Scott, and Kelly Moore, eds. 2005. *The New Political Sociology of Science*. University of Wisconsin Press.

Friedman, Avram. 2007. A Call to Reason on Energy Issues Pending in the North Carolina Legislature. avram.sustainablewnc.org/.

Friedman, Brad. 2011. Audio: Chris Christie Lets Loose at Secret Koch Brothers Confab. http://motherjones.com/.

Friedman, Milton. 1987. Outdoing Smoot-Hawley. *Wall Street Journal*, April 20.

Friends of the Earth. 2009. Friends of the Earth Statement on the Kerry-Boxer Draft Climate Bill (revised). www.foe.org.

Fritsch, Michael, and Andreas Stefan. 2005. Regionalization of Innovation Policy: Introduction to Special Issue. *Research Policy* 34 (8): 1123–1127.

Furtado, Celso. 1968. *The Economic Growth of Brazil: Survey from Colonial to Modern Times*. University of California Press.

Galbraith, Kate. 2009. First Biodiesel Pipeline Starts Operations. *New York Times* Green blog, July 2. green.blogs.nytimes.com.

Galbraith, Kate. 2010. Made in the U.S.A.: Efficiency Materials. *New York Times* Green blog, March 12. green.blogs.nytimes.com.

Galbraith, Kate. 2011. As Governor, Perry Backed Wind, Gas, and Coal. *New York Times*, August 21.

Gallucci, Maria. 2011. Maine Governor Proposes 63 Clean Energy and Environment Reversals. insideclimatenews.com.

Galpern, Steven. 2009. *Money, Oil, and Empire in the Middle East: Sterling and Postwar Imperialism, 1944–1971.* Cambridge Unviersity Press.

Garrett, Paul. 2011. Anti-Cape Wind Alliance Challenges PPA in Court. *Windpower Monthly*, September. www.windpowermonthly.com.

Geels, Frank. 2002. Technological Transitions as Evolutional Reconfiguration Processes: A Multi-level Perspective and a Case Study. *Research Policy* 31: 1257–1274.

Geels, Frank. 2005. The Dynamics of Transitions in Socio-technical Systems: A Multilevel Analysis of the Transition Pathway from Horse-drawn Carriages to Automobiles (1860–1930). *Technology Analysis and Strategic Management* 17 (4): 445–476.

Geels, Frank. 2007. Feelings of Discontent and the Promise of Middle Range Theory for STS: Examples from Technology Dynamics. *Science, Technology & Human Values* 32 (6): 627–651.

Geels, Frank. 2011. The Multi-Level Perspective on Sustainability Transitions: Responses to Seven Criticisms. *Environmental Innovation and Societal Transitions* 1 (1): 24–40.

Geertz, Clifford. 1973. *The Interpretation of Cultures.* University of Chicago Press.

Gelman, Emmaia, ed. 2009. Green Jobs, Green Homes New York. Center for American Progress. www.americanprogress.org.

Gelman, Emmaia. 2011. Green Jobs, Green New York. Presentation in Taking It to the States panel at Good Jobs, Green Jobs conference, Washington.

Geothermal Energy Association. 2011. Geothermal Basics—Employment. www.geo-energy.org.

Gerard, Leo. 2008. China Trade Promises All Snake Oil—Fair Trade Crucial. Huffington Post, August 4. www.huffingtonpost.com.

Gibson, Lay. 1988. Economic Development: The University and Commercialization. *Economic Development Review* 6 (2): 7–12.

Glasmeier, Amy. 2000. Economic Geography in Practice: Local Economic Development Policy. In *The Oxford Handbook of Economic Geography*, ed. G. Clark, M. Feldman, and M. Gertler. Oxford University Press.

GlobalConnect. 2007. Clean Tech Industry: An Assessment of Assets and Capabilities in San Diego. www.sandiego.gov.

Global Insight. 2008. U.S. Metro Economies: Current and Potential Green Jobs in the U.S. Economy. U.S. Conference of Mayors. www.usmayors.org.

Goetz, Stephen, and Hema Swaminathan. 2006. Wal-Mart and County-Wide Poverty. *Social Science Quarterly* 87 (2): 211–226.

Goetz, Stephen, and Anil Rapasingha. 2006. Wal-Mart and Social Capital. *American Journal of Agricultural Economics* 88 (5): 1304–1310.

Gold, Rachel, Steven Nadel, John Laitner, and Andrew deLaski. 2011. Appliance and Equipment Efficiency Standards: A Money Maker and Job Creator. American Council for an Energy-Efficient Economy. www.aceee.org.

Goldman, Charles, Jane Peters, Nathaniel Albers, Elizabeth Stuart, and Merrian Fuller. 2011. Energy Efficiency Services Sector: Workforce Training and Education Needs. Lawrence Berkeley Livermore Laboratory, LBNL-33163E. eetd.lbnl.gov.

Goldschmidt, Walter. 1978. *As You Sow: Three Studies in the Social Consequences of Agribusiness*. Allanheld, Osmun.

Goldstein, Benjamin. 2010. Implementing the Recovery Act Buy-American Provisions. Presentation at annual Good Jobs, Green Jobs conference, Washington.

Gomory, Ralph, and William Baumol. 2001. *Global Trade and Conflicting National Interests*. MIT Press.

GOP.gov. 2010. CBO Says Kerry-Lieberman Is Multi-Billion Dollar National Energy Tax. www.gop.gov.

Gottlieb, Robert. 1993. *Forcing the Spring*. Island.

Gottlieb, Robert. 2001. *Environmentalism Unbound*. MIT Press.

Gould, Kenneth, Tammy Lewis, and J. Timmons Roberts. 2004. Blue-Green Coalitions: Constraints and Possibilities in the Post-911 Political Environment. *Journal of World-systems Research* 10 (1): 91–116.

Graven, Sal. 2009. Partnerships among NYSERDA, Center for Economic Growth, and Small Business Development Center will Assist Business Expansion and Job Creation Efforts. www.nyserda.org.

Green for All. 2009. Washington Senate Bill 5649. www.greenforall.org.

Green for All. 2010. Clean Energy Works Portland: A National Model for Energy Efficiency Retrofits. www.greenforall.org.

Green for All. 2011. Green Economy Roadmap: The Stories. www.greenforall.org.

Greenpeace. 2011. Case Study: Koch Front Groups Attack RGGI—the Northeast Regioanl Greenhouse Gas Initiative. www.greenpeace.org.

Gregg, Deirdre. 2009. Ray of Light in Washington State's New Energy Law. *Puget Sound Business Journal*, May 1. seattle.bizjournals.com.

Hall, Simon. 2010. China Protests U.S. Green-Energy Probe. *Wall Street Journal*, November 18.

Hamilton, Alexander. 1913. Report on Manufactures: Communication to the House of Representatives, December 5, 1791. U.S. Treasury Department.

Hansen, James. 2009. *Storms of My Grandchildren: The Truth about the Coming Climate Catastrophe and Our Last Chance to Save Humanity*. Bloomsbury.

Harold, Rebecca. 2009. 10 Smart Grid Consumer-to-Utility Privacy Concerns: Are There More? www.realtime-itcompliance.com.

Harrison, Sheena. 2011. Xunlight Lays Off 30 Local Workers After Customer Fails to Pay $5M Order. *Toledo Blade*, April 12. www.toledoblade.com.

Harvey, David. 2005. *A Brief History of Neoliberalism*. Oxford University Press.

Harwood, John. 2010. 53% in U.S. Say Free Trade Hurts Country: NBC/WSJ Poll. www.cnbc.com, September 28.

Hawkins, William. 2005. China Pursues Manifest Destiny Through New Mercantilism. www.americaneconomicalert.org.

Haxeltine, Alex, Tom Hargreaves, Noell Longhurst, and Gill Seyfang. 2011. Where Does Change Come From? Theoretical and Conceptual Framings for Research on the Role of Civil Society in Changing Social Practices and Socio-Technical Transitions. Presented at annual meeting of Sustainable Consumption Research and Action Initiative, Princeton.

Heckscher, Eli. 1935. *Mercantilism*. George Unwin and Allen.

Herring, Horace, ed. 2009. *Energy Efficiency and Sustainable Consumption: The Rebound Effect*. Palgrave Macmillan.

Herzenberg, Stephen. 2010. Pennsylvania's Industry Partnerships—Foundation for a Competitive and Prosperous Pennsylvania. Testimony for Public Hearing on House Bill 2230, Labor Relations Committee, Pennsylvania House of Representatives, February 24.

Hess, David. 2005. Technology- and Product-Oriented Movements: Approximating Social Movement Studies and STS. *Science, Technology & Human Values* 30 (4): 515–535.

Hess, David. 2007a. *Alternative Pathways in Science and Industry: Activism, Innovation, and the Environment in an Era of Globalization*. MIT Press.

Hess, David. 2007b. What Is a Clean Bus? Object Conflicts in the Greening of Urban Transit. *Sustainability: Science, Practice, and Policy* 3 (1): 1–14.

Hess, David. 2009. *Localist Movements in a Global Economy: Sustainability, Justice, and Urban Development in the United States*. MIT Press.

Hess, David. 2010. Sustainable Consumption and the Problem of Resilience. *Sustainability: Science, Practice, and Policy* 6 (2): 1–12.

Hess, David. 2011. Electricity Transformed: Neoliberalism and Local Energy in the United States. *Antipode* 43 (4): 1056–1077.

Hess, David. 2012. Sustainable Consumption, Energy, and Failed Transitions: The Problem of Adaptation. In *Sustainable Lifestyles in a New Economy*, ed. M. Cohen. Edward Elgar.

Hess, David, and Anna Lamprou. 2012. When Nanotechnology Meets Solar Energy: Environmental Social Theory and Problems of Policy. In *Nanotechnology and Society*, ed. D. Maclurcan. CRC Press.

Hess, David J., David A. Banks, Bob Darrow, Joseph Datko, Jaime D. Ewalt, Rebecca Gresh, Matthew Hoffmann, Anthony Sarkis, and Logan D. A. Williams. 2010. Building Clean-Energy Industries and Green Jobs: Policy Innovations at the State and Local Government Level. Research report, Science and Technology Studies Department, Rensselaer Polytechnic Institute. www.davidjhess.org.

Hielscher, Sabine, Gill Seyfang, and Adrian Smith. 2011. Community Innovation for Sustainable Energy: Growing Alternative Consumption Practices Through Civil Society Movements? Presented at annual meeting of Sustainable Consumption Research and Action Initiative, Princeton.

Hindery, Leo Jr. 2010. China Trade Reform: Mission (Not Yet) Accomplished. www.huffingtonpost.com.

Hirsh, Richard. 1999. *Power Loss: The Origins of Deregulation and Restructuring in the American Electric Utility System.* MIT Press.

H.I.S. Global Insight. 2009. Contributions of the Natural Gas Industry to the U.S. National and State Economies. www.anga.us.

Hodur, Nancy. F. Larry Leistritz, and Donald Senegal. 2009. Economic Impacts of Increasing the Ethanol Blend Limit. www.growthenergy.org.

Holmes, William. 2010a. Massachusetts Suspends In-State Requirement for Renewable Energy Generation and Modifies Solar Carve-Out. Renewable + Law blog, June 22. www.lawofrenewableenergy.com.

Holmes, William. 2010b. TransCanada Challenges Massachusetts RPS. Renewable + Law blog, April 22. www.lawofrenewableenergy.com.

Holt, Mark, and Carol Glover. 2006. Energy Policy Act of 2005: Summary and Analysis of Enacted Provisions. CRS Report for Congress, Order Code RL33302. www.ncseonline.org.

Home Performance Resource Center. 2010a. Best Practices for Energy Retrofit Program Design. www.hprcenter.org.

Home Performance Resource Center. 2010b. Domestic Manufacturing Shares of Common Energy Remodeling Products. www.hprcenter.org.

Howell, Katie. 2009. Exxon Sinks $600M in Algae-Based Biofuels in Major Strategy Shift. Greenwire, July 14. http://www.eenews.net.

Howell, Katie. 2010. Is Algae Worse Than Corn for Biofuels? *Scientific American* website. www.scientificamerican.com.

Huang, Ming-Yuan, Janaki Alavalapati, Douglas Carter, and Matthew Langholtz. 2007. Is the Choice of Renewable Portfolio Standards Random? *Energy Policy* 35 (11): 5571–5575.

Hudson, Michael. 1975. *Economics and Technology in 19th Century American Thought: The Neglected American Economists.* Garland.

Hudson, Michael. 2003. *Super Imperialism: The Origin and Fundamentals of U.S. World Dominance.* Pluto.

Hudson, Michael. 2005. *Global Fracture: The New International Economic Order.* Pluto.

Hudson, Tim, and Judson Edwards. 2000. The Roots of State Involvement in Industrial Development: Mississippi's Balance Agriculture with Industry Program, 1936–1940. *Economic Development Review* 17 (2): 55–61.

Hufbauer, Gary, and Jeffrey Schott. 2009. Buy American: Bad for Jobs, Worse for Reputation. Policy brief 09-02, Peterson Institute for International Economics. www.iie.com.

Hughes, Thomas. 1987. The Evolution of Large Technological Systems. In *The Social Construction of Technological Systems*, ed. W. Bijker, T. Hughes, and T. Pinch. MIT Press.

Hull, Dana. 2010. The Coalition to Defeat Prop. 23 Has a Formidable Weapon in Its Arsenal: Republican Gov. Arnold Schwarzenegger. *San José Mercury News*, October 12.

IBISWorld. 2011. U.S. Industry Reports. www.ibisworld.com.

Imbroscio, David. 1997. *Reconstructing City Politics: Alternative Economic Development and Urban Regimes*. Sage.

Independent Petroleum Association of America. 2010. 2009–2010 IPAA Oil and Gas Producers in Your State. www.ipaa.org.

Institute for Building Efficiency. 2010. Property-Assessed Clean Energy Bonds: Alive and Well in the Commercial Sector. www.institutebe.com.

Institute for Economic Competitiveness. 2009. Metro Orlando Cleantech: Assets, Capabilities, Presence, and Potential. University of Central Florida. www.bus.ucf.edu.

Jacobs, Jane. 1969. *The Economy of Cities*. Vintage Books.

Jacobs, Jane. 1984. *Cities and the Wealth of Nations*. Random House.

Jacques, Peter, Riley Dunlap, and Mark Freeman. 2008. The Organization of Denial: Conservative Think Tanks and Environmental Skepticism. *Environmental Politics* 17 (3): 349–385.

Jefferson, Thomas. 1787. Notes on the State of Virginia. In *Thomas Jefferson: Writings*, ed. M. Peterson. Library Classics of the United States.

Jefferson, Thomas. 1793. Report on the Privileges and Restrictions on the Commerce of the United States in Foreign Countries. In *Thomas Jefferson: Writings*, ed. M. Peterson. Library Classics of the United States.

Jefferson, Thomas. 1816. Letter to Benjamin Austin, January 9. In *Thomas Jefferson: Writings*, ed. M. Peterson. Library Classics of the United States.

Johnson, Tom. 2011. Bill Would Benefit Solar Installers that Build Panels in New Jersey. *New Jersey Spotlight*, March 8. www.njspotlight.com.

Jørgensen, Ulrik. 2012. Forthcoming. Mapping and Navigating Transitions: The Multi-level Perspective Compared with Arenas of Development. *Research Policy*.

Jørgensen, Ulrik, and Ole Sorensen. 1999. Arenas of Development: A Space Populated by Actor Worlds, Artefacts, and Surprises. *Technological Analysis and Strategic Forecasting* 11 (3): 409–429.

Karlsson, Charlie, ed. 2008. *Handbook of Research on Cluster Theory*. Edward Elgar.

Kaufman, Leslie. 2011a. Push in States to Deregulate Environment. *New York Times*, April 16.

Kaufman, Leslie. 2011b. Stung by President on Air Quality, Environmentalists Weigh Their Options. *New York Times*, September 4.

Kemp, René, and Jan Rotmans. 2009. Transitioning Policy: Co-Production of a New Strategic Framework for Energy Innovation Policy in the Netherlands. *Policy Sciences* 42 (4): 303–322.

Kemp, René, Johan Schot, and Remco Hoogma. 1998. Regime Shifts to Sustainability through Processes of Strategic Niche Formation: The Approach of Strategic Niche Management. *Technology Analysis and Strategic Management* 10 (2): 175–195.

Kemp, René, and Haro Van Lente. 2011. The Dual Challenge of Sustainability Transitions. Presented at annual meeting of Sustainable Consumption Research and Action Initiative, Princeton.

Kerry, John. 2010. Kerry, Lieberman—American Power Act Will Secure America's Energy, Climate Future. kerry.senate.gov.

Khosla, Vinod. 2006. Biofuels: Think Outside the Barrel. Google Tech Talk, March 28. video.google.com.

Kiely, Pam. 2007. New Energy Economy One Step from Governor's Desk. Environment Colorado, March 15. www.environmentcolorado.org.

Kinchy, Abby, Daniel Kleinman, and Roby Autry. 2008. Against Free Markets, Against Science? Regulating the Socio-economic Effects of Biotechnology. *Rural Sociology* 73 (2): 147–180.

Kinchy, Abby, and Simona Perry. 2011. Knowledge Investments during the Marcellus Shale Gas Rush: A Study of Public and Private Efforts to Monitor Water Quality. Presented at Conference on the Political Sociology of Science and Technology, Rensselaer Polytechnic Institute.

King, Neil, and John Miller. 2009. The Stimulus Package: Obama Risks Flap on Buy American. *Wall Street Journal*, February 4.

Kinner, Mary-Sarah. 2011. Sandoval Speaks at Clean-Energy Summit. Office of the Governor, Nevada. gov.nv.gov.

Klas, Mary. 2011. Scott Wants to Reduce Energy Efficiency Rules and Push Cost-Effective Renewables. *Miami Herald*, June 24. www.miamiherald.com.

Kleindienst, Linda. 2008. Economic Growth Plan Taps State Pension Fund. *Sun Sentinel*, May 3.

Knutson, Ryan. 2009. Oregon Looks to Clean Tech for Revival. *Wall Street Journal*, August 28.

Koshmri, Mike. 2011. Renewable Energy: Where the States Are Headed. www.Sustainablebusiness.com.

Krapels, Edward. 2008. Mercantilism and the Green Energy Debate. *Boston Globe*, March 3.

Krebs, Brian. 2009. Smart Grid Raises Security Concerns. *Washington Post*, July 28.

Krugman, Paul. 2010. Chinese New Year. *New York Times*, January 1.

Kucinich, Jackie. 2011. Romney's Rhetoric Differs from Mass. Record. *USA Today*, September 8.

Labor Research Organization. 2004. Wages and Benefits: Real Wages (1964–2004). www.workinglife.org.

La Capra Associates, GDS Associates, and Sustainable Energy Advantage. 2006. Analysis of a Renewable Energy Portfolio Standard for North Carolina. North Carolina Utilities Commission. www.ncuc.net.

LaFleur, Paul. 2010. Geochemical Soil Gas Survey: A Site Investigtaion of SW30-50-13-W2M. Weyburn Field, Saskatchewan. www.ecojustice.ca.

Laird, Frank. 2001. *Solar Energy, Technology Policy, and Institutional Values.* Cambridge University Press.

Lantz, E., and S. Tegan. 2009. Economic Development Impacts of Community Wind Projects: A Review and Empirical Evaluation. Conference paper NREL/CP-500-45555, National Renewable Energy Laboratory. www.nrel.gov.

Lapoksy, Issie. 2011. Electric Paradise? Why Portland Could be the EV Promised Land. *Inc.*, February: 23–24.

Laranja, Manuel, Elvira Uyarra, and Kieron Flanagan. 2008. Policies for Science, Technology, and Innovation: Translating Rationales into Regional Policies in a Multi-Level Setting. *Research Policy* 37 (5): 823–835.

Lawrence Berkeley National Laboratory, Renewable Funding, and Clinton Climate Initiative. 2011. Property Assessed Clean Energy (PACE) Financing: Update on Commercial Programs. eetd.lbl.gov.

Lee, Annabelle, and Tanya Brewer. 2009. Draft NISTR 7628: Smart Grid Cybersecurity Strategy and Requirements. csrc.nist.gov.

Leffingwell, Lee. 2010. State of the City Address. *Austin Chronicle*, February 5 www.austinchronicle.com.

Leiserowitz, Anthony, Edward Maibach, Connie Roser-Renouf, and Jay Hmielowski. 2011. Politics and Global Warming: Democrats, Republicans, Independents, and the Tea Party. Yale University and George Mason University. environment.yale.edu.

Lian, Ruby, and Donny Kwok. 2011. ENN Group to Invest $8 Billion in Clean Energy: Report. Reuters, September 1.

Lifsher, Marc. 2011. Utilities: Gov. Seeks to Extend Energy Levy. *Los Angeles Times*, August 25.

Little, Amanda. 2011. Tennessee Governor's Race: Haslam vs. McWherter. *Grist*, October 28. www.grist.org.

Los Angeles Apollo Alliance. 2009. Los Angeles Adopts Landmark Green Jobs Ordinance. www.scopela.org.

Los Angeles Apollo Alliance. 2011. City of Los Angeles Green Retrofit and Workforce Development Program. www.scopela.org.

Lowe, Marcy, Soari Tokuoka, Kristen Dubay, and Gary Gereffi. 2010. U.S. Manufacture of Rail Vehicles for Intercity Passenger Rail and Urban Transit. Duke University Center on Globalization Governance and Competitiveness. www.cggc.duke.edu.

Lugar, Richard. 2011. Senator Lugar's Practical Energy and Climate Plan. lugar .senate.gov.

Luke, Peter. 2009. Granholm Signs Auto Battery Tax Credits. *Michigan Political Report*, April 6. mlive.com.

Lustgarten, Abrahm. 2011. Pennsylvania Limits Authority of Oil and Gas Inspectors. *ProPublica*, March 31. www.commondreams.org.

Mader, Robert. 2010. Independent Opposition Builds to Home Star Bill. *Contractor Magazine*, July 7. contractormag.com.

Marchetti, Nino. 2011. Green Jobs in Obama's Speech If You Look for Them. Reuters, September 12. www.reuters.com.

Marshall, Alfred. 1890. *Principles of Economics*, vol. 1. Macmillan.

Massachusetts Community Labor United. 2009. Victory for Green Justice Coalition: New Mass. Energy Efficiency Plan Will Help Revise Working Class Neighborhoods. www.openmediaboston.org.

Massachusetts Technology Collaborative. 2009. Welcome to the Massachusetts Technology Collaborative. www.masstech.org.

Matsui, Doris. 2010. Rep. Matsui Introduces Legislation to Bolster Local Clean-Tech Industry. www.matsui.house.gov.

Mattera, Philip. 2009. High Road or Low Road? Job Quality in the New Green Economy. www.goodjobsfirst.org.

Matthews, Dylan. 2011. Rick Perry's Environmental Record. Ezra Klein's Wonkblog, August 15. www.washingtonpost.com.

Mayer, Brian. 2008. *Blue-Green Coalitions: Fighting for Safe Workplaces and Healthy Communities. Cornell Univeristy Press.* ILR Press.

Mayer, Jane. 2010. Covert Operations. *The New Yorker*, August 30: 45ff.

Mayrl, Matthew, Phil Mattera, Andrea Buffa, and Elena Foshay. 2010. Winning the Race: How America Can Lead the Global Clean Energy Economy. Apollo Alliance and Good Jobs First. www.goodjobsfirst.org.

Mazmanian, Daniel, and Michael Kraft. 1999. *Towards Sustainable Communities: Transitions and Transformations in Environmental Policy.* MIT Press.

Mazza, Patrick. 2008. Community Wind 101: A Primer for Policymakers. Energy Foundation. www.ef.org.

Mazza, Patrick, and Roel Hammerschlag. 2004. *Carrying the Energy Future: Comparing Hydrogen and Electricity for Transmission, Storage, and Transportation.* Institute for Lifecycle Environmental Assessment.

McDermott, Deborah. 2011. Automatic Phone Calls on Green Bill Raise Ire. www.seacoastonline.com.

McDonnell, Bob. 2011. Environment. www.bobmcdonnell.com.

McGeehan, Patrick. 2011. Albany Mulls Altering Ways State Permits Power Plants. *New York Times*, June 23.

McGowan, Elizabeth. 2010. Montgomery Country Carbon Tax Law Could Set Example for Rest of Country. insideclimatenews.org.

McGowan, Richard, and Thomas Vaughan. 1988. Deciphering the Japanese Automobile Import Quota. *Policy Studies Journal: the Journal of the Policy Studies Organization* 16 (3): 413–425.

McGreevy, Patrick. 2011. State Boosts Mandate for Green Power. *Los Angeles Times*, April 11.

Meadows, Donella, Jørgen Randers, and Dennis Meadows. 2004. *Limits to Growth: The Thirty-Year Update*. Chelsea Green.

Meehan, Andrew. 2007. New Law Aims to Promote Renewable Energy for North Carolina Customers. *Carolina Country*, October: 10.

Mehta, Shyam. 2011. Solar Summit 2011: Is PV Manufacturing Doomed to Failure? *Green Tech*, March 7. www.greentechmedia.com.

Michigan League of Conservation Voters. 2011. How Green Is Your Governor? www.michiganlcv.org.

Michigan Policy Network. 2011. Rick Snyder's Michigan Economic Development Corporation: What's the Incentive? www.michiganpolicy.com.

Midwestern Governors' Association. 2009. Midwestern Energy Infrastructure Accord 2009. www.midwesterngovernors.org.

Miller, Stewart. 2007. Energy Mercantilism: Is Private Oil Threatening the NYMEX? www.investmentu.com.

Mills, Karen, Elisabeth Reynolds, and Andrew Reamer. 2008. Clusters and Competitiveness: A New Federal Role for Stimulating Economies. www.brookings.edu.

Minnesota Project. 2009. Lessons and Concepts for Advancing Community Wind. www.mnproject.org.

Mitchell, Katrina. 2009. Current Structures, Strategies, and Examples for Green Economic Development. BlueGreen Alliance Foundation. www.bluegreenalliance.org.

Mitchell, Stacy. 2006. *Big-Box Swindle: The True Cost of Mega-Retailers and the Fight for America's Independent Businesses*. Beacon.

Mitchell, Stacy. 2011. Crowdfunding Bill Would Allow People to Invest in Local Businesses. New Rules Project. www.newrules.org.

Mitchell, Tim. 2009. Carbon Democracy. *Economy and Society* 38 (3): 399–432.

Mol, Arthur. 1995. *The Refinement of Production: Ecological Modernization Theory and the Chemical Industry*. International Books.

Mol, Arthur, and Gert Spaargaren. 2000. Ecological Modernisation Theory in Debate: A Review. *Environmental Politics* 9 (1): 17–49.

Mol, Arthur, and Gert Spaargaren. 2005. From Additions and Withdrawals to Environmental Flows: Reframing Debates in the Environmental Social Sciences. *Organization & Environment* 18 (1): 91–108.

Montgomery, Charlie, Pam Kiely, Phil Hayes, and Mary Broderick. 2011. Raising the Colorado Renewable Energy Standard: Lessons Learned from a Blue-Green Collaboration. Panel presentation at annual Good Jobs, Green Jobs conference, Washington.

Mooney, Nan. 2008. *(Not) Keeping Up With Our Parents: The Decline of the Professional Middle Class.* Beacon.

Moore, Kelly, Scott Frickel, David Hess, and Daniel Kleinman. 2011. Science and Neoliberal Globalization: A Political Sociological Approach. *Theory and Society* 40 (5): 505–532.

Morales, Alex, and Louise Downing. 2011. A Bright Outlook for Energy Efficiency Plays. *Bloomberg Businessweek*, February 7–13: 53.

Morici, Peter. 2011. The Fed Is Out of Tricks to Jump-Start the Economy. www .AmericanEconomicAlert.org.

Morse, Steve. 2011 Session in Review. looncommons.org.

Motoyama, Yasuyuki. 2008. What Was New about the Cluster Theory? *Economic Development Quarterly* 22 (4): 353–363.

Moyer, Bill, with JoAnn McAllister, Mary Lou Finley, and Steven Soifer. 2001. *Doing Democracy: The MAP Model for Organizing Social Movements.* New Society.

Mufson, Steven. 2010. China Denounces U.S. Trade Ruling on Steel Pipes. *Washington Post*, January 1.

Mulkern, Anne. 2010. Rival Ethanol Groups Campaigning to Woo Senators, Clobber Each Other. Greenwire, April 13. http://www.eenews.net.

Mulvaney, Dustin. 2011a. Are Green Jobs Just Jobs? Innovation, Environmental Justice, and the Political Ecology of Photovoltaic (PV) Life Cycles. Presented at School of International Development, University of East Anglia.

Mulvaney, Dustin. 2011b. Looking for Environmental Justice in Clean-Energy Metrics: The Case of Solar Photovoltaics. Ms., Environmental Studies, San José State University.

Mulvaney, Dustin. 2011c. Prospecting the Solar Frontier: Decarbonization, Sputnik Moments, and the Political Ecology of the Green New Deal. Presented at annual meeting of Society for Social Studies of Science, Cleveland.

Muro, Mark. 2010. America COMPETES: Pass It, Nevertheless. *New Republic*, December 21. www.tnr.com.

Muro, Mark, and Bruce Katz. 2010. The New Cluster Moment: How Regional Innovation Clusters Can Foster the Next Economy. Brookings Institution. www .brookings.edu.

Muro, Mark, and Sarah Rahman. 2009. Seattle's Green Building Capital Initiative: Partnering for Citywide Retrofits. Metropolitan Policy Program, Brookings Institution. www.brookings.edu.

Muro, Mark, Jonathan Rothwell, and Devashree Saha. 2011. *Sizing the Clean Economy: A National and Regional Green Jobs Assessment.* Brookings Institution.

National Biofuels Energy Lab. 2011. NextEnergy Lab Takes 1st Step to Biodiesel Standard. engineering.wayne.edu.

National Institute of Standards. 2009. NIST Framework and Roadmap for Smart Grid Interoperability Standards. Release 1.0 (Draft). www.nist.gov.

National Venture Capital Association. 2008. NVCA Recommendations to Obama Administration and New Congress on Energy Policy: A Perspective on a U.S. Economic Recovery Package. www.nvca.org.

Navarro, Mireya. 2011a. Calling for Achievable Target, Christie Plans Cuts in State's Renewable Energy Goals. *New York Times*, June 8.

Navarro, Mireya. 2011b. Christie Pulls New Jersey From 10-State Climate Initiative. *New York Times*, May 27.

Nearing, Brian. 2009. State Pension Fund Turning Green. *Albany Times Union*, September 15.

Nelson, Richard, and Sidney Winter. 1982. *An Evolutionary Theory of Economic Change*. Belknap.

Nester, William. 1998. *A Short History of American Industrial Policies*. St. Martin's.

Network for New Energy Choices. 2010. Freeing the Grid: Best Practices in State Net Metering Policies and Interconnection Procedures. www.newenergychoices. com.

Neville, Patrick. 2008. Climate Action and Green Jobs. www.apolloalliance.org.

New Economy Network. 2011. Network History and Structure. www.neweconomynetwork.org.

New Jersey's Clean Energy Program. 2011. Renewable Energy Manufacturing Incentive. www.njcleanenergy.com.

Newkirk, Margaret, and Frank Bass. 2011. Does Right-to-Work Actually Work? *Bloomberg BusinessWeek*, October 24: 32.

New Rules Project. 2011. Local Purchasing Preferences. www.newrules.org.

New York Battery and Energy Storage Consortium. 2010. Annual Conference Proceedings 2010. www.ny-best.org.

New York State Energy Research and Development Authority (NYSERDA). 2009. Toward a Clean Energy Future: A Three Year Strategic Outlook, 2009–2012. www.nyserda.org.

New York State Energy Research and Development Authority (NYSERDA). 2010. Green Jobs – Green New York Annual Report. www.nyserda.org.

New York State. Foundation for Science, Technology, and Innovation. 2009. 2009 Annual Report. www.nystar.state.ny.us.

New York State Smart-Grid Consortium. 2009. Strategic Smart Grid Vision and Technical Plan Report. www.nyssmartgrid.com.

Next10. 2009. Many Shades of Green. www.next10.org.

North Carolina Sustainable Energy Association. 2008. 2007–2008 Annual Report. energync.org.

North Carolina Sustainable Energy Association. 2009. A Citizen's Guide: The North Carolina Renewable Energy and Energy Efficiency Standard. energync.org.

Norton, Paul. 2003. A Critique of Generative Class Theories of Environmentalism and of the Labor-Environmental Relationship. *Environmental Politics* 12 (4): 96–119.

Notthoff, Ann, Sara Letourneau, Mike Mielke, Erin Rogers, and Ian Kim. 2011. Leaving Prop 23 Behind and Forging Ahead in California: The Fight to Defend California's Landmark Clean Energy Policies. Panel presentation at annual Good Jobs, Green Jobs conference, Washington.

Nugent, James. 2011. Changing the Climate: Ecoliberalism, Green New Dealism, and the Struggle Over Jobs in Canada. *Labor Studies Journal* 36 (1): 56–82.

Obach, Brian. 2004. *Labor and the Environmental Movement: The Quest for Common Ground.* MIT Press.

O'Carroll, Eoin. 2009. Does Wind Power Really Provide More Jobs Than Coal? *Christian Science Monitor*, January 31. www.csmonitor.com.

Office of the United States Trade Representative. 2011. China Ends Wind Power Equipment Subsidies in Challenge Filed by the United States in WTO Trade Dispute. www.ustr.gov.

Ohio Green Pathways. 2009. Green Pathways: University System of Ohio Green Catalog. www.uso.edu.

Ohio Third Frontier. 2008. Ohio Third Frontier Annual Report 2008. development.ohio.gov.

Open Secrets. 2011. Lobbying: Ranked Sectors. www.opensecrets.org.

Orcutt, Mike. 2011. Experts Criticize Evidence used to Diagnose a Suspected Leak at One of the World's Largest CO_2 Storage Sites. www.scientificamerican.com.

PACENow. 2011a. Commercial PACE Launches in San Francisco, Sacramento, and South Florida. www.pacenow.org.

PACENow. 2011b. What Is PACE? www.pacenow.org.

Partnership for Communities. 2009. Green Jobs on the Way for Low-Income Workers. www.thepartnershipfornewcommunities.org.

Pasqualetti, Martin. 2002. Living with Wind Power in a Hostile Landscape. In *Wind Power in View: Energy Landscapes in a Crowded World*, ed. M. Pasqualetti, P. Gipe, and R. Righter. Academic Press.

Pawlenty, Tim. 2006. Governor Pawlenty Signs Executive Order Increasing Use of Renewable Fuels by State Agencies. Office of the Governor, Minnesota. www.leg.state.mn.us.

PDX Lounge. 2011. About Us. www.pdxlounge.com.

Peck, Jamie, and Adam Tickell. 2002. Neoliberizing Space. *Antipode* 34 (3): 380–404.

Pellow, David, Allan Schnaiberg, and Adam Weinberg. 2000. Putting the Ecological Modernization Theory to the Test: The Promises and Performances of Urban Recycling. *Environmental Politics* 9: 109–137.

Pelosi, Nancy. 2011. Make It in America. U.S. House of Representatives. www .democraticleader.gov.

Persky, Joseph, and Wim Wiewel. 1994. The Growing Localness of the Global City. *Economic Geography* 70 (2): 129–143.

Persky, Joseph, David Ranney, and Wim Wiewel. 1993. Import Substitution and Local Economic Development. *Economic Development Quarterly* 7 (1): 18– 29.

Pew Center on Global Climate Change. 2009. Key Provisions: American Recovery and Reinvestment Act. www.pewclimate.org.

Pew Center on Global Climate Change. 2011. Climate Action Plans. www .pewclimate.org.

Pew Charitable Trusts. 2009. The Clean Energy Economy: Repowering Jobs, Business, and Investment across America. www.pewcenteronthestates.org.

Pew Charitable Trusts. 2010a. *Global Clean Power: A $2.3 Trillion Opportunity.* Pew Charitable Trusts.

Pew Charitable Trusts. 2010b. *Who's Winning the Clean-Energy Race: Growth, Competition, and Opportunity in the World's Largest Economies.* Pew Charitable Trusts.

Pew Charitable Trusts. 2011. *From Barracks to the Battlefield: Clean-Energy Innovation and America's Armed Forces.* Pew Charitable Trusts.

Pew Research Center for the People and the Press. 2010. Americans Are of Two Minds on Trade. pewresearch.org.

Pike Research. 2010. PACE Financing for Commercial Buildings to reach $2.5 Billion by 2015. www.pikeresearch.com.

Pinderhughes, Raquel. 2007. Green Collar Jobs: An Analysis of the Capacity of Green Businesses to Provide High Quality Jobs for Men and Women with Barriers to Employment. bss.sfsu.edu.

Piore, Michael, and Charles Sabel. 1984. *The Second Industrial Divide: Possibilities for Prosperity.* Basic Books.

Pleven, Liam, and Russell Gold. 2011. U.S. Nears Milestone: Net Fuel Exporter. *Wall Street Journal,* November 30.

Plosila, Walter. 2004. State Science- and Technology-Based Economic Development Policy: History, Trends and Developments, and Future Directions. *Economic Development Quarterly* 18 (2): 113–126.

Podobnik, Bruce. 2006. *Global Energy Shifts: Fostering Sustainability in a Turbulent Age.* Temple University Press.

Pollin, Robert, Heidi Garrett-Peltier, James Heintz, and Helen Scharber. 2008. Green Recovery: A Program to Create Good Jobs and Start Building a Low-Carbon Economy. Center for American Progress and University of Massachusetts at Amherst. www.peri.umass.edu.

Pool, Sean. 2010. First Energy Regional Innovation Cluster Announced. thinkprogress.org.

Porter, Michael. 1990. *The Competitive Advantage of Nations*. Free Press.

Porter, Michael. 2000. Location, Competition, and Economic Development: Local Clusters in a Global Economy. *Economic Development Quarterly* 14 (1): 15–34.

Porter, Michael. 2003. The Economic Performance of Regions. *Regional Studies* 37 (6&7): 549–578.

Portes, Alejandro. 1994. When More Can Be Less: Labor Standards, Development, and the Informal Economy. In *Contrapunto: The Informal Sector Debate in Latin America*, ed. C. Rakowski. State University of New York Press.

Portes, Alejandro, and Bryan Roberts. 2005. The Free-Market City: Latin American Urbanization in the Years of the Neoliberal Experiment. *Studies in Comparative International Development* 40 (1): 43–82.

Power, Thomas Michael. 1996. *Lost Landscapes and Failed Economies: The Search for a Value of Place*. Island.

Powers, Mary. 2011. Pa. GOP Lawmakers Eye Changes in Renewables, Efficiency Mandates. www.plattsenergyweektv.com.

Prasso, Sheridan. 2010. American Made . . . Chinese Owned. *Fortune*, May 24: 84–92.

PriceWaterhouseCoopers. 2009. The Economic Impacts of the Oil and Natural Gas Industry on the U.S. Economy: Employment, Labor Income, and Value Added. American Petroleum Institute, www.api.org.

Prosper. 2009. Prosper's SEC Registration Declared Effective. www.prosper.com.

Provance, Jim. 2011. Ohio Renewable Energy Law in Danger. *Toledo Blade*, September 12. www.toledoblade.com.

Province of Ontario. 2009. SmartPrivacy for the Smart Grid: Embedding Privacy into the Design of Electricity Conservation. Information and Privacy Commissioner, Province of Ontario, and the Future of Privacy Forum. www.futureofprivacy.org.

Puget Sound Regional Council. 2009. Clean Tech Cluster Analysis Update for the Puget Sound Region. psrc.org.

Quinlan, Paul. 2010. The North Carolina Cases (2006–2007). In *Renewable Energy Systems: The Choice and Modeling of 100% Renewable Solutions*, ed. H. Lund. Academic Press.

Quinlan, Paul. 2011. North Carolina's Renewable Energy and Energy-Efficiency Portfolio Standard. Presented at meeting of Tennessee Solar Energy Industries Association.

Quinn, Elias. 2009. Privacy and the New Energy Infrastructure. Center for Energy and Environmental Security, University of Colorado Law School. papers.ssrn.com.

Ramsey, Duane. 2009. State Awards Solar Research Grant to UT, BGSU. *Toledo Free Press*, October 12. www.toledofreepress.com.

Randall, Willard. 1993. *A Life*. Henry Holt.

Rao, Maya. 2011. Christie Rolls Out Energy Plan; Reversing Renewable Goals, It Has a Basket of Options. *Philadelphia Inquirer*, June 8.

Redman, Elizabeth. 2009. Building the East Bay Green Economy: Critical Steps for Supporting and Engaging East Bay Green Businesses. Oakland Metropolitan Chamber of Commerce and the East Bay Green Corridor Partnership. www.oaklandpartnership.com.

Reece, Ray. 1979. *The Sun Betrayed: A Report on the Corporate Seizure of Solar Energy*. South End.

Rees, Jonathan. 2005. Why We Need a Little Ronald Reagan-Style Protectionism. *History News Network*, November 28. hnn.us.

Regional Greenhouse Gas Initiative. 2011. Investment of Proceeds from RGGI CO2 Allowances. www.rggi.org.

Renewable Energy Research Institute. 2009. Colorado Renewable Energy Laboratory. University of Colorado. rasei.colorado.edu.

Renewable Fuels Association. 2010a. Climate of Opportunity. www.ethanolrfa.org.

Renewable Fuels Association. 2010b. Policy Positions: The Need for Higher Ethanol Blends. www.ethanolrfa.org.

Renner, Michael, Sean Sweeney, and Jill Kubit. 2008. *Green Jobs: Towards Decent Work in a Sustainable, Low-Carbon World*. Worldwatch Institute and United Nations Environmental Program.

Reopelle, Keith. 2011. Suspension of Wind Siting Rules Kills Brown County Wind Project. www.greenbayprogressive.com.

Resch, Rhone. 2011. SEIA Statement on Expected Petitions for the U.S. Government to Investigate Chinese Trade Practices. Solar Energy Industries Association. www.seia.org.

Righter, Robert. 1996. Renewable Energy: Pioneering in Wind Energy. The California Experience. *Renewable Energy* 1–4: 781–784.

Rip, Arie, and René Kemp. 1998. Technological Change. In *Human Choice and Climate Change*, volume 2: *Resources and Technology*, ed. S. Rayner and E. Malone. Battelle Press.

Roberts, Dexter. 2010. Closing for Business? *Bloomberg BusinessWeek*, April 5: 32–37.

Robyn, Dorothy. 2011. Statement of Dr. Dorothy Robyn, Undersecretary of Defense (Installations and Environment). Senate Armed Services Committee, Subcommittee on Readiness and Management Support. www.dod.gov.

Rodrik, Dani. 2004. Industrial Policy for the Twenty-First Century. ideas.repec.org.

Rodrik, Dani. 2009. Mercantilism Reconsidered. www.project-syndicate.org.

Rodrik, Dani. 2011. Growth After Crisis. In *Aftermath: A New Global Economic Order?* ed. C. Calhou and G. Derluguian. Social Science Research Council and New York University Press.

Romm, Joe. 2010. Senior Military Leaders Announce Support for Climate Bill. thinkprogress.org.

Roosevelt, Margot. 2010. Election 2010: Assessing the Results. Prop. 23 Fight Marks New Era in Eco-Politics. *Los Angeles Times*, November 4.

Rose, Fred. 2000. *Coalitions Across the Class Divide: Lessons from the Labor, Peace, and Environmental Movements*. Cornell University Press.

Rose, James. 2010. Freeing the Grid: Best Practices in State Net Metering Policies and Interconnection Procedures. Network for New Energy Choices. www .newenergychoices.org.

Rotmans, Jan, René Kemp, and Marjolein van Asselt. 2001. More Evolution than Revolution: Transition Management in Public Policy. *Foresight* 3 (1): 1–17.

Runge, C. Ford. 2010. The Case Against Biofuels: Probing Ethanol's Hidden Costs. *Environment 360*, March 11. e360.yale.edu.

Rutland, Ted, and Sean O'Hagan. 2007. The Growing Localness of the Canadian City, or, On the Continued (Ir) relevance of Economic Base Theory. *Local Economy* 22 (2): 163–184.

Sadowski, Dennis. 2009. Faith Communities Push for Creation of Green Jobs as Economy Recovers. *Catholic Review*, October 17: 1.

Samuelson, Robert. 2007. The End of Free Trade. *Washington Post*, December 26.

Samuelson, Robert. 2011. At War with China. *Washington Post*, October 17.

Sanders, Robert. 2007. BP Awards $500 Million for Clean Energy Research. www.universityofcalifornia.edu.

Sandro, Phillip. 1994. Jobs and Buy Local Programs: Expected Employment Effects of Public-Sector Import Substitution in Chicago. *International Journal of Public Administration* 18 (1): 199–225.

Sanger, David. 2009. Senate Agrees to Dilute "Buy America" Provisions. *New York Times*, February 5.

Saxenian, Annalee. 1996. *Regional Advantage: Culture and Competition in Silicon Valley and Route 128*. Harvard University Press.

Scheinberg, Anne. 2003. The Proof of the Pudding: Urban Recycling in North America as a Process of Ecological Modernization. *Environmental Politics* 12 (4): 49–75.

Schnaiberg, Allan, and Kenneth Gould. 1994. *Environment and Society: The Enduring Conflict*. St. Martin's.

Schumpeter, Josef. 1942. *Capitalism, Socialism, and Democracy*. McGraw-Hill.

Schwartz, David. 2011. Governor Vetoes Controversial Last-Minute Energy Bill. *Las Vegas Sun*, June 17. www.lasvegassun.com.

Scott, Allen. 1988a. *Metropolis: From the Division of Labor to Urban Form*. University of California Press.

Scott, Allen. 1988b. *New Industrial Spaces: Flexible Production Organization and Regional Development in North America and Western Europe*. Pion.

Scott, Robert. 2011. *Growing U.S. Trade Deficit with China Cost 2.8 Million Jobs Between 2001 and 2010.* Economic Policy Institute.

Seldon, Shawna. 2011. Suspension of Wind Power Siting Rules Threatens to Shut Door on Wind Power in the State. American Wind Energy Association. www .awea.org.

Shoemaker, Jessica, and Christie Brekken. 2006. Community Wind: A Review of Select Federal and State Policy Incentives. Farmers' Legal Action Group. www .flaginc.org.

Shuman, Michael. 2006. *The Small Mart Revolution: How Local Businesses Are Beating the Global Competition.* Berrett-Koehler.

Shuman, Michael. 2009. Local Stock Exchanges and National Stimulus. *Community Development Investment Review* 5 (2): 81–84.

Shuman, Michael. 2011. Don't Occupy Wall Street, Ditch It! Post-Carbon Institute. www.postcarbon.org.

Sierra Club. 2007. Sierra Club Statement on S.3. sierraclubnc.blogspot.com.

Silicon Valley Leadership Group. 2010. Silicon Valley Leadership Group Opposes Prop. 23. svlg.org.

Silicon Valley Toxics Coalition. 2009. Toward a Just and Sustainable Solar Energy Industry. svtc.org.

Silverfarb, Bill. 2011. Solar Tax Incentive Bill Signed. *Daily Journal* (San Mateo County), June 29. www.smdailyjournal.com.

Simmie, James. 2008. The Contribution of Clustering to Innovation: From Porter I Agglomeration to Porter II Export Base Theories. In *Handbook of Research on Innovation and Clusters,* ed. C. Karlsson. Edward Elgar.

Simmons, Jill. 2010. Community Power Works: High Road Agreement to Leverage $20 Million in Federal Stimulus Dollars Awarded to Seattle. www.runtanews .com.

Simon, Stephanie. 2010. Even Boulder Finds It Isn't Easy Going Green. *Wall Street Journal,* February 13.

Sirkin, Harold, Michael Zinzer, and Douglas Hohner. 2011. Make It in America, Again. Boston Consulting Group. www.bcg.com.

Smil, Vaclav. 2010. *Energy Transitions: History, Requirements, Prospects.* Praeger.

Smith, Adam. 1904. *An Inquiry into the Nature and Causes of the Wealth of Nations.* Methuen.

Smith, Adrian, Jan-Peter Voss, and John Grin. 2010. Innovation Studies and Sustainability Transitions: The Allure of the Multi-Level Perspective and Its Challenges. *Research Policy* 39 (4): 435–448.

Solar Energy Industries Association. 2009. U.S. Solar Industry: Year in Review, 2009. www.seia.org.

Solar Energy Industries Association. 2010. U.S. Solar Industry: Year in Review, 2010. www.seia.org.

Solar Energy Industries Association. 2011a. Facts on America's Solar Industry. www.seia.org.

Solar Energy Industries Association. 2011b. U.S. Solar Energy Industry Trade Assessment 2011. www.seia.org.

Solar Foundation. 2010. National Solar Jobs Census. www.thesolarfoundation .org.

Southern Alliance for Clean Energy. 2011. Two 1-Megawatt Solar Projects Are Largest Yet in TVA Region. Footprints on the Path to Clean Energy. blog.cleanenergy.org.

Sovacool, Benjamin. 2011. *Contesting the Future of Nuclear Power*. World Scientific Press.

Spence, Michael, and Sandile Hlatshwayo. 2011. Jobs and Structure in the Global Economy. www.project-syndicate.org.

Stagliano, Vito. 2001. *A Policy of Discontent: The Making of a National Energy Strategy*. PennWell.

Stanko, Greg. 2011. U.S. Solar Cell Manufacturers Respond to Chinese Commerce Ministry Statement. Coalition for American Solar Manufacturing. www .americansolarmanufacturing.org.

State of California. 2005. California Treasurer Phil Angelides' Green Wave Initiative. www.treasurer.ca.gov.

State of California. 2009a. California Green Jobs Corps: Award List and Project Summaries. Employment Development Department. www.edd.ca.gov.

State of California. 2009b. California Green Corps: Putting Federal Economic Stimulus Dollars to Work Training California's Youth to Excel in Emerging Green Jobs. Office of the Governor. gov.ca.gov.

State of Illinois. 2009. Bill Status of HB 3990. www.ilga.gov.

State of Iowa. 2009. Governor Culver Requests Federal Government for E-15 Ethanol Waiver. www.governor.iowa.gov.

State of Iowa Department of Economic Development. 2010. Grow Iowa Values Fund Financial Assistance Program. www.pdiowa.com.

State of Kentucky. 2009. Kentucky, Argonne Partner to Help Build Domestic Battery Industry. governor.ky.gov.

State of Maryland. 2011. Governor O'Malley's 2011 Legislative Agenda. www .governor.maryland.gov.

State of Michigan. 2009. Michigan Green Jobs Report 2009: Occupations and Employment in the New Green Economy. Department of Energy, Labor, and Economic Growth, Bureau of Labor Market Information and Strategic Initiatives. www.milmi.org.

State of Minnesota. 2008. Governor Pawlenty Unveils "Green Jobs Investment" Initiative. Office of the Governor. mn.gov/governor/.

State of New Mexico. 2009. New Mexico's Green Economy: Capitalizing on Assets and Opportunities. www.gonm.biz.

State of New Mexico. 2010. Green Jobs Guidebook. www.gonm.biz.

State of Ohio. 2009. An Update on Ohio's Fuel Cell Map. Department of Development. www.development.ohio.gov.

State of Oregon. 2011. The Oregon Energy Efficiency and Sustainable Technology Program (EEAST). Department of Energy. www.oregon.gov.

State of Texas. 2011. Texas Emerging Technology Fund. governor.state.tx.us .ecodev.

State of Washington. 2009. The Washington Innovation Economy: New Strategy for Economic Development. Washington Economic Development Commission. www.wedc.wa.gov.

State of Washington, Office of the Governor. 2011. Governor Gregoire Signs Landmark Legislation to Transition State off of Coal Power. www.governor .wa.gov.

Stein, Peter. 2010. Bloomberg to America: Lay Off the Chinese. *Wall Street Journal* Metropolis blog, November 16. blogs.wsj.com.

Steinhauer, Jennifer, and Mark Landler. 2011. Senate Proposes Punishing China for Low Currency Value. *New York Times*, October 4.

Stewart, Terence, and Elizabeth Drake. 2009. Buy America: Key to America's Economic Recovery. Alliance for American Manufacturing. assets.usw.org.

Stewart, Terence, Elizabeth Drake, Amy Dwyer, and Ping Gong. 2011. Rare Earths, an Update. A Fresh Look at the Suppliers, the Buyer(s), and the Trade Rules. Law Offices of Stewart and Stewart. www.stewartlaw.com.

Stone, Brad. 2008. Lending Alternative Hits Hurdle. *New York Times*, October 15.

Streater, Scott. 2010. Feinstein Bill Attempts to Reconcile Landscape Protection, Clean Energy. Greenwire, January 7. http://www.eenews.net.

Stroupe, Joseph. 2006. Russia Tips the Balance. The New World Oil Order, Part 2. *Asia Times*, November 23. www.atimes.com.

Styles, Geoffrey. 2010. Renewable Energy and Domestic Content. Energy Outlook. energyoutlook.blogspot.com.

Sullivan, Colin. 2010. Jerry Brown's Environmental Record Runs Deep. Greenwire, October 8. http://www.eenews.net.

Sustainable Business. 2011a. Around the States, February 9. www.sustainable-business.com.

Sustainable Business. 2011b. Around the States, June 17. www.sustainablebusiness.com.

Syracuse Center of Excellence in Environmental and Energy Systems. 2009. History. www.syracusecoe.org.

Szasz, Andrew. 2007. *Shopping Our Way to Safety*. University of Minnesota Press.

Taylor, Margaret. 2008. Beyond Technology-Push and Demand-Pull: Lessons from California's Solar Policy. *Energy Economics* 30 (6): 2829–2854.

Tellus Institute. 2011. Integrated Scenarios. www.tellus.org.

Thornley, Taylor. 2010. Governor McDonnell Signs Green Energy Legislation at Old Dominion University. Commonwealth of Virginia Department of Natural Resources. www.naturalresources.virginia.gov.

Thornton, Mark, and Robert Ekelund, Jr. 2004. *Tariffs, Blockades, and Inflation: The Economics of the Civil War*. SR Books.

Thrush, Glenn. 2009. Microsoft, Nike, Dow Urge Obama to Seal C'hagen Deal. www.politico.com.

Toke, David, Sylvia Breukers, and Maarten Wolsink. 2008. Wind Power Deployment Outcomes: How Can we Account for the Differences? *Renewable & Sustainable Energy Reviews* 12 (4): 1129–1147.

Tolbert, Charles. 2005. Minding Our Own Business: Local Retail Establishments and the Future of Southern Civic Community. *Social Forces* 83 (4): 1309–1328.

Tolbert, Charles, Michael Irwin, Thomas Lyson, and Alfred Nucci. 2002. Civic Community in Small-Town America: How Civic Welfare Is Influenced by Local Capitalism and Civic Engagement. *Rural Sociology* 67 (1): 90–113.

Tomain, Joseph. 2010. Dirty Energy Policy. In *Economic Thought and U.S. Climate Change Policy*, ed. D. Driesen. MIT Press.

Tödtling, Franz, and Michaela Trippl. 2005. One Size Fits All? Towards a Differentiated Regional Innovation Policy Approach. *Research Policy* 34 (8): 1203–1209.

Udall, Tom. 2011. Senate Passes Udall-Schumer Buy American Solar Amendment for Defense Dept. tomudall.senate.gov.

Union of Concerned Scientists. 2006. Summary of the 2005 Energy Bill. www.ucsusa.org.

United Steelworkers. 2010a. United Steelworkers' Section 301 Petition Demonstrates China's Green Technology Violate WTO Rules. assets.usw.org.

United Steelworkers. 2010b. USW Files Trade Case to Preserve Clean, Green Manufacturing Jobs in America. www.usw.org.

United Steelworkers. 2011. USW Applauds Obama Administration Success Ending China Subsidies in Wind Energy Sector Following Section 301 Petition. www.usw.org.

University of California Merced. 2009. U.C. Merced to Lead Multicampus Research Program on Solar Energy. www.ucmerced.edu.

University of Central Florida. 2009. UCF Gets $2.8M from DOE for Solar Network. *UCF Today*, October 16. today.ucf.edu.

University of South Carolina. 2009. COEE-IP-Incubation. www.sc.edu.

Urbanchuk, John. 2011a. Contribution of the Ethanol Industry to the Economy of the United States in 2010. Renewable Fuels Association. www.Ethanolrfa.org.

Urbanchuk, John. 2011b. Economic Impact of Removing the Biodiesel Tax Credit for 2010. National Biodiesel Board. www.biodiesel.org.

US Bureau of Labor Statistics. 2009. B-2. Average Hours and Earnings of Production and Nonsupervisory Workers on Private Nonfarm Payrolls by Major Industry Sector, 1964 to Date. ftp.bls.gov.

US Bureau of Labor Statistics. 2011. Employment, Hours, and Earnings from the Current Employment Statistics Survey (National). Manufacturing. data.bls.gov.

US Census Bureau. 2007. Historical Income Tables—People. www.census.gov.

US Chamber of Commerce. 2009a. Reject Buy American Rules. www.uschamber.com.

US Chamber of Commerce. 2009b. Trade Action—Or Inaction: The Cost for American Workers and Companies. www.uschamber.com.

US Congress. 2010. Letter to the President, September 28. waysandmeans.house.gov.

US Department of Energy. 2009. Energy Frontier Research Centers. www.science.doe.gov.

US Department of Energy. 2010. Report to Congress: Dedicated Ethanol Pipeline Feasbility Study. www1.eere.energy.gov.

US Department of Energy. 2011a. Better Buildings. www1.eere.energy.gov.

US Department of Energy. 2011b. FY 2009 Congressional Budget Request: Budget Highlights. www.cfo.doe.gov.

US Department of Energy. 2011c. FY 2011 Congressional Budget Request: Budget Highlights. www.cfo.doe.gov.

US Department of Energy. 2011d. History. Loan Programs Office. lpo.energy.gov.

US Department of Energy. 2011e. Key Federal Legislation. Energy Efficiency and Renewable Energy, Alternative Fuels and Advanced Vehicles Data Center. www.afdc.energy.gov.

US Department of Energy. 2011f. Our Projects. lpo.energy.gov.

US Department of Labor. 2010a. U.S. Department of Labor Announces $100 Million in Green Jobs Training Grants Through Recovery Act. www.dol.gov.

US Department of Labor. 2010b. U.S. Department of Labor Announces $150 Million in "Pathways out of Poverty" Training Grants for Green Jobs. www.dol.gov.

US Department of Labor. 2010c. U.S. Department of Labor Announces Nearly $190 Million in State Energy Sector Partnership and Training Grants for Green Jobs. www.dol.gov.

US Department of Labor. 2011. Recovery Act: Slow Pace Placing Workers into Jobs Jeopardizes Employment Goals of the Green Jobs Program. Report 18-11-004-03-390, Employment and Training Administration. www.oig.dol.gov.

US Energy Information Administration. 2010. Coal Mining Productivity by State and Mine Type. www.eia. gov.

US Environmental Protection Agency. 2010. Administrator Jackson Announces $2 Million in Brownfields Job Training Funds to Clean up Our Communities. yosemite.epa.gov.

US International Trade Commission. 2010. U.S. Trade Balance, by Partner Country, 2010. dataweb.usitc.gov.

U-SNAP Alliance. 2009. EPRI and U-SNAP Alliance Establish Liaison Agreement in Effort to Standardize the Interface for Smart Appliances. www.usnap .org.

Vachon, Stephan, and Fredric Menz. 2006. The Role of Social, Political, and Economic Interests in Promoting State Green Electricity Policies. *Environmental Science & Policy* 9 (7–8): 652–662.

Vail, Jeff. 2006. Energy Mercantilism on the March. Post-Carbon Institute Energy Bulletin, November 22. www.energybulletin.net.

Van der Brugge, Rutger, Jan Rotmans, and Derek Loorbach. 2005. The Transition in Dutch Water Management. *Regional Environmental Change* 5: 164–176.

Van Dyke, Nella, and Holly McCammon, eds. 2010. *Strategic Alliances: Coalition Building and Social Movements.* University of Minnesota Press.

Van Nostrand, James. 2011. Legal Issues in Financing Energy Efficiency: Creative Solutions for Funding the Initial Capital Costs of Investments in Energy Efficiency Measures. Journal of Energy and Environmental Law Winter: 1–16.

Verbong, Geert, and Frank Geels. 2006. The Ongoing Energy Transition: Lessons from a Socio-Technical, Multi-level Analysis of the Dutch Electricity System (1960–2004). *Energy Policy* 35 (2): 1025–1037.

Verbong, Geert, and Frank Geels. 2010. Exploring Sustainability Transitions in the Electricity Sector with Socio-Technical Pathways. *Industrial Engineering (American Institute of Industrial Engineers)* 77 (8): 1214–1221.

Victor, Peter. 2008. *Managing Without Growth: Slower by Design, Not Disaster.* Edward Elgar.

Vlasic, Bill. 2011. Carmakers Back Strict New Rules for Gas Mileage. *New York Times*, July 29.

Wald, Matthew. 2011. EPA Approves Use of More Ethanol in Gasoline. *New York Times*, January 22.

Wald, Matthew, and Charlie Savage. 2011. Furor Over Loans to Failed Solar Firm. *New York Times*, September 15.

Washington Post. 2010. *Washington Post*–ABC News Poll, June 6.

Washington State Legislature. 2010. SB 5649-2009-10. apps.leg.wa.gov.

Way, Ron. 2008. Minnesota's Corn Ethanol Industry Blends Subsidies, Politics, and Lobbying. *Minneapolis Post*, January 7. www.minnpost.com.

Weinrub, Al. 2011. Community Power: Decentralized Renewable Energy in California. Local Clean Energy Alliance. www.localcleanenergy.org.

Weiss, Daniel, Rebecca Lefton, and Susan Lyon. 2010. Dirty Money: Oil Companies and Special Interests Spend Millions to Oppose Climate Legislation. Center for American Progress. www.americanprogressaction.org.

Welna, David. 2011. Democrats, Republicans at Odds over Stopgap Bill. National Public Radio, September 21. www.npr.org.

Wesoff, Eric. 2011. The Reality of China's Billions in Solar Loans. Greentech Media. www.greentechmedia.com.

Wheeland, Matthew. 2009. What Obama's New Order Means for Green Buildings, Green IT. www.greenbiz.com.

Wheeler, Jacob. 2009. American-Made Streetcars: Portland Company Rebuilds Lost Industry. apolloalliance.org.

White House. 2010. Fact Sheet: $2.3 Billion in New Energy Advanced Manufacturing Tax Credits. www.whitehouse.gov.

White, Sarah, and Jason Walsh. 2008. Greener Pathways: Jobs and Workforce Development in the Clean Energy Economy. Apollo Alliance, Center on Wisconsin Strategy, and Workforce Alliance. www.greenforall.org.

Williams, Colin. 1994. The Role of the Service Sector in Revitalising Local Economies. *Local Economy* 9 (1): 73–82.

Williams, Colin. 1997. Rethinking the Role of the Retail Sector in Economic Development. *Service Industries Journal* 17 (2): 205–220.

Williams, Dave. 2009. Biofuel Pipeline to Serve Atlanta. *Atlanta Business Chronicle*, January 30. bizjournals.com.

Willon, Phil. 2009. Green Jobs Plan Announced. *Los Angeles Times*, September 9.

Windustry. 2011. Community Wind Toolbox. www.windustry.org.

Wines, Michael, and Xiyun Yang. 2010. China Escalates Fight with U.S. on Energy Aid. *New York Times*, October 18.

Winslow. 2011. Winslow Green Mutual Funds: Overview. www.winslowgreen.com.

Woody, Todd. 2009a. Desert Vistas v. Solar Power. *New York Times*, December 22.

Woody, Todd. 2009b. The Wind v. Coal Jobs Debate. thegreenwombat.com.

Wolsink, Maarten. 2006. Wind Power Implementation: The Nature of Public Attitudes: Equity and Fairness instead of "Backyard Motives." *Renewable & Sustainable Energy Reviews* 11 (6): 1188–1207.

World Commission on Environment and Development. 1987. Our Common Future. Oxford University Press.

York, Richard, and Eugene Rosa. 2003. Key Challenges to Ecological Modernization Theory. *Organization & Environment* 16 (3): 273–288.

Zito, Kelly. 2008. Air Quality District Votes to Make Polluters Pay for Carbon Emissions. *San Francisco Chronicle*, May 22.

Index

Advanced Research Project Agency—Energy, 58, 96, 128
Alliance for American Manufacturing, 87
American Energy Innovation Council, 58
American Legislative Exchange Council, 202
American Recovery and Reinvestment Act, 53, 58–61, 66, 85–89, 93–96, 101, 138, 161, 182
Americans for Prosperity, 195, 202, 210
Apollo Alliance, 52, 53, 60, 96, 139, 156, 174–184
Austin, 115, 116, 134

Batteries and energy storage, 130–138
Biofuels policy, 43–46, 57, 58, 94, 110, 111, 121, 122, 129, 134, 142, 187, 201, 214–220
Bioregionalism, 5
Bloomberg, Michael, 81, 115
BlueGreen Alliance, 52, 53, 77, 173–178, 184, 194. See also Labor-environmental coalitions
Boston, 134, 135
Boulder, 114
Bourdieu, Pierre, 17, 18
Brown, Halina, 16
Brown, Jerry, 41, 201–203
Bush, George H. W., 42
Bush, George W., 42, 48, 95

Business Alliance for Local Living Economies, 26, 150–155
Buy American policy. See Trade

California policy, 41, 57, 105, 112–115, 121, 129, 134–142, 159–161, 172–174, 182, 195, 201–206
Carter, Jimmy, 40, 41, 46, 89
Chang, Ha-Joon, 10–12, 121, 217
Chicago, 60, 119, 135, 139, 152
China, 1, 2, 6, 7, 55, 73–85, 95–99, 192–194, 219
Clean tech, 1, 23, 56–58, 83, 98, 130–138, 145, 201, 227. See also Manufacturing
Climate science and denial, 92, 171, 188, 196–198, 210
Coal. See Fossil fuels
Colorado policy, 129, 135, 142, 159–161, 175, 176, 204–208
Community choice, 158, 159
Connecticut policy, 204
Cooke, Philip, 127–129
Countervailing power, 17–19, 49, 57, 87, 92, 93, 184, 189, 214, 218, 225

Daly, Herman, 24
Debt and deficits, 7, 34, 191, 210, 220, 225
Demand policies, 27, 38, 41, 55–58, 90–95, 100–122, 160–162

Democratic Party, 59, 62, 68, 73, 85, 183–211, 215–218
Developmentalism, 3–18, 31–39, 54–56, 68, 69, 78, 88, 123, 145, 171, 172, 191, 209–229
Domestic content programs, 12, 75, 80–89, 183, 226

Ecological modernization, 21
Economic development policy, 34–39, 103, 123, 130–154. *See also* Industrial policy
Eisinger, Peter, 37–45
Electricity industry, 42, 49, 50, 104–107, 144, 156, 157
Electric vehicles, 94, 109, 117, 119, 129–133, 194, 195, 205
Ella Baker Center, 59–61, 139, 173–175
Energy efficiency policy, 90–99, 107–109, 176–181, 203–208, 220, 221. *See also* Retrofitting
Energy independence, 31, 40, 41, 45, 90, 91, 187
Energy Regional Innovation Cluster, 128, 141, 215
Environmental movement, 51–55, 91, 92, 104–106, 154, 173–180, 196, 200
Environmental policy, 68, 171, 199–201. *See also* Renewable energy policy
Environmental Protection Agency, 92, 94, 96, 195
Evans-Pritchard, Ambrose, 77, 78

Farrell, John, 157, 158
Field theory, 17–22, 213
Fitzgerald, Joan, 68
Florida policy, 113, 121, 129, 136, 143, 196
Ford, Gerald, 32, 39, 40
Fossil fuels
  as bridge technology, 49
  coal, 49–51, 91, 104, 105, 148, 200, 219, 220

geographical concentration of, 45, 214
  natural gas, 42, 49–51, 104, 105, 197, 198, 219, 220
  petroleum, 31, 32, 45–51, 187, 218–220, 228
  political influence of, 19–27, 45–51, 66, 73, 91–96, 105, 123, 133, 173–210, 214–221
Framing of policies, 2, 20, 48, 68, 90, 114, 171–174, 186–194, 209–211, 220, 225
Fuel cell industry and policy, 83, 97, 108, 117, 129–143
Fuel efficiency standards, 40, 43, 48, 195

Geels, Frank, 14–16
Gerard, Leo, 1, 2, 52, 76, 77, 177
Glasmeier, Amy, 38
Global economy, 2–13, 28–34, 99, 154, 213–221, 226, 227
Goldschmidt, Walter, 150
Gottlieb, Robert, 47
Gould, Kenneth, 20, 24
Green energy transition. *See* Technological transition
Green For All, 59, 60, 96
Green jobs, definitions of, 49, 50, 53, 54, 63–68, 155, 156, 165, 166
Green Jobs Act of 2007, 60, 96
Green transition coalitions, 21, 48–63, 81, 90–93, 100, 105, 106, 155, 167, 172–188, 215–218
Green, types of, 22–24, 56, 57, 61, 62, 104–111, 228, 229

Hamilton, Alexander, 10–12
Hawaii policy, 203, 204
Hawkins, William, 76
"High road" agreements, 177, 181, 182
Hindery, Leo, 75
Hudson, Michael, 11, 39
Hughes, Thomas, 13, 14

Illinois policy, 119–121
Import substitution, 9–12, 31, 44, 94, 100, 117–123, 152–157, 165, 174, 187, 204, 214, 215
Industrial policy, 3–6, 37–45, 58, 59, 69, 89–104, 133–145, 154, 198, 214–216. *See also* Demand policies; Investment policies; Supply policies opposition to, 140, 191–194, 211, 220, 227
procurement preferences in, 119–123, 149, 150
Institute for Local Self-Reliance, 119, 157
Investment policies, 56–58, 67, 68, 84, 85, 89, 90, 133–138, 162–165, 193, 194
Iowa policy, 137, 143, 199

Jacobs, Jane, 128, 152
Japan, 32, 33, 74
Jefferson, Thomas, 10, 34
Job estimates, 8, 49, 50, 87, 88, 93, 94, 115, 119, 132–140, 153–156, 173, 177, 182–186, 195, 218
Job training programs, 61, 62, 96, 130, 138–140
Jørgensen, Ulrik, 16

Kerry, John, 48, 90–92, 184
Koch, Charles and David, 51, 197, 198, 210
Kraft, Michael, 68
Krugman, Paul, 74, 75

Labor. *See* Unions
Labor-environmental coalitions, 20, 47, 48, 51–55, 93, 106, 110, 144, 173–186
Labor-localist relations, 154, 165, 166
Localism, 5, 18, 147–150, 165–167, 215
Local living economy, 154–156
Los Angeles, 135, 141, 142, 174, 175
Lugar, Richard, 91

Maine policy, 162, 197
Manufacturing, 2–6, 32–36, 53, 54, 64, 76–89, 95–98, 122, 151, 152, 177, 178, 192, 214–217
Maryland policy, 114, 205–207
Massachusetts policy, 35–37, 120, 121, 131, 176, 177, 199, 205
Mayer, Brian, 20
Mazmanian, Daniel, 68
Mercantilism, 9–11, 73–79, 120–123
Michigan policy, 122, 129–138, 143, 199, 200, 211
Military, 91, 186–189, 228
Minneapolis, 120, 132, 177, 178
Minnesota policy, 117, 135–138, 159, 177, 178, 199, 204
Mississippi policy, 34, 35
Mitchell, Stacy, 150, 151
Morris, David, 157, 158
Multiplier effects, 64, 153
Mulvaney, Dustin, 194

National laboratories, 97–99, 128, 134, 141–144, 156
Neoliberalism, 2–9, 18, 68, 69, 86, 123, 145, 166–171, 191, 211–215, 225–228
Net metering, 43, 158–160, 201–206
Nevada policy, 201
Newark, New Jersey, 60
New Deal, 4, 34, 42, 43, 61, 227
"New economy," 60
New Jersey policy, 122, 197
New Mexico policy, 129–131, 139, 140, 197, 198, 205
New York City, 115, 120
New York (State) policy, 112, 129, 134–136, 142, 178, 179, 203
North Carolina policy, 179–182, 205
Nuclear energy, 47, 91, 95, 104, 144, 180, 194, 199, 204
Nugent, James, 20

Oakland, 59, 134, 135, 139, 175
Obach, Brian, 20, 47, 48, 51, 52

Obama, Barack, 44, 52, 73, 89, 92, 95, 183, 193–195
O'Hagan, Sean, 153
Ohio policy, 105, 131, 132, 137, 139, 140, 143, 198
On-bill financing, 162, 178, 181, 203, 205
Oregon policy, 138, 204, 207

Pennsylvania policy, 104, 105, 198
Persky, Joseph, 153
Philadelphia, 128, 132, 134
Pinderhughes, Raquel, 63
Piore, Michael, 126
Plosila, Walter, 37, 38
Podobnik, Bruce, 99
Political opportunity, 14–27, 49–51, 73, 195, 196, 224
Porter, Michael, 36, 126, 127, 132
Portland, Oregon, 115–117, 132–134, 180, 181
Poverty, 58–63, 96
Property Assessed Clean Energy laws, 160–162, 205–208
Public benefits fund, 103, 113, 202, 203

Rail transportation, 1, 52, 88, 117, 196–200
Rare earth metals, 80, 84, 98
Raven, Rob, 15
Reagan, Ronald, 4, 32, 33, 42, 46
Rebound effect, 107
Regional carbon initiatives, 113, 114, 173, 197–204
Regional differences, 11, 34–36, 40–45, 93, 118–120, 136, 183, 189, 214
Religion, 60, 61
Renewable energy
  geothermal, 95, 96, 105
  hydro, 106, 204
  solar, 82–84, 97, 105, 129, 130, 137, 143, 156–159, 188, 191–202
  wind, 83–88, 105, 121, 122, 129, 130, 156–159, 197–199

Renewable energy industry, 49–51, 55–59, 65, 66, 81–83, 215, 219–221
Renewable energy policy, 40–42, 55–59, 90–96, 105, 175–189, 196–208
Renewable portfolio standard, 90, 103–105, 112, 113, 183–188, 196–211
Republican Party, 68, 91, 140, 184–211, 215–218
Research policy, 83–99, 140–144
Reserve currency, 31, 32, 218–221
Retrofitting of buildings, 59–62, 93, 175–182, 203
Rutland, Ted, 153

Samuelson, Robert, 78
San Diego, 134, 142, 156, 175
San Francisco, 115, 175
San José, 135
Saxenian, AnnaLee, 126
Scott, Alan, 126
Seattle, 116, 182
Service sector, 7, 59, 63–67, 125, 147–154, 218
Seyfang, Gill, 16
Shuman, Michael, 151, 152, 164
Silicon Valley, 39, 125, 126, 151
Small business, 147, 148
Smart grid, 108, 129, 130, 134
Smith, Adrian, 15, 16
Smoot-Hawley Act, 12, 33, 78
Socialism, 5, 18, 34, 158, 191, 214, 215
Social liberalism, 3–9, 18, 59, 68, 69, 91, 122, 139, 145, 167–171, 209–228
Solyndra bankruptcy, 84, 171, 191–193, 211
South Carolina policies, 143, 151
St. Paul, 107, 119, 120, 177, 178
Structural adjustment programs, 12
Supply policies, 95–99, 125–145
Sustainability, 24, 25, 221–225

Tariffs, 79–86, 192, 193
Tea Party movement, 8, 46, 51, 195, 196, 205–210, 226
Technological transition, 2, 13–27, 46, 73, 99, 100, 104, 105, 111, 118, 172, 186, 188, 195, 209, 213–229
Tellus Institute, 189, 229
Tennessee policy, 143, 144, 200
Texas policy, 37, 38, 136, 137, 199
Trade, 32–37, 43–47, 54–56, 219, 220. *See also* Domestic content programs; Smoot-Hawley Act; Tariffs
and competitiveness, 36, 37, 83, 100, 167, 214–227
fair, 155, 165, 166, 226
liberalization of, 5–13, 33, 81, 86, 87, 120, 121, 166, 214–227
protectionism and, 6–12, 32, 33, 44–45, 69, 73–89, 123, 167, 174, 192, 193, 211–219
Transition theory, 2, 13–17, 213, 222. *See also* Technological transition
Transportation, 14, 117, 118, 219, 223. *See also* Biofuels; Electric vehicles; Rail transportation
Treadmill of production theory, 21

Unemployment, 2, 6–8, 59, 66, 67, 78, 87, 132, 173, 202, 226
Unions, 1, 2, 8, 35, 53, 62, 76–80, 86, 87, 154, 165–167, 198, 218, 226. *See also* Labor-environmental coalitions; United Steelworkers
United Kingdom, 10, 11, 31, 99
United States Business and Industry Council, 76
United States Chamber of Commerce, 86, 87, 92
United States Department of Energy, 95–97, 118, 128, 141, 161, 194
United Steelworkers, 1, 20, 48–52, 76–87

Van Jones, Anthony, 59, 60
Venture capital, 134. *See also* Industrial policy
Vermont policy, 204
Virginia policy, 105, 201

Wages, 7, 8, 53
Washington (State) policy, 116, 159, 181, 182, 205–207
Williams, Colin, 153
Wisconsin policy, 143
World Trade Organization, 48, 77–89, 216

Urban and Industrial Environments

Series editor: Robert Gottlieb, Henry R. Luce Professor of Urban and Environmental Policy, Occidental College

Maureen Smith, *The U.S. Paper Industry and Sustainable Production: An Argument for Restructuring*

Keith Pezzoli, *Human Settlements and Planning for Ecological Sustainability: The Case of Mexico City*

Sarah Hammond Creighton, *Greening the Ivory Tower: Improving the Environmental Track Record of Universities, Colleges, and Other Institutions*

Jan Mazurek, *Making Microchips: Policy, Globalization, and Economic Restructuring in the Semiconductor Industry*

William A. Shutkin, *The Land That Could Be: Environmentalism and Democracy in the Twenty-First Century*

Richard Hofrichter, ed., *Reclaiming the Environmental Debate: The Politics of Health in a Toxic Culture*

Robert Gottlieb, *Environmentalism Unbound: Exploring New Pathways for Change*

Kenneth Geiser, *Materials Matter: Toward a Sustainable Materials Policy*

Thomas D. Beamish, *Silent Spill: The Organization of an Industrial Crisis*

Matthew Gandy, *Concrete and Clay: Reworking Nature in New York City*

David Naguib Pellow, *Garbage Wars: The Struggle for Environmental Justice in Chicago*

Julian Agyeman, Robert D. Bullard, and Bob Evans, eds., *Just Sustainabilities: Development in an Unequal World*

Barbara L. Allen, *Uneasy Alchemy: Citizens and Experts in Louisiana's Chemical Corridor Disputes*

Dara O'Rourke, *Community-Driven Regulation: Balancing Development and the Environment in Vietnam*

Brian K. Obach, *Labor and the Environmental Movement: The Quest for Common Ground*

Peggy F. Barlett and Geoffrey W. Chase, eds., *Sustainability on Campus: Stories and Strategies for Change*

Steve Lerner, *Diamond: A Struggle for Environmental Justice in Louisiana's Chemical Corridor*

Jason Corburn, *Street Science: Community Knowledge and Environmental Health Justice*

Peggy F. Barlett, ed., *Urban Place: Reconnecting with the Natural World*

David Naguib Pellow and Robert J. Brulle, eds., *Power, Justice, and the Environment: A Critical Appraisal of the Environmental Justice Movement*

Eran Ben-Joseph, *The Code of the City: Standards and the Hidden Language of Place Making*

Nancy J. Myers and Carolyn Raffensperger, eds., *Precautionary Tools for Reshaping Environmental Policy*

Kelly Sims Gallagher, *China Shifts Gears: Automakers, Oil, Pollution, and Development*

Kerry H. Whiteside, *Precautionary Politics: Principle and Practice in Confronting Environmental Risk*

Ronald Sandler and Phaedra C. Pezzullo, eds., *Environmental Justice and Environmentalism: The Social Justice Challenge to the Environmental Movement*

Julie Sze, *Noxious New York: The Racial Politics of Urban Health and Environmental Justice*

Robert D. Bullard, ed., *Growing Smarter: Achieving Livable Communities, Environmental Justice, and Regional Equity*

Ann Rappaport and Sarah Hammond Creighton, *Degrees That Matter: Climate Change and the University*

Michael Egan, *Barry Commoner and the Science of Survival: The Remaking of American Environmentalism*

David J. Hess, *Alternative Pathways in Science and Industry: Activism, Innovation, and the Environment in an Era of Globalization*

Peter F. Cannavò, *The Working Landscape: Founding, Preservation, and the Politics of Place*

Paul Stanton Kibel, ed., *Rivertown: Rethinking Urban Rivers*

Kevin P. Gallagher and Lyuba Zarsky, *The Enclave Economy: Foreign Investment and Sustainable Development in Mexico's Silicon Valley*

David N. Pellow, *Resisting Global Toxics: Transnational Movements for Environmental Justice*

Robert Gottlieb, *Reinventing Los Angeles: Nature and Community in the Global City*

David V. Carruthers, ed., *Environmental Justice in Latin America: Problems, Promise, and Practice*

Tom Angotti, *New York for Sale: Community Planning Confronts Global Real Estate*

Paloma Pavel, ed., *Breakthrough Communities: Sustainability and Justice in the Next American Metropolis*

Anastasia Loukaitou-Sideris and Renia Ehrenfeucht, *Sidewalks: Conflict and Negotiation over Public Space*

David J. Hess, *Localist Movements in a Global Economy: Sustainability, Justice, and Urban Development in the United States*

Julian Agyeman and Yelena Ogneva-Himmelberger, eds., *Environmental Justice and Sustainability in the Former Soviet Union*

Jason Corburn, *Toward the Healthy City: People, Places, and the Politics of Urban Planning*

JoAnn Carmin and Julian Agyeman, eds., *Environmental Inequalities Beyond Borders: Local Perspectives on Global Injustices*

Louise Mozingo, *Pastoral Capitalism: A History of Suburban Corporate Landscapes*

Gwen Ottinger and Benjamin Cohen, eds., *Technoscience and Environmental Justice: Expert Cultures in a Grassroots Movement*

Samantha MacBride, *Recycling Reconsidered: The Present Failure and Future Promise of Environmental Action in the United States*

Andrew Karvonen, *Politics of Urban Runoff: Nature, Technology, and the Sustainable City*

Daniel Schneider, *Hybrid Nature: Sewage Treatment and the Contradictions of the Industrial Ecosystem*

Catherine Tumber, *Small, Gritty, and Green: The Promise of America's Smaller Industrial Cities in a Low-Carbon World*

Sam Bass Warner and Andrew H. Whittemore, *American Urban Form: A Representative History*

John Pucher and Ralph Buehler, eds., *City Cycling*

Stephanie Foote and Elizabeth Mazzolini, eds., *Histories of the Dustheap: Waste, Material Cultures, Social Justice*

David J. Hess, *Good Green Jobs in a Global Economy: Making and Keeping New Industries in the United States*